T0090654

Praise for THE CHALLENGE FOR AFRICA
and Wangari Maathai

"Admirable. . . . Thorough. . . . A penetrating assessment of the corrosive legacy of Africa's history on its inhabitants, and the failure of most contemporary African leaders to rise to innumerable challenges. . . . *The Challenge for Africa* is a poignant counter to the suggestion that nations can so readily shake off their history."   —*Financial Times*

"[Maathai] offers pragmatic but hopeful advice on resolving the problems of her native continent—from achieving gender equity to saving Congo's forests to removing the stigma of HIV and AIDS and giving victims of the disease the tools to empower themselves."   —*Ms.*

"Wangari Maathai and the Green Belt Movement demonstrate the intimate connection between sustainable management of Africa's rich natural resources, democracy, good governance, and peace. Such are the solutions that will bring new light to Africa. I hope the world will support her vision of hope."
—Nelson Mandela

"*The Challenge for Africa* reads like an African version of *The Audacity of Hope* by Barack Obama. . . . It is both an accessible primer on the challenges facing Africa and a lucid manifesto on how to address them. . . . Maathai's idea, that Africans must look back first, is audacious and noble."   —*The Irish Times*

"Wangari Maathai is the rare leader who knows how to create independence, not dependence."   —Gloria Steinem

"As one of the women leaders that are changing Africa she is an inspiration to us all." —British Prime Minister Gordon Brown

"Maathai's writing is as clear as an African sky. . . . This book represents her accumulated insights, wisdom and recommendations for the continued recovery of the continent. . . . [It] should be placed at every African seat of learning, and should become prescribed reading for every African politician."
—*Cape Times* (South Africa)

"A wide-ranging study of Africa's current predicament and a no-nonsense, tightly argued proposal of the way forward for the continent. Written with a measured tone and in plain, simple language, it would be a mistake to underestimate the book's validity and sheer intellectual power."
—*African Business* (London)

"Wangari Maathai has been a champion of the environment, of women, of Africa, and of anyone concerned about our future security."
—Kofi Annan

"Exposes the most obstinate 'bottlenecks to development,' proposing ingenious initiatives aimed at overcoming a legacy of colonialism, an unforgiving global economy—and, most intractably, a mentality of dependency. In such troubled times, women with experience—and the conviction to match it—offer a hopeful way forward."
—*Vogue*

"From one of Africa's most positive and farsighted thinkers comes a wonderful book combining an elegant critique of Africa's troubled past with a rallying cry for how Africans can use culture, nature and self-belief to reverse their continent's decline. *The Challenge for Africa* is a milestone in African writing that both educates and inspires."
—Tim Butcher, bestselling author of
Blood River: A Journey to Africa's Broken Heart

Wangari Maathai

THE CHALLENGE FOR AFRICA

Wangari Muta Maathai was born in Nyeri, Kenya, in 1940. She is the founder of the Green Belt Movement, which, through networks of rural women, has planted 40 million trees across Kenya since 1977. In 2002, she was elected to Kenya's Parliament in the first free elections in a generation, and in 2003, she was appointed Deputy Minister for the Environment and Natural Resources, a post she held until 2007, when she left the government. The Nobel Peace Prize laureate of 2004, Maathai has been honored around the world for her work, including appointments to the Legion d'Honneur by France and the Order of the Rising Sun by Japan. She is the author of two previous books: *The Green Belt Movement* and *Unbowed*, a memoir. She died in 2011.

www.greenbeltmovement.org

THE CHALLENGE
FOR AFRICA

Wangari Maathai

THE CHALLENGE
FOR AFRICA

Anchor Books

A DIVISION OF RANDOM HOUSE, INC.

NEW YORK

FIRST ANCHOR BOOKS EDITION, MARCH 2010

Copyright © 2009 by Wangari Muta Maathai

All rights reserved. Published in the United States by Anchor Books, a division of Random House, Inc., New York, and in Canada by Random House of Canada Limited, Toronto. Originally published in hardcover in the United States by Pantheon Books, a division of Random House, Inc., New York, in 2009.

The Library of Congress has cataloged the Pantheon edition as follows:
Maathai, Wangari.
The challenge for Africa / Wangari Maathai.
p. cm.
Includes bibliographical references and index.
1. Political leadership—Africa. 2. Africa—Economic conditions—1960–
3. Africa—Social conditions—1960– I. Title.
JQ1875.M33 2009
320.6096—dc22   2008043017

Anchor ISBN: 978-0-307-39028-8

Book design by M. Kristen Bearse

www.anchorbooks.com

146119709

TO ALL THE PEOPLES OF AFRICA

Contents

THE CHALLENGE
FOR AFRICA

ON THE WRONG BUS

FOR THIRTY YEARS, I have worked in the trenches with others to find ways to break the wall that separates the peoples of Africa from justice, wealth, peace, and respect. We have searched for a route out of poverty, ignorance, ill health and early death, violations of basic rights, corruption, environmental degradation, and many other problems associated with Africa. I have done this work through the Green Belt Movement, helping communities plant trees, and so improve their livelihoods, protect their environment, and, in the process, increase their commitment and persistence. It is these experiences at the grassroots level, coupled with my service in the Kenyan government and participation in numerous international efforts to assist Africa and protect the environment, that have shaped my worldview and inform the approaches, examples, analyses, and solutions that I offer in this book.

In the three decades since the Green Belt Movement began its work, some Africans have left the trenches to pursue their own interests and ambitions; others have become disappointed and tired. Some are languishing in their homes or jails; others are homeless or in refugee camps. Some are hoping for leadership to deliver them; others are waiting until it is clear to them that they must save themselves by, in the words of Mahatma Gandhi, being the change they wish to see in the world.

Yet as I seek to show, the challenges before Africa not only stem from national and international policies (although these play an important part in determining Africa's future, as they have its past), but are also moral, spiritual, cultural, and even psychological in nature. As I also illustrate, the condition of Africa is bound to that of the world. We all share one planet and are one humanity; there is no escaping this reality.

I have written *The Challenge for Africa* for all those with an interest in the fate of the African continent, from the general reader to advocates, researchers, development specialists, and government officials, including heads of state. In its pages I hope to explain, elucidate, engage, and, perhaps most important, encourage all concerned to grapple with the challenges facing Africa today.

The Challenge for Africa is divided into five sections: the contemporary face and cultural and historical background of the challenges (chapters 1–2); the economic, political, and international context and dimension of these challenges (chapters 3–5); the challenge of leadership and good governance at the top of society and at the grassroots (chapters 6–7); the complex and problematic relationship of ethnic identity to the nation-state in modern Africa (chapters 8–10); and the centrality of the environment to Africa's development challenges and solutions to them (chapters 11–13), followed by a final chapter on the challenges before individual Africans, at home and abroad.

In chapter 1, I reflect on a woman I saw in Yaoundé, Cameroon, whose subsistence farming techniques were causing soil erosion and water loss. Subsistence farming is how a large majority of Africans make a living, and I consider how the challenges facing that one farmer are, in many ways, a microcosm of the myriad challenges facing the African farmer in particular, and Africa in general.

In chapter 2, I uncover some of the challenging legacies facing Africa, including colonialism. My aim is to show that while colonialism was devastating for Africa, it has become a convenient scapegoat for conflicts, warlordism, corruption, poverty, dependency, and mismanagement in the region. Africa cannot continue to blame her failed institutions, collapsed infrastructure, unemployment, drug abuse, and refugee crises on colonialism; but neither can these issues be understood fully without acknowledging the fact of Africa's past.

In chapter 3, I offer what I believe is a useful metaphor to describe a functioning society and contrast it with the history of Africa after the Cold War.

In chapters 4 and 5 I look at how aid, trade, and debt foster an imbalance in the relationship between Africa and the industrialized world, while in chapter 6 I discuss the deficit of leadership that exists in Africa and what can be done to change it. My concern in chapters 4 and 5 is not simply to criticize the international community for unfair trade practices and the heavy debt burden under which Africans still labor; it is to challenge all Africans to escape the culture of dependency that leads to passivity, fatalism, and failure. Likewise, my aim in chapter 6 is not to shame or blame, but to challenge all of African society, especially its leadership, to break free of the corruption and selfishness that exists, from high offices to the grassroots. Every African, from the head of state to the subsistence farmer, needs to embrace cultures of honesty, hard work, fairness, and justice, as well as the riches—cultural, spiritual, and material—of their continent.

In chapters 7 and 8, I describe in more detail the loss of culture I touch on in chapter 2: the lack of respect for some of the cultures in Africa, and the consequent devastating loss of self-confidence in many ethnic groups—what I call "micronations"—throughout the continent. As I investigate in more detail in chapter 8, my personal recognition of the importance of culture led me to create the Civic and Environmental Education seminars as part of the Green Belt Movement's work.

Through the seminars, I developed a concept that I call "The Wrong Bus Syndrome." Like travelers who have boarded the wrong bus, many people and communities are heading in the wrong direction or traveling on the wrong path, while allowing others (often their leaders) to lead them further from their desired destination. It is my analysis that much of Africa today is on the wrong bus.

Chapters 9 and 10 delve more deeply into the challenges of the African nation-state, or what I term the "macro-nation." For decades, Africans have belittled or ignored the fundamental cultural and psychological importance of micro-national identity, instead using ethnicity for political gain. I call for Africans to rediscover and embrace their linguistic, cultural, and ethnic diversity, not only so their nation-states can move forward politically and economically, but so that they may heal a psyche wounded by denial of who they really are.

Just as cultural diversity is essential for healthy human societies, so, too, is biological diversity. In chapters 11, 12, and 13 I argue for the centrality of the environment in all discussions of, and approaches to, addressing the challenges Africa faces. I look at the issues of land, agriculture, and conservation, particularly of forests. I then explore the enormous task, and necessity, of preserving central Africa's Congo Basin Forest Ecosystem.

Finally, in chapter 14, I reflect on the challenges facing the African family—both in the continent and in the diaspora. I urge Africans to support each other in their efforts to forge their own ways forward, and to believe that they can.

As I write, the world is in a financial crisis, caused in part by lack of oversight and deregulation in the industrialized world. The poor have long experienced the fallout of such greed and selfishness. For decades, Africa has been urged to emulate this financial system and practices acquired from the industrialized world. While this structure has enriched the West, practicing it without caution has only impoverished Africa. The current crisis offers Africa a useful lesson and its greatest challenge: nobody knows the solution to every problem; rather than blindly following the prescriptions of others, Africans need to think and act for themselves, and learn from their mistakes.

One

THE FARMER OF YAOUNDÉ

THE CHALLENGES Africa faces today are real and vast. Just as I began work on this book, my own country of Kenya was plunged into a pointless and violent postelection political conflict and humanitarian crisis that claimed more than a thousand lives and left hundreds of thousands homeless. As I write, internecine fighting still wracks the Darfur region of Sudan, Chad, southern Somalia, the Niger Delta, and eastern Congo. Zimbabwe's most recent election was marred by violence and a failure to tally the vote properly and reach a negotiated political settlement. Meanwhile, a series of violent attacks in South Africa against immigrants from other African countries left more than forty dead and forced tens of thousands to flee from their homes.[1] South Africa, a political and economic beacon in the region, appeared in peril of facing the conflicts many other African nations have experienced.

Drought and floods affect many countries in both western and eastern Africa. Natural resources are still being coveted and extracted by powers outside the region with little regard for the long-term health of the environment or poverty reduction; desertification and deforestation, through logging and slash-and-burn agriculture, are decimating species, water supplies, grazing grounds, and farmland, and contributing to recurring food emergencies. Shifting rainfall patterns, partly as a result of global climate change, directly threaten the livelihoods of the majority of Africans who still rely on the land for their basic needs. At the same time, sub-Saharan African countries are falling short of the benchmarks for health, education, gender equality, and environmental sustainability, which are among the eight Millennium Development Goals agreed on by the United Nations in 2000.

Although poverty rates in Africa have declined over the past decade, they remain stubbornly high.[2] HIV/AIDS, malaria, and tuberculosis—all preventable diseases—still take too many lives. In sub-Saharan Africa, one in six children dies before his fifth birthday, comprising fully half of the world's child deaths.[3] Conflicts ravage too many communities as rival groups vie for political and economic power. And the importance of Africans' cultural heritage to their own sense of themselves still isn't sufficiently recognized.

Nevertheless, in the half century since most African countries achieved independence and in the nearly two decades since the end of the Cold War, the continent has moved forward in some critical areas of governance and economic development. More African countries have democratic forms of governance, and more Africans are being educated. Debt relief has been granted to a number of African states, and international trade policies are now subject to greater scrutiny to assess their fairness, or lack of it. South Africa has made a successful, and peaceful, transition to full democracy from the time of apartheid. In 2002, Kenya held its first genuinely representative elections in a generation. Decades-long civil wars in Angola and Mozambique have ended. Liberia has emerged from a devastating series of internal and regional conflicts. In 2005, it elected to the presidency Ellen Johnson-Sirleaf, the first woman to head a modern African state, and the process of reconciliation and reconstruction is under way. Rwanda, a decade and a half after the 1994 genocide, has a growing economy, and Rwandan women constitute almost half of its parliament, the highest percentage in the world.[4]

After decades of dictatorship, instability, and extreme poverty, and a conflict that has claimed upward of five million lives, in 2006 the Democratic Republic of the Congo held elections overseen by the United Nations that were judged largely free and fair. A fragile peace holds between northern and southern Sudan, and efforts continue to bring an end to the civil war in northern Uganda. Since the early years of this century, a number of African economies have grown at more than 5 percent a year (and some at twice this rate), and African civil society—nongovernmental organizations, trade unions, civic associations, community-based groups, and ordinary citizens—is becoming bolder in speaking out in support of human rights and good governance. These are real achievements, and they belie the idea that Africans cannot take charge of their own affairs.

Of course, throughout the continent there are instances where forward motion and stasis are occurring simultaneously: efforts to battle corruption have been waged, but often incompletely; principled and visionary leaders are still too few in number; and while the world increasingly recognizes that Africa will be hit hard by climate change, the transfer of "green" technology from industrialized nations to the continent is slow, and forests in Africa continue to shrink.

MOVING BEYOND SUBSISTENCE

One morning in early September 2007, I stepped through the front door of my hotel in Yaoundé, the capital of Cameroon. I was there because the ten governments of Central Africa had appointed me the Goodwill Ambassador for the Congo Basin Forest Ecosystem in 2005, and I had come to familiarize myself with the secretariat of the Congo Basin Forest Partnership (CBFP) and the Commission for the Forests of Central Africa

(COMIFAC), headquartered in Yaoundé, and to meet the governments' ministers responsible for the economy and management of the forests.

Yaoundé is a metropolis whose 1.4 million people live among seven hills between the Nyong and Sanaga rivers in the south-central part of the country. The hotel was beautiful, modern, and clean; its location was similarly attractive, perched on one of those hills overlooking the city, with a view of Mount Cameroon, West Africa's tallest peak.

As I stood outside, I happened to look across from the hotel and saw a group of farmers on one of the hills, which was covered in thick vegetation except where the few men and women were working. It looked like they had planted a few banana and what appeared to be cassava trees, and were preparing the ground for more crops. As a light rain fell, I noticed that the farmers were making small depressions in the soil and then molding it into rows that were parallel to the gradient of the hill. I thought to myself, *Those people should not be working on such a steep slope, because they are very quickly going to lose all that soil when it rains.* Anxiously, I turned to ask the guards at the gate of my hotel why one of these farmers—a woman on whom my eyes had settled—was cutting the furrows downward, instead of against the gradient. "That way, when the rains come the water will run along the furrow and not disturb the crops," one of the young men replied, without hesitating.

Seeing the women and men on the hillside in Yaoundé didn't surprise me. Such a sight is not uncommon in many other cities and towns throughout the vast African continent. Whether it is in the middle of a big city like Yaoundé, Johannesburg, Dar es Salaam, or Nairobi, or in the countryside, the story is the same: slash and burn, plant, harvest once or twice, and move on to new land to repeat the same unsustainable process.

What amazed me, though, was the guard's response, although it could have come from any African in any country south of the Sahara. Yet this method of farming directly contradicted every principle of soil and species conservation I knew. Instead of making furrows across the gradient of the hill so the rainwater would pool in the small depressions and sink into the ground, where it would replenish belowground reservoirs, this farmer was doing just the opposite. She was guaranteeing that the soil, one of her most precious natural resources and one she'd so carefully formed and so desperately needed to make her crops grow, would be swept down the hillside when the rains fell—in the very furrows she had just dug! Not only was the woman making it easier for what she had planted to be washed away; she was also creating the perfect environment for the erosion of precious topsoil and loss of rainwater, making it less likely that *anything* would grow on the hillside in the future. And the hotel guards had no idea of the damage she was doing; they assumed that this was how farming was done. The tragedy is they are not alone.

I was struck by the irony of the situation. I was in Cameroon, a guest of the state, sleeping in a luxurious hotel and waiting for a car to take me to meetings to discuss how to safeguard the Congo Basin forests—an ecosystem of seven hundred thousand square miles in Central Africa. It is the second-largest intact expanse of forest in the world, after the Amazon rainforest, and is often referred to as the world's "second lung." I would be visiting government ministers, international donors, and officials of COMIFAC. All of us are charged with the responsibility of ensuring that the forests are sustainably managed for the benefit of everyone, including those subsistence farmers on the hill.

Whatever the outcome of our discussions, I knew one essential fact: no matter what else we were doing, unless those of us assembled at the COMIFAC headquarters could work with that farmer—multiplied by several million in Cameroon, and several million more in the ten countries of the Congo Basin region and, indeed, throughout Africa—not only would we not save the Congo forests, but we might also be unable to halt the rapid desertification under way across the continent.

Of course, the farmers I observed, and others like them, aren't the primary threats to the Congo Basin forests. Mining and timber concessions that feed the seemingly insatiable global demand for raw materials, as well as residual conflict and ongoing illegal logging in the eastern part of the region, are more directly destructive. But once the timber trucks and mining companies have literally made their inroads into the forests and cleared the trees, it is people such as these farmers who follow. They carve out small plots and cut the remaining vegetation for charcoal or small-scale subsistence agriculture, engage in poaching and the trade in bush meat, and complete the destruction.

Often, the soil in tropical forests is not well suited to agriculture and can be farmed for only a few years. Unless the subsistence farmers practice good land management, the soil degrades quickly, and they are forced to encroach further into the forests and grasslands. When rains fall, the earth is washed into the rivers, leaving barren land behind. As the trees are cut, the landscape is transformed, and the risks of soil erosion and desertification increase. In this way, a cycle is set in motion that not only threatens the survival of the people who rely on the ecosystems' resources—its watersheds and rainfall patterns, its flora and fauna—but also has the potential to endanger the climatic systems on which the entire planet depends.

To be sure, individuals such as myself—government ministers, university professors, civil society activists, and development specialists—need to be involved in crafting policies and legislation both within and across our countries' borders for utilizing natural resources sustainably and sharing them more equitably. But sometimes when we do our work in high-level meetings, we're not making changes where they really matter—in this case, in the world where that farmer places her blade in the soil. If she's not given assistance to stop farming the way she was on that hillside, she'll finish the business of destruction begun by the previous generation and exacerbated by poor governance, expanded by globalization, and intensified by the failure in Africa to focus on development that benefits the African people.

I don't blame the farmer for attempting to eke out a living. Because of my work with the Green Belt Movement planting trees with communities in Kenya, including many in the country's Central Highlands, I know how hard it is to grow anything on a slope! But, as I stood there that morning, the woman on the hillside in Yaoundé came to represent to me the collective challenges that face many African countries.

I wondered how much of the revenue of the hotel—which was owned by a foreign corporation—was making its way into the government's coffers, and then, in turn, how much of that money the government was investing in its agricultural sector, including in an extension service, that could educate the woman and assist her in farming more sustainably. I thought about what the farmer's situation might have been fifty or a hundred years earlier, when there were fewer people, stronger social and community networks, and no hotels, and whether a woman of that generation—someone not unlike my own mother, who grew her own food for almost her entire life—would have considered herself happier or wealthier than her fellow African subsistence farmer of today.

If the African states' agricultural extension services had not been underfunded or neglected in the decades since African nations became independent, this farmer not only might have learned the right way to prepare the soil for planting, she also might have had access to information, modern equipment, and governmental support that would have enabled her to farm more efficiently and less destructively. Perhaps she might even have had extension or agricultural cooperative officers who would have assisted her, instead of exploiting her and taking advantage of her poverty, illiteracy, and powerlessness. If, in turn, development practitioners and international agencies had, in their work with national governments, given more priority to investing in Africa's farmers, the continent's agriculture might not be in such poor condition today. And that woman farmer might not be practicing such destructive agriculture.

If African states had prioritized the budgets and work of the ministries of agriculture and environment instead of defense and internal security—indeed, if governments had concentrated on practical measures that helped their people rather than, at times, investing in grandiose, attention-seeking projects or misguided attempts to satisfy the demands of outside investors, often at the expense of their own peoples—then perhaps long ago the woman would have been provided with land more suitable for farming than that hillside.

If the continent's governments had organized their development priorities so that productive land itself had been used more wisely, natural resources conserved, and suitable urban planning undertaken, the farmer might not have been forced up that hillside. If they had addressed the inequities of land distribution left over from the colonial period, then not only might many of the conflicts that have plagued the continent been avoided or lessened in intensity, but this woman might not have been tilling that steep slope. If they had advocated more forcefully for the industrialized nations to reduce their own agricultural subsidies, and had argued for fairer trading terms, then this farmer might have had a greater number of markets and a better price for her produce.

If the African leaders had invested more in education, the creation of sustainable employment options, and inclusive economies, and if they had been more concerned with the welfare of their people and not with their own enrichment, then perhaps this farmer would have gone to school. Perhaps she would not have been a subsistence farmer but instead a manager for a larger, more efficient farm that could have freed her from grinding poverty.

I also asked myself this: How many people concerned with the continent's development—Africans and non-Africans alike—would even have noticed such a woman on the hillside? Although many of the politicians and others who work in the various ministries of the environment, public works, human development, or health throughout Africa are intelligent and educated, and may be highly motivated, how many even see farmers such as the ones I saw that day? Shuttled from hotel to conference center and back in luxury cars, accustomed to high-powered meetings with donors or officials, many policymakers may not take the time to recognize how hard the people of Africa are working to make a living in circumstances that are getting more difficult, day after weary day.

I may notice individuals like this woman because I have worked with people like her in the Green Belt Movement tree-planting campaign. I strongly believe that if Africa, particularly that part of the continent south of the Sahara, is to progress so it is no longer dependent on aid from the international community, or if it is to cease being a byword for poverty, conflict, and corruption, it is on hillsides like these and with women such as that farmer that we must work. That's where those of us concerned about the fate of Africa and her citizens must focus our energies, for it is where the vast majority of Africa's peoples are, and it is with their lives that we must engage.

Unless that farmer—and millions of others like her—acquires what she needs to develop her skills and educate herself and her children, and is encouraged to make decisions that can take her on a different path, then future generations will look back fifty or a hundred years from now and shake their heads. They'll experience expanding deserts and degraded lands, and increased numbers of displaced people migrating in search of food, water, and greener pastures, sometimes across national borders. They'll suffer through the inevitable conflicts that occur when people scramble for scarce resources.

THE LEADERSHIP REVOLUTION

The Challenge for Africa lays down a set of principles for what it will take to change the life of that farmer, who represents the 65 percent of Africans who continue to rely on subsistence agriculture; to avoid the crises of the future; and to ensure that Africans alive today experience good governance, basic freedoms that include respect for human rights, development that's both equitable and sustainable, and peace. Some of the measures I suggest to counter Africa's many challenges are practical—an engagement in grassroots democracy and the strengthening of civil society, so people's energies can be released to shape their own lives and development priorities, and governments can support them in realizing their vision.

Other measures are less tangible. Fundamentally, I argue, Africa needs a revolution in leadership—not only from the politicians who govern, but from an active citizenry that places its country above the narrow needs of its own ethnic group or community. Those in power—the presidents, prime ministers, politicians, and other elites—have to recognize that the way Africa has been conducting its affairs of state has neither protected nor promoted the welfare of the continent's citizens nor provided for the long-term growth and stability of its nations. This ought to be unacceptable to the new leadership in Africa.

The revolution I propose requires the development of policies that work for the benefit of all citizens rather than the advantage of a few. It necessitates standing up to international interests that seek access to the considerable natural resources with which Africa is blessed for less than their fair market value. It entails implementing decisions that encourage the dynamism and entrepreneurship of African peoples, protecting them from unfair competition, and nurturing economies that add value to the commodities the rest of the world desires so much.

The revolution demands that its leaders not merely support honesty and transparency in government from the president and the highest ministerial level to the grassroots, but embody it in their behavior as well. No longer should African leaders or their supporters play politics with ethnicity, grab public lands, sell off national resources, and loot the treasury—or tolerate such actions by others. They must foster values such as fairness, justice, and working for the common good rather than turning a blind eye to violence and exploitation, or promoting narrow self-interest and opportunism.

Perhaps the most important quality that the African leadership needs to embrace, and which is desperately lacking across the continent, is a sense of service to their people. Too many Africans still live in hope that their leaders will be magnanimous enough not to take advantage of their weakness and vulnerability, and instead to remove the causes for why so many continue to live in fear.

The revolution in leadership and the need to instill a sense of service cannot be confined only to those at the top of African societies, however. Even the poorest and least empowered of Africa's citizens need to rid themselves of a culture that tolerates systemic corruption and inefficiency, as well as self-destructive tendencies and selfishness. They must grasp the available opportunities and not wait for someone else magically to make development happen for them; they must realize that, no matter how meager their capacities and resources, they have the means to protect what is theirs. Africa's peoples, wherever they are in society, need to hold politicians and themselves accountable, value long-term sustainability over short-term gain and instant gratification, and plan wisely for an uncertain future rather than settle for an expedient present. Instead of milking the cow called *Africa* to death, everyone should feed, nurture, and love her so she can thrive and provide.

Africa has been on her knees for too long, whether during the dehumanizing slave trade, under the colonial yoke, begging for aid from the international community, paying now-illegitimate debts, or praying for miracles. At both the top and the bottom, all Africans must change the mind-set that affects many colonized peoples everywhere. They must believe in themselves again; that they are capable of clearing their own path and forging their own identity; that they have a right to be governed with justice, accountability, and transparency; that they can honor and practice their cultures *and* make them relevant to today's needs; and that they no longer need to be indebted—financially, intellectually, and spiritually—to those who once governed them. They must rise up and walk.

In confronting these challenges, the environment needs to be at the center of all decision making. Neither Africa nor the world can afford for the continent to continue to be solely the resource base for the industrialization and development of countries outside her borders—whether in Europe, the Americas, or Asia. Instead, together, African countries and the international community should enable the African peoples to protect their precious ecosystems—the land, wetlands, fisheries, rivers, lakes, forests, and mountains—and use them responsibly, equitably, and sustainably. Development practices must be conceived and implemented holistically.

If a critical mass of Africans adopts an attitude of preservation over exploitation, collective responsibility over individual gain, and common feeling for the continent rather than narrow ethnic nationalism, they will have a chance to survive. They will also have an opportunity to experience an African revival such as what I believe Thabo Mbeki, the former president of South Africa, envisioned when he invoked the African Renaissance.

My concern for an African revival is personal. As I described in my autobiography, *Unbowed,* my life represents the aspirations—as well as the complexities—of the contemporary African citizen. Unlike many others who write about or lead large-scale efforts in support of Africa, I am not an economist, a social scientist, or a political theorist. I haven't worked on the staff of a donor agency or large international development organization. Just about all my life has been spent in Kenya. By training, I am a biological scientist and taught for many years at the University of Nairobi. For five years I served in Kenya's parliament, as well as in the government of President Mwai Kibaki as an assistant minister for Environment and Natural Resources. But for more than thirty years I have remained a keen member of civil society, especially through my work with the Green Belt Movement.

I was raised in central Kenya in a rural village with no modern amenities. I grew up in the shadow of both Mount Kenya and colonialism's last throes. My community, the Kikuyus, was adversely affected by colonial expansion: traumatized by physical displacement, the gradual and systematic extermination of many good aspects of our culture, and the oppressive reaction to the Mau Mau struggle for self-determination and Kenya's independence. This history has challenged the community's ability to raise subsequent generations of children, many of whom have drifted onto the streets or are members of the outlawed Mungiki sect. Many African peoples experienced similar assaults on their societies over the course of several centuries. Such deculturation has left many Africans ill-equipped to deal with the forces of modernity, principally political and economic systems that are still alien to them, and may not be in their, or Africa's, best interests.

Yet I'm also someone who benefited extensively from the opportunities provided by a Western model of education, introduced by the colonial administration. I know firsthand how the liberating self-determination of Western culture can act as a positive force in one's life. (Without it, I probably wouldn't be writing this book and sharing my thoughts.) Nevertheless, I believe passionately in the need for African communities to discover the value of embracing their *own* destiny and determining their *own* futures, rather than solely and passively relying on outside forces.

My dual identities—both "Western" and "African," local and international, a member of the elite and someone from a rural background—capture the essence of what might be perhaps the deepest and most complex issue of all facing Africa: what it means to be an African today. Part of this identity is one not determined by Africans themselves. Too often, it seems, Africa has been seen as ungovernable, incomprehensible, and immune to the efforts of more enlightened nations' attempts to civilize it—in short, as unable to help itself. Africans too often have allowed themselves to be defined by these retrogressive stereotypes and have not seen themselves as they are: a spectacularly varied and dynamic cluster of what I call "micro-nations"—communities bound together by their environment, experiences, culture, and history that interact with other communities within the larger nation-state and region. Africans must reclaim and embrace their diversity if they are to flourish.

As the title of this book suggests, the work that needs to

be done will be hard, for those who lead as well as for those who are led. And while Africans should continue to welcome the international agencies, donor nations, and private ventures that have expressed an interest in helping the continent develop in a manner both sustainable and just, ultimately the fate of the continent depends on its citizens. It cannot be overemphasized: Africans must decide to manage their natural resources responsibly and accountably, agree to share them more equitably, and use them for the good of fellow Africans. Otherwise, they will continue to allow outside forces to seduce or bully their governments into arrangements that allow those resources to be removed from the continent for a pittance. It is for Africans to determine whether they will work hard to build up their own talents and abilities, strengthen their democracies and institutions of governance, and foster their peoples' creativity and industry. Or, instead, whether they will continue to nurture a culture of dependency through the acceptance of loans and development assistance, which has resulted in too many Africans waiting for outside help instead of unleashing their energies and capabilities and taking actions today that will improve their lives in the future.

Only Africans can resolve to provide leadership that is responsible, accountable, and incorruptible. It is they who must embrace their cultural diversity, restore their sense of self-worth, and use both to create thriving nations, regions, and the continent itself. It is they who must begin the revolution in ethics that puts community before individualism, public good before private greed, and commitment to service before cynicism and despair.

Of course, these challenges apply not only to Africa but to the world as a whole. It is a simple, although often overlooked, fact that the planet's biological resources are finite, and that the current development path is imperiling the ecosystems on which human life and livelihoods depend. Reimagining ways of relating to the environment must become the major concern of the citizens of every country on this planet. This is especially important now that the scientific consensus is that climate change is already upon us and that Africa in particular will be negatively impacted. The challenge for Africa is, therefore, a challenge for all of us, too.

Two

A LEGACY OF WOES

ONE OF THE major tragedies of postcolonial Africa is that the African peoples have trusted their leaders, but only a few of those leaders have honored that trust. What has held Africa back, and continues to do so, has its origins in a lack of principled, ethical leadership. Leadership is an expression of a set of values; its presence, or the lack of it, determines the direction of a society, and affects not only the actions but the motivations and visions of the individuals and communities that make up that society. Leadership is intimately influenced by culture and history, which determine how leadership perceives itself and allows itself to serve: whether it has self-respect, and how it shapes public and foreign policy. I have no doubt that independent African states would have made far more progress if they had been guided by leaders motivated by a sense of service to their people and who therefore practiced better governance, creating opportunities for their people to prosper.

Of course, poor leadership isn't an African invention, or a solely African reality. Colonizers, oppressors, and violators of human rights are to be found throughout history. In the modern era, dictatorships, military juntas, oligarchies, kleptocracies, and "Big Men" have bedeviled many nations in the world, as they have in Africa. These regimes have betrayed the aspirations and violated the rights of their people with impunity; they plundered national treasuries and resources, often plunging their citizens into fruitless wars, both civil and cross-border.

Many people who care about the fate of Africa question why so many postcolonial African leaders treated their citizens so cruelly, and why after nearly half a century of independence so many African countries still remain bywords for failure, poverty, and dysfunction. As with many issues associated with the condition of Africa, no simple answers exist. However, a number of factors can be pointed to that suggest why the continent continues to have a considerable leadership deficit. Among these are the legacy of colonialism, the Cold War, postcolonial governance structures, and cultural destruction.

BEYOND THE CONGRESS OF BERLIN

An important milestone in the creation of the modern leadership dilemma in Africa was the Berlin Conference in 1884–85.[1] Here, Great Britain, Germany, France, Italy, Portugal, and King Leopold II of Belgium, among others, carved up the African continent into spheres of influence. The European powers were seeking to establish not merely outposts from which they could launch campaigns against each other to preserve their geopolitical dominance, but also new sources for the raw materials they needed to expand their industrial economies—or, in Leopold's case, a personal fiefdom in Congo.[2] The territories established after the Berlin Conference served the interests of the colonial powers well. The administrations they set up were not interested in the genuine development of an empowered local populace; they were there either to ensure the flow of raw materials to the mother countries or to provide representation and organizational capacity for the white settlers who were encouraged to colonize the new territories, in the name of developing them, and to "civilize" and Christianize the native peoples.

As in any society, some natives, especially those in trouble with the local establishment, cooperated with the newcomers, sharing the community's secrets and lifestyle. In return for their "generosity," these collaborators (many of them outcasts) were elevated to the positions of chiefs, scouts, or church elders: positions that they would never have held in the traditional societies. This deliberate practice of ignoring or misunderstanding the complex and subtle existing leadership structures in favor of selecting leaders and imposing them on the population was the cornerstone of the colonial administration. Though they were members of the community, such chiefs and their assistants were de facto agents and information gatherers for the imperial powers. These local autocrats did everything they could to promote the oppressive, exploitative, and undemocratic authority of the colonial government and ruled their own people with even greater cruelty than the colonizers. In turn, they were empowered to arrest and detain any member of the community, regardless of that individual's standing. The colonial authorities' elevation of these individuals, and the imposition of them on an unwilling community, laid the foundation for an oppressive provincial administration that undermined indigenous systems of governance and justice. These newly powerful men became the new African elite.

The colonial administration could also confiscate the local population's most valued assets—land and livestock—especially from those who did not cooperate, thereby damaging both the basis of the local economies and Africans' right of ownership, their honor and honesty. Without any means of redress or restitution, communities' existing systems of justice and sense of fairness, including a traditional respect for privately held property, were rendered irrelevant: the power of the gun was the new form of administering "justice." In this way, a dictatorial regime was cultivated, imposed, and, in time, increasingly tolerated.

By the end of World War II, however, the economies of the European powers lay in ruins, and the imperial project of the previous four centuries was not only exhausted but also unsustainable. Many Africans who had been drafted and had fought for the colonial forces returned to their home countries with their horizons broadened and their "masters" ever so slightly demystified, and with a knowledge of guerrilla warfare. As a result, many colonized or conquered peoples throughout the world, including in Africa, were inspired to start campaigns to liberate themselves. In Kenya, this experience led to the Mau Mau freedom struggle. At the same time, within the United Nations, several individuals, including the American Ralph Bunche, head of the Department of Trusteeship and later undersecretary-general, put the issue of decolonization on the UN's agenda.

To a number of African men fell the task of freeing their peoples from the yoke of colonialism, humiliation, and exploitation. These men struggled and fought, with their people behind them, and with the example of those who had waged similar struggles against slavery and exploitation, especially in the Americas. (Although women participated in liberation efforts, they generally were not at the forefront and rarely held real power.) Over a period that spanned four decades, the peoples of Africa gained political independence. Many believed, often wrongly, that economic wealth would follow automatically.

Unfortunately, only a few leaders served and honored their long-suffering peoples by putting them first once independence was achieved. Many lacked principles and true leadership qualities; indeed, many were just ordinary men who happened to be in the right place at the right time. They dishonored the trust their people placed in them, and instead of standing up for them, many turned against the very individuals on whose shoulders they had stood to acquire power and the extensive privileges that came with it.

It is perhaps hard, looking back, to capture the excitement of the early years of independence, and how rapidly the transition took place. In January 1966, when I was twenty-five, I returned to Kenya, having completed my undergraduate and master's degrees in the United States. Six years earlier, I had gone to the United States as part of the Kennedy "lift," a visionary attempt to educate a generation of East African leaders to meet the challenges of independence. The initiative was supported by the U.S. Department of State and members of the prominent U.S. political family the Kennedys.

When I left Kenya, Jomo Kenyatta, the president of the Kenya African National Union (KANU), then a leading pro-independence political party, was still in internal exile, and the country was under a state of emergency imposed in 1952 by the British colonial administration after the outbreak of the Mau Mau war of liberation. When I returned, Kenya was independent, and Kenyatta was its first president. During the years I was away, Nigeria, Mauritania, Sierra Leone, Tanzania, Rwanda, Burundi, Algeria, Uganda, Malawi, Zambia, the Gambia, Botswana, and Lesotho also achieved independence. I remember the exultation that I and many other young Africans felt then and the commitment we shared to build the newly emerging countries that were now fully ours, on a continent returning to African control.

Disappointment lay ahead. By and large, newly independent nations made no efforts to change the inherited colonial systems of governance, even though they had been designed, principally, to facilitate the continued exploitation of human and natural resources of the colonies for the benefit of the colonial motherland. And, although they were relinquishing direct rule over their colonies, the European powers were eager to maintain economic ties with the new states and ensure a steady supply of the raw natural resources that had provided their countries with such wealth during the colonial period. The

departing administrators made sure that the leaders who eventually held power in the former colonies were as cooperative
politically as they were pliant economically. For all practical
purposes, it was simply a change of guards. Those leaders, like
Julius Nyerere of Tanzania, who sought to remain nonaligned
and who tried to forge a different path of development were iso-
lated, vilified, and denied support.

At the same time, those leaders who toed the line were
rewarded with political protection from would-be plotters of
coups d'états. They were given economic assistance they did
not have to account for, such as opportunities to open secret
bank accounts or purchase expensive villas in foreign capitals.
Their armies were well supplied with weapons and equipment,
which were used mostly to silence their own citizens. These
regimes violated human rights and remained unquestioned
even by those colonial powers that considered themselves
defenders of freedom and democracy.

Such was the legacy of colonialism in the newly independent states of Africa: it left the African people chained to a new
form of oppression. Throughout the first half of the twentieth
century, many colonial administrations had deliberately kept
local Africans undereducated and prevented them access to the
professional classes in order to avoid unnecessary competition
and to ensure that the new managers of the state could not
lead on their own. This helped maintain Africans' dependency.
The rapid withdrawal of colonial administrators left newly
independent countries with relatively few local people quali-
fied to manage the inherited colonial bureaucracies, or medical and service professionals to operate health services, the
business sector, schools, and other institutions. For example,
when Zambia achieved independence in 1964 there were only
about a hundred university graduates in the country.[3] It translated into a long delay before the new African nations and
citizens could develop the mechanisms of government that

would allow it and other institutions to function efficiently and independently. Unable to compete, but preferred by the nation-state when business licenses were issued, some Africans quickly succumbed to corruption and easy money. They often became so-called sleeping partners, who received dividends as nominal co-owners, while doing little for the business. Eventually, many failed and never caught up.

A further impediment to genuine autonomy was the fact that the countries of Africa became independent during the Cold War, which in Africa was far from cold. The United States and the Soviet Union and their allies not only were determined to maintain their axes of influence in Southeast Asia, Latin America, and the Caribbean, but also saw African nations as bulwarks against either Communism or U.S. expansionism. As a result, from the outset, countries throughout the continent were forced to ally themselves with either the Eastern or Western blocs. These divisions stifled any efforts to foster the cooperation, development, and unity that many Africans of my generation had hoped for and expected. Dictators and bad governance were at best ignored and at worst promoted. Those who refused to cooperate sometimes "disappeared" or were made irrelevant.

It was, therefore, hardly a surprise that barely six months after achieving independence from the Belgians in 1960, the Republic of the Congo's democratically elected prime minister, Patrice Lumumba, was overthrown in a coup, widely alleged to have been backed by a foreign government. Lumumba was said to have been murdered by forces loyal to then colonel Joseph-Désiré Mobutu, who would lead his own coup in 1965 and hold power for the next thirty years as president of the country he later renamed Zaire. The years I was away in the United States saw instability in a number of the new African states.[4] In the year 1965 alone, civil war broke out in Chad; the Southern Rhodesian government under Ian Smith unilaterally declared independence from Britain (only a guerrilla war would eventually achieve black majority rule in 1980, when the country was renamed Zimbabwe); and Pierre Ngendandumwe, the first Hutu prime minister of Burundi, was assassinated by a Tutsi extremist—a sign that the animosity between Hutus and Tutsis in both Burundi and Rwanda, fostered over generations by the colonial authorities, would not be "solved" even by self-government.

Following my return to Nairobi in January 1966, the governments of the Central African Republic, Upper Volta (Burkina Faso), and Nigeria were overthrown in military coups. A second coup in Nigeria the following year led to the Biafran War, which over three years killed an estimated three million people. The conflict in Sudan that had broken out between the mainly Muslim north of the country and the mainly Christian south shortly before independence in 1956 continued, and would lead to a series of civil wars that lasted until 2005. In February 1966, another coup allegedly backed by a foreign power ousted the founding president of Ghana, Kwame Nkrumah, forcing him into exile. Today, many Ghanaians and other Africans realize he was a wasted talent.

Nkrumah and other first-generation postcolonial leaders had recognized that the economic and political strength of their new nations would be enhanced if they worked collectively rather than separately. To that end, in 1963 the countries of Arabic-speaking North Africa and sub-Saharan Africa came together to create the Organization of African Unity (OAU), the precursor of the current African Union. The leaders identified three major goals: to decolonize the entire continent; to promote unity; and to effect economic and social development in order to rid Africa of ignorance, disease, and poverty. These were monumental tasks, perhaps beyond the scope of some of these leaders, especially given the inherited legacies of the slave trade, colonialism, and the burden of the Cold War between the United States, the Soviet Union, and their allies.

Rejecting the direct and indirect meddling by foreign powers in the politics of independent African nations, the OAU made efforts to exert some sovereignty and committed itself to a policy of nonintervention in the internal affairs of member states. Ultimately, this decision, while understandable in the historical circumstances in which it was made, would paralyze the organization's ability to stop gross human rights violations within Africa by African leadership. Perhaps it was also a clear reflection of the lack of financial and military means at the disposal of the OAU that would have been necessary to give weight to any actions against those considered rogue leaders. There were also many points of nonconvergence: history, language, ethnicity, race, culture, religion, and national boundaries. Even the difference between Francophone and Anglophone black Africa was a factor. It was hard for the OAU to establish a single identity, and not long after its inception it splintered into unofficial factions, rendering it largely ineffective.

Through the 1970s and '80s, the struggle for influence in Africa between the East and West intensified, precipitating some of the most devastating internal wars for political and economic control African nations had ever experienced. For instance, proxy wars consumed Angola and Mozambique for years, during which more than a million people lost their lives. Tragically, the power blocs of both West and East also used the Cold War to justify the tolerance throughout Africa of dictatorial leaders who oppressed and facilitated the exploitation of their people politically and economically, and who routinely violated the rights of any citizen who dared to ask questions or dissent. The superpowers and their allies supported these leaders with a combustible mix of development aid and massive quantities of weaponry. In subsequent years these arms not only helped to silence citizens, but whether in the hands of the state police or used by self-styled (and sometimes politically sponsored) street militias, they caused further carnage in the streets of many African cities.

THE CRACKED MIRROR

Another reason—both more nuanced and yet perhaps even more devastating—for the dearth of good leadership in Africa was the destruction of Africans' cultural and spiritual heritage through the encounter with colonialism. This experience, commonly shared among colonized peoples, is not widely acknowledged in analyses of the problems facing the continent of Africa, which tend to be economic or political in orientation. However, the lack of self-knowledge that comes from Africans' cultural deracination is one of the most troubling and long-lasting effects of colonialism. Like other peoples who experienced not only physical colonization but also what might be called a colonization of the mind, Africans have been obscured from themselves. It is as if they have looked at themselves through another person's mirror—whether that of a colonial administrator, a missionary, a teacher, a collaborator, or a political leader—and seen their own cracked reflections or distorted images, if they have seen themselves at all.

For five centuries, the outside world has been telling Africans who they are. In much the same way as happened with the Aborigines in Australia, the native peoples of North America, and the indigenous peoples of Amazonia, Africans were told that their societies were backward, their religious traditions sinful, their agricultural practices primitive, their systems of governance irrelevant, and their cultural norms barbaric.

It is only relatively recently that the work of archaeologists and historians has slowly been replacing long-held European preconceptions about Africa as the "dark continent." These scholars have discovered that the continent in the centuries before the arrival of the Europeans had sophisticated civilizations, substantial governance structures, and cultural artifacts to rival any in the Europe of that time. For example, the central African kingdom of Kongo, which spanned 130,000 square miles and contained over half a million people, survived for centuries until the Portuguese slave trade reduced it to a virtual vassal state. The Mali Empire during the fourteenth century was larger than western Europe and, according to some contemporaries, one of the richest states in the world. During the time of its successors, the Songhai of the fifteenth and sixteenth centuries, the renowned University of Sankore at Timbuktu, one of the oldest seats of learning in the world, reached the heights of its achievements.

The Ashanti dominated West Africa from the seventeenth to the nineteenth century. The kingdom of Benin spread south and west to the Niger Delta during the fifteenth century, while Dahomey (in modern-day Ghana and Benin) flourished from the sixteenth to the end of the nineteenth century. The Zulu nation resisted the British and Boer expansion into southern Africa; Zanzibar traded spices with India and the Arab world; and the city of Great Zimbabwe was a center of commerce that archaeological evidence suggests may have done business with Arabia—and, if the discovery of pottery shards from Nanjing is any indication, possibly with China as well.

To be sure, some of these states, like those of their eventual European conquerors, were imperialist, collected tributes, and engaged in slavery, across both the Atlantic Ocean and the Arabian Sea. However, contrary to the image of Africans perpetually at war with each other, there is no evidence that these civilizations were any more aggressive or perpetrated more atrocities than the colonialists who subdued them. Indeed, until the expansion of the slave trade in the eighteenth and nineteenth centuries, when as many as twenty-five million people were removed from Africa's shores (and new diseases wiped out both people and livestock), Africans had seen their wealth increase along with advances in technology, learning, and the arts. Some communities possessed huge herds of cattle and had mastered the ability to refine precious metals and mineral deposits.[5]

Given that advanced indigenous African civilizations were a reality, why were most African societies so vulnerable to European powers? One obvious factor was that African leadership and the slave traders developed an insatiable greed as the demand for slaves increased across the Atlantic. Another was the products of the Industrial Revolution and the advances of Western medicine that followed the debilitating effects of slavery. Ordinary Africans were awestruck at the power, knowledge, and skills displayed by the colonial administrators and missionaries; dazzled by the healing power of their medicines; and stunned by the speed of their transportation when horses, rickshaws, and, later, trains ("fire-spitting snakes") and cars arrived. All of these new technologies overwhelmed the native peoples, whose technology was demonstrably less developed.

Most impressive of all, however, was the power of the gun, which was presented to the African populations as the white man's magic and witchcraft—and a very strong witchcraft at that. For the colonial powers, everything depended on intimidating the natives through the display and use of force, because if the local peoples had been less impressed, they would have been harder to subdue and exploit.

Nonetheless, in spite of the often terrible and disproportionate retribution for opposing the colonial powers, many African nations resisted the foreign intrusion and acquisition of their lands and property wherever they could. The Ashanti waged four wars with the British during the nineteenth century; Samory Touré fought French expansion in western Africa and the Sudan for decades, while the Zulus famously battled the British in 1879; and the Hehes of German East Africa (who live in what is now modern-day Tanzania) fought the colonial administration in the early years of the twentieth century. Some African communities played imperialist forces off each other in a desperate attempt to ensure their survival as the Great Powers fought for control of the continent's human beings, rubber, gold, ivory, diamonds, cacao, timber, and fertile lands. Nevertheless, the gun proved far superior to magic, or the spear, shield, and bow and arrow. Tens of thousands of native Africans were killed mercilessly so the newcomers could access their wealth or settle on their lands. Eventually, the military power of the intruders overwhelmed Africa, and the Europeans carved its territory into spheres of control. Overwhelmed, many Africans were hauled onto reservations.

Perhaps nothing from the West, however, had greater power over conquered natives worldwide than the legal and economic systems the imperial powers imposed, along with exposure to the Bible. Before the missionaries came to sub-Saharan Africa in the mid- to late nineteenth century, contact beyond the coasts had mainly involved trade in slaves and ivory; Islam, which had been in Africa almost since its beginning in the seventh century CE, generally remained confined to the regions north of the Sahel and on the coast; and neither Arabs nor Europeans made much effort to introduce their cultures to the natives in the hinterlands.

Culture in Africa had remained mostly oral, with the tenets, triumphs, and troubles of its peoples transmitted from generation to generation through word of mouth or tradition. When written culture finally arrived in sub-Saharan Africa, especially with the missionaries, Africans were mesmerized by the records that were proclaimed to be the words of God.

While the native peoples knew and worshipped God, they didn't know that anything had been written about him. The

Bible was presented to the inhabitants as more relevant to their lives than the oral knowledge, traditions, and wisdom of the culture that had sustained them up to that point. They were told that Christianity not only represented a better expression of devotion than their own cultural practices, but indeed was the true faith; to question its authority or that of those who interpreted it was a sin and indeed heretical. To local peoples all around the world, including Africa, the Bible became the entry point to a new way of life that was guided by a new priesthood, whose power and authority were reinforced by the conquerors' guns. If some parts of the Bible contradicted the traditional wisdom of the local community's ancestors or were incomprehensible, what was needed, the natives were told, was not any effort to explain God's mysteries, but faith, and faith alone.

Missionaries certainly provided an opportunity for communities to become literate—though only the Bible was available to read. Rather than take the foreign scriptures as works of human beings inspired by the Divine, however, the native peoples took them to be the literal words of God, whether dictated or even written by God himself. Neither the missionaries nor teachers saw the need to correct such misinformation; often they believed it themselves.

However well-meaning the missionaries may have been in spreading what they perceived to be the Good News of Jesus Christ, the result of their evangelism was the beginning of a deep cultural inferiority complex among their African converts. Many assumed that God favored them less; that God had decided not to reveal himself to them directly but only to others—the Europeans—who were now offering them God's messages. If the favored communities, such as the colonialists and missionaries, had been chosen to receive the holy inspiration from God and offer it to other peoples, it was self-evident that their way of life, culture, and mores were superior, and that native life and culture would have to change. Moreover, went Africans' reasoning, not only would they be welcomed into a superior culture should they accept the teachings of the Book, but they also would be blessed in the eyes of God.

Africans' acceptance of their own "inferiority" partly explains why, in spite of the political and armed resistance they marshaled, so many cultures fell to the gunboats and missionaries in the latter half of the nineteenth and early years of the twentieth centuries. Within a few decades, everything foreign—that which the colonial administrators and missionaries brought forth—became synonymous in the local peoples' minds with what was more advanced, closer to God's wishes, and in all ways preferable to their previous way of life and values. The existence they had led before the arrival of the colonial powers and missionaries became not only unworthy, but sinful. Some peoples were even encouraged to consider themselves the children of Ham, who saw his father, Noah, naked and was cursed (see Genesis 9:22). Christianity would lift this curse Africans had lived under for centuries without their knowing it; they were baptized children of God and finally available for his mercy.

It didn't occur to the local communities or even the bearers of this message that, in the same way the Israelites were the children of their God, so were they of theirs. The idea that God speaks and inspires all peoples and gives them what they need to lead them through life was lost to the missionaries. Where there had been priests, teachers, and wisemen and -women, who carried with them the knowledge required to sustain the people and recollect their history in order to teach future generations, all local populations became perpetual students of the new knowledge and wisdom. Inherent in the very nature of being a learner and not a teacher is an inability to be master of one's own world. One is forever being led, forever having to look for guidance from someone else, forever vulnerable to a master's misinformation or exploitation.

As Christianity became embedded in Africa, so did the idea that it was the afterlife that was the proper focus of a devotee, rather than this one—a legacy that continues to affect development. Putting so much emphasis on the delights of heaven and making it the ultimate destination devalues life in the present. It is as if all happiness and satisfaction, as well as relief from material wants and needs, will be found in heaven, not on Earth.

In my view, such an attitude allows institutions (such as the church) and powerful people (a member of parliament or other politician) to encourage people to remain passive. The people come to believe, in effect, that they will ultimately be saved by an outside force rather than by the sum of their actions. They may know they have a problem, for instance, with soil being swept into rivers when the seasonal rains come, or their sand dams being blocked. They may understand that they can change their situation, since neither planting trees nor scooping excess soil from the river requires heavy machinery or advanced technical skills. Yet they sit and wait for their MP, the church, an aid agency, or a foreign government to solve the problem. They devalue their own capacity and responsibility to act. This legacy of colonialism persists and remains devastating.

A further cause of vulnerability is the fact that those communities whose cultures and religions are oral rather than written and institutionalized are always likely to be more susceptible to the destabilizing forces of colonialism, unrest, or war. Across Africa, over the course of several decades, the cultures of many communities were pushed into irrelevance. The wisdom-keepers were dismissed as sorcerers and witches, and what they knew about their communities—the ceremonies, symbols, stories, dances, folklore—died with them.

The indigenous priesthood was replaced by a Christian one, which was defined as innately superior. The ways communities had learned about the land they lived on, the peoples who surrounded them, the God they worshipped, and their own reasons for being were lost as missionary schools replaced traditional systems of learning.

The Bible and the gun were not the only ways to impress the natives. There were the cotton clothes that replaced the wearing of animal skins. There was soap and salt and sugar. The use of stone and cement was a very new technology that allowed the building of large rectangular houses with many rooms, as opposed to traditional circular homes built with mud and thatch. There were also household goods that replaced calabashes, earthen pots, straw trays, and a whole range of artifacts. Instead, there came the glamour of official clothing, accoutrements, and mannerisms. All these were forceful symbols of the intruders' self-image and power and were embraced as tokens of modernity, gentility, and success.

This impressive materialism and social advantage stood to be acquired by the locals if they allowed the newcomers to settle on their lands and teach them the new ways of life. To inherit all these, the communities needed to accept the world of the missionaries and denounce their own culture. Furthermore, the colonialists and the missionaries didn't always have to push their ideas down the throats of the colonized population; once subdued, the public on their own accepted opportunities to become followers and collaborators. Some of the missionaries were welcomed into communities and naturalized by the elders, and lived among them as one of their own.

For most Africans, the imposition of colonialism—whether through conquest, immigration, or the demands of an unfair trading system—in the nineteenth and twentieth centuries happened too fast for them to be able to adopt the new way of life and at the same time control the loss of their cultures and civilizations. For some communities in Africa, though, the colonial experience was limited or short-lived, such as in Ethiopia and Botswana. Others were marginalized or ignored. For example, the pastoralist Maasai were stubborn in their unwillingness to cooperate with the colonial authorities, which were mainly interested in acquiring land for commercial farming. In Kenya, the Maasai were moved from much of their land and restricted to reservations that other Africans needed special permission to enter. As their interaction with the colonial authorities and missionaries was limited, the Maasai were able to keep their culture more intact. Ironically, it is the Maasai who are proud symbols of Kenya to tourists, precisely because they didn't surrender their culture and accept the vision presented to them through the cracked mirror.

Perhaps the ultimate irony of the arrival of the Bible and the gun in Africa rests in the fact that it's almost exclusively because of the writings of the missionaries, the colonialists, and the Western social historians—those who largely dismissed the traditions of Africans as primitive tribal customs—that we know anything about many of the cultural practices of precolonial African peoples. When Africans desire to rediscover and reclaim their own culture, they're often obliged to travel to European and American libraries and archives for the information. It isn't unusual to find that foreigners know more about the native peoples than the latter know about themselves. Such is often the fate of the colonized.

Africans have been shaped by many experiences: invasion, the slave trade, liberation, discrimination, and apartheid; the arrival of literacy, Christianity, and Islam; and deculturalization and displacement. Some were beneficial and revolutionized the African way of life; others were destructive.

All these experiences have touched and shaped the African psyche. Perhaps because of the intensity, frequency, and persistence of these challenges, it has been more difficult for the

African spirit to overcome them than it has been for other peoples who experienced similar upheavals. The African leadership often failed to help its people deal with the impact of these experiences and instead tended to deny that they ever happened. Because Africa has not had a culture of writing, it has been easy to promote a culture of forgetting.

For instance, few Africans fully understand the history of the Atlantic slave trade, because for many generations this period was kept out of oral or written history and is largely unspoken of in Africa, even though Africans were the victims. If history is not passed orally from generation to generation, and it is not written in history books so that it is deliberately taught to the next generation, it quickly disappears from memory. Those who wrote the history of Africa that is taught in schools were often the perpetrators of the wrongs that were done and wrote from their perspective. Quite obviously, they preferred to "forget and move forward."

It is often outside Africa that Africans begin to discover the untold story of slavery and other terrible deeds done to and by them on the continent. Many Africans are shocked when they discover the truth about their ancestors during the slave trade and colonial expansion. Now, finally, a more balanced history is being written by researchers who can access classified information, which may have been state secrets until recently.

THE NEW NATION-STATES

As hurriedly and haphazardly as the European powers drew lines across the map of Africa in 1885, so in the 1950s and '60s did they retreat from their colonies. They coalesced groups of people to form nation-states, and many groups found themselves herded together into these new entities and identities. In eastern Africa, for instance, the Maasai were placed in Kenya and Tanzania; the Teso in Kenya and Uganda; the Somalis in

Kenya, Ethiopia, and Somalia; and the Luos in Kenya, Uganda, and Tanzania. The new nation-states were given a name, a flag, and a national anthem, and then handed over to a select group of Western-educated elites, most of whom were sympathetic to the colonial administration, whether they had been groomed for leadership by them or imprisoned or exiled instead.

The process of deculturization continued after independence, as the division between the new African elites and the peoples they governed continued to widen. The peoples of Africa were very disadvantaged—economically, in terms of education, and with their cultures destroyed. As a result, they were not in a position to hold their leaders accountable, and unfortunately their leaders took advantage of that fact. In addition, many of the new African states retained many elements of colonial governance, which leaders used to the same ends as the colonialists. They exploited their peoples in the name of progress, employment, and a better quality of life, and accumulated wealth for themselves, their families, and their friends, often corruptly and at the expense of the majority of their citizens. They adopted the attitude of the former European masters and did whatever they deemed necessary to maintain power. They took advantage of their peoples and then shed crocodile tears over their continued poverty, conflicts, and all the other ills associated with the continent.

Such wholesale robbery and destruction could have been achieved only through continuing to cultivate the culture of disempowerment, learned from the colonizers, that kept the great mass of people ignorant, fearful, passive, and obedient. The people's ignorance was promoted through the direct control of the flow of information. The national radio and television networks were monopolized and controlled. Public meetings and gatherings were disallowed so that citizens heard and did only what the state machinery let them hear and do.

The provincial administration, an agent of oppression and

one of the worst holdovers of colonial times, addressed the local people in languages that they did not fully comprehend; the people, either out of politeness or out of fear for their own safety, pretended they understood their new masters and applauded enthusiastically at the end of public speeches. Meanwhile, the leaders promised the show of good government. The citizens clapped with much enthusiasm at the empty assurances, and thanked the leaders for goods and services they never received. For the many peoples of Africa, the dreams of the postcolonial era were shattered.

Like many Africans, I have a deep ambivalence toward Africa's "founding fathers," to say nothing of the second generation of political leadership. I am aware that, whatever their flaws or crimes, the first generation of postindependence leaders were all born subjects of European powers. The land of their fathers had been invaded and occupied, and their people subdued and colonized. One might argue that, when they looted the treasury and the natural resources at the expense of their own people and country, or made it easy for others to do the same, they were only doing what their former masters had taught them to do. And the people so wanted to believe in their indigenous African leaders that they might not have been willing to acknowledge the scale of the crimes committed against them, or feel they had the moral authority or the right to hold their leaders accountable.

Perhaps even more troubling than the heads of state themselves were their inner circles, the local administrators, and politicians, many of whom in the decades before independence had been collaborators with the colonial administration. As such, they had never had their own peoples' best interests at heart, but, rather, actively worked against them. At independence, many of these men were not held accountable for what they had done but instead were rewarded with political and economic power, which they continued to wield against their peoples during the Cold War, and even after it ended. One wonders how many potential postindependence leaders who did not cooperate with the colonial authorities were sidelined or even executed by those same authorities, and who might have provided, in the end, better leadership for their people. It's a question that now, of course, can't be answered.

The gulf between the elites and the mass of the people still remains wide—not least concerning cultural identification. Even today, many African elites in government and elsewhere continue to trivialize their indigenous cultures and consider them retrogressive and irrelevant in today's world. At the national level, the continent's varied micro-national heritages are deliberately defined very narrowly to mean, for instance, traditional dances performed for politicians during ceremonial occasions or for tourists looking for the "authentic" or "exotic" Africa. In schools, on the radio, and on television, little of African culture is given serious attention, while other peoples' heritages are glorified. Many Africans very quickly embrace alternative cultures, principally from the West. For many today, that is all they know. It is a reflection of their society's material, political, and spiritual impoverishment.

Few African leaders recognize that what they call the "nation" is a veneer laid over a cultureless state—without values, identity, or character. Those who would promote local cultures and practices are still accused of fostering "tribalism" and division rather than unity. They are urged to shed the identity of their micro-nations and become citizens of the new modern state, even though no African really knows what the character of that modern state might be beyond a passport and an identity card.

Nearly fifty years from the time when we young Africans (including a Kenyan named Barack Obama Sr.) boarded planes for further study in the United States, none of us could have imagined the conflicts, the coups, the civil wars, and the corruption of the imperial presidencies that would dog our continent for decades to come, or that the promise of Africa, which seemed almost inevitable at the time, would remain unfulfilled. The challenge continues for each new generation of Africans.

Three

PILLARS OF GOOD GOVERNANCE:
THE THREE-LEGGED STOOL

IN THE 1960s, those of us Africans who entered the professions—medicine, teaching, business, and the civil service—felt confident that our continent was on the move, in spite of the emerging instability. Humanitarian and development arms of the international community did too, at least enough to advance substantial amounts of aid, technical assistance, and technology, and, at times, to adopt policies that urged more accountability in the management of state affairs. In 1964, western Europe and North America gave grants and inexpensive loans to sub-Saharan African nations amounting to more than $1 billion.[1] Huge potential existed to develop Africa's natural resources, such as bauxite, uranium, gas, oil, gold, and diamonds. Indeed, in the 1960s, growth in many African economies was robust.

ECONOMIC DECLINE

It was in the 1970s, however, that the continent's economic fortunes began to decline. In an analysis published in 2003, the National Bureau of Economic Research, a U.S. nongovernmental organization (NGO), indicated that while the world economy grew by an average of almost 2 percent a year between 1960 and 2002, in Africa GDP growth was negative from 1974 to the mid-1990s.[2] By 2003, average sub-Saharan GDP was 11 percent lower than thirty years previously. Whereas in the early 1960s only 10 percent of the world's poor were African, by the year 2000 50 percent were.

In the forty-year period between 1960 and 2001, according to the World Bank, the Republic of Korea's average per capita annual growth rate was 5.8 percent a year, while China's and Singapore's was 5.6 percent. By contrast, over the same period, Côte d'Ivoire's rate was only half a percent, Zimbabwe's a third of a percent, and Nigeria's a fifth of a percent. Conversely, average per capita annual growth rates in Ghana, Senegal, Chad, the Central African Republic, Zambia, Sierra Leone, Madagascar, Niger, Liberia, and the Democratic Republic of the Congo were all negative. Given the fact that the population of the continent increased more than threefold, from 277 million in 1960 to over 900 million in 2008, not even those economies that grew were able to meet the basic needs of their people. Botswana, whose economy expanded by an average of 6.4 percent per year from 1960 to 2001, remains an exception to the anemic economic performance of the rest of continental sub-Saharan Africa.[3]

Like other developing regions, Africa has had to contend with a set of external conditions imposed by the industrialized world that were meant to combat poverty and foster growth, even though they sometimes had precisely the opposite effect. For decades, African states were offered or even urged to accept loans to finance large-scale development projects. Many of these were inappropriate to Africa's needs or simply fronts for official corruption. As the debt and interest payments mounted, African states were more often than not returning more funds to the industrialized countries than they were receiving in aid. In spite of their demonstrable corruption and lack of democratic bona fides, many leaders of African countries continued to receive funding from international agencies and donor nations, inhibiting the prospects for development and further impoverishing the African people.

In the 1980s, in part as a response to the vicious cycle of indebtedness that had been created between the rich and poor worlds, the international financial institutions, principally the World Bank and the International Monetary Fund, launched "structural adjustment policies." In order to receive more loans or development aid, states were required to drastically cut back government expenditures, privatize state-owned companies, reduce inflation, charge fees for services like health care and education, and endeavor to create export-oriented economies rather than focus on the immediate needs of their people for food and essential services. While these policies were, in part, an effort to root out the corruption that by this time riddled many government agencies in Africa and elsewhere, the budgetary austerity forced on poor nations often led to the gutting of essential services like agricultural extension, infrastructure, health, and education. Despite the broad application of structural adjustment, from the perspective of most African citizens, governance did not measurably improve. Nor did the quality of their lives.

HOPE RENEWED: THE END OF THE COLD WAR

The fall of the Berlin Wall in November 1989 and the collapse of the Soviet Union in 1991 removed one of the blockages to development in Africa. African leaders no longer had to pledge allegiance to either the Soviet or the American axis—whether they had an ideological commitment or not. These events put African governments on notice that even they could not continue to deny democratic space to their citizens indefinitely. The two superpowers encouraged leaders to accept, in theory at least, the proposition that the one-party rule that had been the norm for decades hadn't fulfilled the aspirations of the

African peoples, and that multipartism was worth trying. This was initially resisted. The reintroduction of multipartism in many African nations resulted from demands by donor nations, as well as from the many years of struggle by African civil society for better governance.

Another powerful sign that the Cold War was over and that entrenched systems could change was the release of Nelson Mandela in February 1990 after twenty-seven years in prison, followed by the formal end of apartheid in South Africa four years later. Mandela's release also fulfilled one of the main aims of the much-maligned Organization for African Unity: the political decolonization of the entire African continent.

The end of apartheid heartened citizen-activists in Africa and, indeed, around the world. In many African nations, civil society intensified its challenge to the policies of dictatorial governments and engaged in opposition politics. Citizens of the industrialized nations also grew less accepting of their governments' support for despotic regimes, particularly as details of some of the leaders' depredations became more widely known. Governments began to deliver loans and aid to African heads of state with demands that they respect human rights, improve governance, end one-party political rule, curtail corruption, and focus on poverty reduction.

During this period, some of the "Big Men" whose personas came to dominate the political life of their country were leaving the stage: President Félix Houphouët-Boigny, who had ruled Côte d'Ivoire for more than thirty years, died in 1993, and Hastings Banda, Malawi's leader for three decades, was defeated in a democratic election the following year. In 1991, presidents Kenneth Kaunda of Zambia and Mathieu Kérékou of Benin allowed multipartism and soon after left office. (Kérékou was reelected to the presidency in 1996, and served for a further decade.) Others had their power wrested from them by other would-be Big Men: Muhammed Siad Barre of Somalia and Mengistu Haile Mariam of Ethiopia were both forced from power in 1991; in Zaire, the ailing Mobutu Sese Seko was forced to give way in 1997 to the rebel fighters of Laurent Kabila.[4]

However, while the iron grip of the first generation of African Big Men and their successors loosened, it was not fully freed. Nor was Africa's crisis of leadership over. The relieving of tensions frozen by the Cold War and the end of some regimes threatened the very existence of a number of nation-states. Some collapsed, while, uncertain and threatened, those in charge of such weakened states succumbed to corruption. More and more, African states came to resemble a crumbling house from which both the owner and the onlookers scrambled to escape with whatever could be looted. Citizens became prisoners and refugees within their own borders, denied freedom of speech, movement, assembly, and association, and treated with less respect than foreigners in their own land.

Governments that felt at risk from a stronger civil society and growing demands both domestically and internationally to open their political systems responded by, in some cases, using ethnicity to set communities against each other. This was the situation in Kenya throughout the 1990s and, on a far more devastating scale, in Rwanda in 1994. No one was safe. Leaders tried to hold on to resources that had become personal fiefdoms.

Along with the political changes brought about by the end of the Cold War, a new economic consensus emerged that free markets and free societies would reinforce each other and that the integration of the global economy through trade and information sharing ("globalization")—now unhindered by the long-standing barriers between West and East—would lift poor countries, along with eastern Europe and the nations of the former Soviet Union, out of their economic doldrums.

Throughout the 1990s, Africa and other poor regions were assisted by donors and encouraged by development agencies to accept the free trade agenda of the newly formed World Trade Organization. In effect, this meant orienting their economies to increase exports, while further opening their markets to foreign goods. When such largely unregulated liberalization failed to make much of a dent in poverty or spur high rates of growth, however, the IMF, World Bank, and the U.S. Treasury Department prescribed new measures. In what became known as the Washington Consensus, poor countries were encouraged—in some cases mandated—to further liberalize their policies on trade and the free flow of capital. In order to accelerate GDP growth, nations were urged to continue privatization programs, curtail government functions, and deregulate their industries.

In the 1990s and the early years of the twenty-first century, some African economies did begin to grow. But by 2001, the number of people in Africa living in extreme poverty had nearly doubled to 316 million, from 164 million twenty years before.[5] And along with international campaigners advocating fair trade and working against debt and poverty, a growing number of economists, among them the Nobel laureate Joseph Stiglitz, began to view the prescriptions of the Washington Consensus as neither concerned enough with equity—who benefited from these policies—nor focused sufficiently on the economic sustainability of global GDP growth and its political, social, and environmental ramifications.

As the twenty-first century began, many African nations had relatively new heads of state. These rulers, a number of whom came to power through coups or civil wars or both, may not have been as oppressive to their peoples as those they succeeded, but they did not usher in the needed revolution in leadership. In 1999, Côte d'Ivoire underwent a military coup followed by a civil war that pitted the north against the south in what was once considered one of Africa's most successful nations (its capital, Abidjan, was long known as the Paris of

Africa). From the late 1990s to early in the twenty-first century, Africa's first "world war" consumed the Democratic Republic of the Congo, eventually including soldiers from nine other African nations. The toll was grisly: while many combatants were killed, civilians were the prime victims; thousands of women were raped as a tactic of war; hundreds of thousands of men, women, and children are still in refugee camps; and five million or more have succumbed to basic diseases or malnutrition that went unaddressed.[6]

In the main, however, Africa's current heads of state are an improvement over those of the previous four decades. Few African leaders today dare to be as autocratic as their predecessors. In nearly all sub-Saharan African countries, democratic space has increased and opposition movements are stronger than they were (although, of course, this varies by region and country). More leaders than ever before in postindependence Africa have their actions scrutinized or checked by an increasingly vocal and sophisticated civil society, and a freer and at times vibrant press. In addition, more heads of government have their time in office limited by set terms and elections— although these are not always accepted to be free and fair, as recent votes in Ethiopia, Guinea, Nigeria, Kenya, Togo, and Zimbabwe demonstrate.

Despite the emergence of more responsive leadership on the continent, the benefits Africans see in democratic countries in other parts of the world have yet to become tangible. Although in 2008 the average growth rate across sub-Saharan African economies was expected to reach 6.7 percent[7]—above the global average—the fruits of better management of state affairs have yet to reach most people and are not spread equally around the continent or even within countries. Unlike in China and India, millions have not been lifted out of poverty.

As of 2005, half the population of sub-Saharan Africa (approximately 380 million) live on the equivalent of $1.25 a day or less—a proportion that matches the 1981 level.[8] Average income in the countries of sub-Saharan Africa is about what it was in the 1970s.[9]

In 2006, the United Nations Children's Fund (UNICEF) reported that a quarter of African children under five were underweight. Because of the AIDS pandemic, average life expectancy in sub-Saharan Africa has increased by only seven years (to forty-seven) since 1960. According to the World Health Organization, nearly twenty-five million people in sub-Saharan Africa are living with HIV.[10] Botswana, so long a beacon of political stability and economic growth, is challenged by the fact that a quarter of its citizens are HIV positive, a key factor in the decline of the average life expectancy from sixty-five years in 1995 to forty years in 2005.[11]

In the 2007/2008 UN Human Development Report, all of the twenty-two lowest-ranked countries—in terms of life expectancy at birth; adult literacy rates; combined gross enrollment ratio for primary, secondary, and tertiary education; GDP per capita; life expectancy index; education index; and GDP—were from Africa south of the Sahara. Alone of sub-Saharan African states, the island nations of Mauritius and the Seychelles were ranked in the top one hundred of the report's Human Development Index.[12]

REMAKING THE THREE-LEGGED STOOL

A definite hunger for the reintroduction of democracy exists among African peoples after being denied it for so many years. At the same time, some of the current so-called democracies are deliberately weak or still unfolding. Too often, the term "democracy" has simply become a bromide offered during voting, rather than a means of enhancing the capacities of governmental and nongovernmental institutions, providing basic services to the people, and empowering them to be active partners in development.

All political systems, institutions of the state, and cultural values (as well as pathways toward, and indicators of, economic growth) are justifiable only insofar as they encourage basic freedoms, including human rights, and individual and collective well-being. In that respect, democracy doesn't solely mean "one person, one vote." It also means, among other things, the protection of minority rights; an effective and truly representative parliament; an independent judiciary; an informed and engaged citizenry; an independent fourth estate; the rights to assemble, practice one's religion freely, and advocate for one's own view peacefully without fear of reprisal or arbitrary arrest; and an empowered and active civil society that can operate without intimidation. By this definition, many African countries—and, indeed, many societies in both the developing and developed worlds—fall short of genuine democracy. Likewise, "development" doesn't only entail the acquisition of material things, although everyone should have enough to live with dignity and without fear of starvation or becoming homeless. Instead, it is a means of achieving a quality of life that is sustainable, and of allowing the expression of the full range of creativity and humanity.

In trying to explain both my work and my philosophy in the wake of being awarded the Nobel Peace Prize, I was reminded of the traditional African stool, which is comprised of a seat and three legs. The first leg represents democratic space, where rights—whether human, women's, children's, or environmental—are respected. The second leg symbolizes the sustainable and accountable management of natural resources both for those living today and for those in the future, in a manner that is just and fair, including for people on the margins of society. The third leg stands for what I term "cultures of peace." These take the form of fairness, respect, compassion, forgiveness, recompense, and justice.

Just as the African stool is made out of a single block of wood, each leg, or pillar, is reinforced by the others and formed from the same grain, so the issues must be addressed together and simultaneously. For instance, the responsible and accountable management of resources, as well as the sharing of them equitably, can be accomplished only if there is democratic space, where rights are respected. In a dictatorial or one-party system, resources cannot be shared equitably and sustainably, because the political leaders tend to apportion them among themselves, their cronies, and their supporters. Since only the elite have access to the wealth of the country, the vast majority of the population is excluded and dissenting voices have little power to bring about change. Where democratic space has been created, however, cultures of peace are more likely to be built and to flourish; when such space is constrained or nonexistent, peace will likewise be elusive and conflict more likely.

The three legs of the stool support the seat, which in this conception represents the milieu in which development can take place. Citizens, feeling secure that the three legs are in place—that their country has robust democratic principles, equitable distribution of resources, and strong cultures of peace—can be educated, productive, and creative. In this situation, the spirit of the citizenry not only welcomes development, but drives it itself, because individually and collectively the people feel they have an opportunity to contribute. A secure seat also provides the environment in which a government can receive funds from multilateral agencies, lending institutions, or private donors, and use them accountably and responsibly—free of corruption—for the benefit not of the few, but of the many.

In Africa today, a number of countries are trying to balance on two of the stool's three legs. Some are teetering on only one leg; a few have none whatsoever and have collapsed. Because citizens in such states live in fear, they are reluctant to take steps to hold their leaders accountable, which means those leaders can, and often will, do what they want with whatever funds flowing into their countries. The democratization process is frustrated, political and economic leadership is destructive, and conflict and insecurity are entrenched.

Whether we work in development agencies, international institutions like the United Nations and the World Bank, or NGOs, or are simply individuals who wish to improve the lot of the very poor in Africa or elsewhere, it is crucial to approach development from this perspective, in which an environment is created for citizens to engage productively. It is essential to recognize when one or more of the three pillars is absent, and accept that, no matter how many funds are provided, in a country that is balancing on two, one, or no legs, the money may not only be wasted or have only a temporary effect, but may even contribute to the continuing instability of that society. The forces responsible for breaking and twisting the stool are still present and, in many countries, still powerful. Having a stable stool means ensuring that a holistic approach to development is adopted, placing a priority on democratic governance and respect for human and other rights; equitable, sustainable, and accountable use of all resources; and managing affairs of state in an accountable and responsible way. When all these facets are in place, the stool is secure, the state has stability, and peace and development can occur.

The appreciation and acknowledgment of these three pillars of development must, however, be combined with a recognition that the current stool did not just appear by magic. In many African countries, there was once a fully formed stool— before the corruption and poor governance, before the destabilization of Cold War politics, and, to a greater or lesser extent, before societies were uprooted and pulled apart by the forces of slavery, colonialism, and modernity. In the intervening years the stool has been bashed, its legs broken and then reconstituted with weak or pliable plastic that is easily twisted and not integral to the piece of wood itself. The meaning is clear: all blame aside, it is essential to accept the truth of the history of Africa and admit that the contemporary stool has been altered drastically. It is also crucial to take on the challenge of trying to imagine what the original stool could have looked like, in what ways its pillars served the people, and how those pillars might be reenvisioned for the challenges of today.

No nation has developed these three pillars without the people themselves chiseling them, sometimes at a great price. In Africa, independence movements throughout the continent struggled to free their fellow citizens from colonialism and imperialism—including those led by Jomo Kenyatta, Patrice Lumumba, Kwame Nkrumah, Nelson Mandela, and Walter Sisulu. One is reminded of the courage and determination of those who fought for women's suffrage in the early part of the twentieth century; Mahatma Gandhi's campaign for Indian independence, which mobilized hundreds of thousands of individuals in nonviolent resistance to British rule; and the civil rights movement in the United States, for which many people gave their lives. All these movements included in their ranks many whose names aren't recorded by history, or whose bones still lie unburied in the forests where they fell fighting for their land and freedom, or who are interred in unmarked graves.

Without citizen participation and an active civil society, prospects for sustainable, equitable development are bleak. The stool will not be created or strengthened without citizens' engagement, because how else will governments be held accountable for their actions? Even today, most governments in Africa (as in other regions) will not respond to the needs of their people unless they see that if they do not, their time in office will be short.

It is in no one's interest to have governments threatened by guns, or coups, or civil wars. Instead, governments need to be "threatened" by votes, cast in free and fair elections. If leaders think their people will not reelect them because the people are unhappy about how they are managing the affairs of the state, leaders will (or should) respond to the wishes of their citizenry. This is also why empowering local communities, promoting local democracy, and decentralizing power into, for example, parliamentary constituencies is so important. (I write more about my personal experience of this process, and ideas for its wider application, in chapter 7.) In the process of engaging civil society, the three legs of the stool can be strengthened: governance becomes more open, transparent, and accountable; equity and fairness are promoted; and prospects for peace are bolstered.

At the moment, in too many African countries, concepts of civil society and democratic space are merely theoretical or abstract. However, while many Africans are not willing to enthusiastically embrace the *concepts* of accountability and transparency, it is clear that when Africans *practice* and *live* them, they realize the need for them and value them deeply. This is why in order for any vision of development to work, those who believe in transparency and accountability must communicate it to the people. Thus, while Africans need to take the lead role in supporting and strengthening civil societies—and many already are—there is a place for the international community, if it approaches development holistically, with a view to accelerating this process through moral support and financial assistance.

The practical challenge, of course, is to determine what responsibilities the international institutions concerned with development and human rights and governance (whether African or otherwise) have to those societies that are balancing on two, one, or perhaps none of the legs. Should we isolate those countries until they rebuild their stool on their own, and in the meantime leave ordinary people to suffer the consequences of violence, bad governance, and the theft of national resources?

It appears that while it would not be responsible to deliver large sums of aid money to those countries ruled by autocrats, citizens ought not to be forgotten until they get themselves out of their difficulties. This isn't simply a matter of protecting the human rights of individuals; it is also about acknowledging the potential knock-on effects of dysfunctional governments. The selling off of natural resources for the personal enrichment of a small elite, suppressing democratic activities and harassing members of civil society, fomenting violence between communities or political parties, mismanaging the economy, and neglecting basic services—all these contribute to the likelihood that the state will eventually collapse.

If it does, a country can be taken over by warlords, factions, or clans that seek whatever they can get in the short term, without regard for the long-term prospects of the nation. (Economist Paul Collier has calculated that the average civil war costs a country and neighboring nations about $64 billion, and that the main risk factors for civil wars and coups are low income and growth levels, both of which are widespread in Africa.[13]) Once the vicious cycle of violence, vengeance, and hatred starts, it can quickly become unstoppable. And the consequences will last for years, if not decades, spilling over into other countries and causing instability and further human misery. We have seen this tragedy in Somalia, Congo, and the Darfur region of Sudan.

In these situations, other African countries, the African Union, and the international community ought to remain engaged in dialogue with leaders and civil society groups and urge reforms, containing the damage as much as possible. Judicious application of international and local sanctions that target the perpetrators of injustices while not deepening the people's suffering offer a way to apply pressure to governments that ignore the plight of their people, as do arms embargoes and freezing the bank accounts of such leaders. These, of course, are tools and not panaceas; all nation-states have their own interests to pursue, and international cooperation over the crises in Darfur, Congo, and Zimbabwe has been inadequate, to say the least. But such engagement might go some way toward assisting countries to get out of their morass. And, in the long run, if citizen activists are supported, interacted with, and provided with the opportunities to learn from civil society leaders in other countries who have dealt with oppressive regimes, the pillar of democratic space would be strengthened and the stool's other two essential pillars could be put back in place and, crucially, maintained.

Four

AID AND
THE DEPENDENCY SYNDROME

IN RECENT YEARS, the emerging consensus within and outside Africa on the importance of democratic space for the continent has coincided with increased interest within East Asia and the West in helping the poorest one billion individuals, many of whom are concentrated in sub-Saharan Africa, to reach at least the lowest rung of the development ladder, from which they can climb higher. Elected leaders, senior diplomats, economists, and celebrities have helped to place the issues of Africa's dehumanizing poverty, HIV/AIDS crisis, food security, and debt relief on the international community's agenda.

DEALING WITH MALARIA AND DEPENDENCY

In January 2005, I attended the World Economic Forum, a gathering of heads of state, entrepreneurs, economists, and public figures that is held every year in Davos, Switzerland. In one session, I listened as then Tanzanian president Benjamin Mkapa addressed the theme "Funding the War on Poverty" on a panel that included President Luiz Inácio Lula da Silva of Brazil; Domenico Siniscalco, Italy's then minister of economy and finance; Gordon Brown, then the UK's chancellor of the exchequer; American economist Jeffrey Sachs; and Bill Gates, the founder of Microsoft.[1] President Mkapa made a passionate appeal for the global North (the wealthy, industrialized countries, which are mainly located in the northern hemisphere) to cancel the debts that his country owed, which, he said,

severely hampered his government's ability to make investments in public health, including, for example, providing bed
nets to protect Tanzanian children from malaria-infected
mosquitoes.

During the question-and-answer period that followed, an
audience member, the American actress Sharon Stone, told
President Mkapa how moved she'd been by his speech and
that she wished to help him save Tanzanian children from
malaria. She immediately made a pledge of $10,000 to buy bed
nets. She then turned to others in the room and asked them to
do the same. I could hear the urgency in her voice to solve right
there and then what for her seemed an eminently preventable
problem: children were dying of malaria for lack of bed nets. I
could empathize; all of us feel pain when we hear that children
are suffering. Within a short time, Ms. Stone had received a
number of pledges, totaling $100,000.[2] The funds would be
donated to the Global Fund to Fight AIDS, Tuberculosis, and
Malaria.

It is always inspiring to watch famous or wealthy people stretch out their hands to help the poor. There are few
well-known Africans who could command the same level of
attention from the international media, donor agencies, or governments as Ms. Stone and others like her from the United
States or Europe can. Some celebrities, such as Bob Geldof and
Bono, who was also in the room that day, speak out forcefully
about how current economic and political systems continue to
harm Africa—views that they can take to any elected leader in
the world and get some results. Nevertheless, once such international personalities have done their part, it is up to the
African leadership and people to make sure the resources that
result are used appropriately.

Still, while sufficient funding is important—for instance, to
purchase bed nets—in my experience development success
isn't only about money; if it were, Africa would have solved

many of her problems years ago. Since 1960, the Organisation for Economic Co-operation and Development (OECD), for example, has provided more than $650 billion in development assistance to sub-Saharan Africa.[3] And yet, every year, approximately eighty thousand children below the age of five in Tanzania die as a result of malaria;[4] one-fifth of all child deaths in Africa are caused by malaria;[5] and in 2005, according to the World Health Organization, 90 percent of the nearly 900,000 deaths from malaria were in sub-Saharan Africa.[6]

Why is preventing and treating malaria not a major concern of African governments? Does any government or individual in Africa need to be persuaded to protect children from preventable diseases? Why do individuals not develop policies and habits that are sustainable and effective for dealing with the disease?

The reason for this examination is that much of sub-Saharan Africa has an environment conducive to mosquitoes and the malarial parasite. In fact, it's been suggested that the spread of Islam in Africa southward beyond the Sahel was curtailed by the incidence of malaria. Bed nets save lives, and they should be widely available throughout Africa; the same is the case for twelve-cent antimalarial medicines.[7] Yet, up to now, it seems as if ordinary Africans have not understood the value of bed nets in preventing malaria—especially for their children— enough to purchase them, if they can afford the four dollars, or to seek them out from government health workers if they cannot. Cultural norms at the local level may dictate that only the man of the household, or only the adults, can use bed nets, even though the principal objective of making the nets available is to protect the children. Communities also may not be aware that bed nets don't offer perpetual protection: if they tear, they need to be repaired or replaced, which may put them out of the reach of poor households.

This lack of attention or understanding appears to be the case with many African governments and media as well. Why

haven't governments directed that information about the importance of bed nets in preventing childhood malaria be part of
the school curriculum in the countries of Africa where malaria
is common, so that children, their parents, and communities
all understand that malaria is a killer and that combating it
requires embracing a set of actions to protect themselves?

It is clear that a gap exists between the concern expressed
about preventable diseases in Africa by development experts
and that evidenced by African governments and the peoples
themselves. In my experience, both middle-class urban-dwellers
and rural parents have not taken seriously the need to prevent
these diseases, and, if an infection occurs, to seek immediate
treatment, including for children. Likewise, the leadership in
Africa has not paid enough attention to these diseases, or successfully sensitized a critical mass of the African people about
their deadly nature and encouraged them to take steps to
reduce the toll.

Most Africans rarely hear about such illnesses from their
ministers of health unless an international development expert
comes bearing money or bed nets—at which point the minister
is eager to talk about the particular disease the donor is concerned about. One might ask: Why do diseases seem to hit the
national headlines only when there is an unusual outbreak, or
a new donor-funded effort has been launched, as opposed to
being a significant issue for journalists to report on regularly?
Why should it take foreign experts working for foreign development agencies and funded by foreign donors to convince the
majority of Africans that they should take the problem of
deadly but preventable diseases seriously? There are doctors
and nurses and community health workers in Africa, but one
doesn't see them breaking down the doors of their respective
governments to make the case for urgent action to combat
malaria and other preventable diseases.

Contrast this with African governments' more recent

emphasis on, and urgency about, the deadliness of HIV/AIDS, which—after a terrible conspiracy of silence—has led to an increase in awareness and in people taking steps to protect themselves and others. In the case of diseases like malaria, unlike with HIV/AIDS, we see the crisis mentality that colors much development assistance, as opposed to putting a priority on prevention, strengthening health systems, and implementing policies to improve the basic health of Africans, which would make them more resilient in the face of preventable yet debilitating illnesses.

While this does not mean we should abandon attempts to broaden the use of any mitigating aids like bed nets and drugs, other policies ought to be adopted that would address the causes of these diseases. One such measure that has been advocated by the Green Belt Movement (GBM) and others is to end the production of thin plastic bags. These bags break easily and are almost always thrown away after a single use. Water pools in them and can provide a breeding ground for mosquitoes. Furthermore, the bags are unsightly—discarded ones "bloom" by the millions along roadsides and in gutters, bushes, shrubs, and even national parks throughout Africa—and they pose a risk to domestic and wild animals if eaten.

It was partly to combat the increase of malaria-bearing mosquitoes in parts of Kenya that GBM and other groups began a campaign to end the production and use of these plastic bags. GBM has been encouraging people to carry groceries and goods in bags and baskets made from sisal and other materials. These containers are durable, biodegradable, and indigenous. By reducing waste and resource use, they also help the environment.

In doing this work, GBM has been careful not to say that these plastic bags *cause* the spread of malaria, because there is no way to prove that the malaria-infected mosquitoes are breeding in the pools provided by the bags. Nor is banning the bags (as a growing number of municipalities and countries have done on ecological grounds) on its own going to solve the problem of malaria. But it is important for African governments and peoples to preempt by all possible means the likelihood of malarial infection.

Every African schoolchild should know that standing water provides a breeding ground for mosquitoes, including those that carry malaria. However, what hasn't been created in most African nations is a practice of eliminating pools of stagnant water near homes. If communities and individuals took preventative measures, it's likely that fewer curative solutions would be needed. Similarly, African governments could revise their building codes and require that all windows and doors have permanent screens on them to keep mosquitoes (and other insects) out. Even if people have bed nets, they and their children are not shielded from malaria-carrying mosquitoes in their homes during the hours between sunset and bedtime. Since evening is also the time when mosquitoes are at their most active, screens on windows and doors would offer some immediate and affordable protection.

The lack of preventative measures and awareness around malaria and other diseases is an example of three central problems in the delivery of development aid: one, African governments and individuals themselves often aren't the active partners in development; two, aid can induce a culture of dependency; and finally, a crisis mentality persists that emphasizes immediate results over long-term prevention.

When communities are offered either technology (bed nets) or ideas about a set of positive behaviors (having all of their children, or, better yet, the whole family, sleep under bed nets), it's my experience that unless they understand the intrinsic value of what they've been given and embrace it as their own, the minute the direct assistance is withdrawn and donors go home, individuals will lapse back into their previous patterns.

The boreholes and health clinics go unattended, the new tractors break down and are not repaired, and the loose taps leak or rust. Instead of a mind-set that looks to prevent problems, the culture of dependence on foreign aid continues with no one taking responsibility for communities' continued development.

Without community buy-in, donors come to be seen as Santa Claus, bringing with them money, materials, and inputs. From the governmental to the community level, individuals will throw open their doors, even when the ideas or approaches being offered by the donors are not necessarily extraordinary. The people will clap and dance in welcome, until the tap dries up, which, with donor funding, happens (as it should).

At the same time, donors' money can further corrode responsibility. Even today, among many current African governments and their citizens, an attitude exists that one doesn't have to be as responsible with, or accountable for, the use of funds or materials that have originated outside the country from a donor agency or private philanthropist. Individuals and governments completely misunderstand or subvert the donors' intention in providing the money in the first place. "If the money doesn't belong to anyone in particular," goes the reasoning, "why should it matter how it's being used? It might as well belong to me."

Some development analysts have suggested that requiring people to purchase an antimalarial net, for instance, creates a sense of investment that will encourage them to use it for the purposes for which it was intended—instead of, as has been reported of bed nets given out for free, employing or selling them as fishing nets or bridal veils. I disagree. It is not necessary for people to have to pay for something to care about it, or for that product to reach the specific demographic that it is intended to help. Rather, a community and individuals must recognize the utility and value of the item in question, regardless of who pays for it. Simply put, unless the people understand that they are expected to empower themselves after the donors are gone, they will not take the appropriate steps: not because they don't like what the donors are doing, or because the help was given to them for free, but because they don't see its value.

Of course, it is the *perception* of the threat and not the reality of malaria that I am examining. There is no question that malaria is a debilitating disease; I have seen for myself its negative effects on people and communities. While the numbers of malaria deaths in Africa have been declining in recent years since bed-net manufacture and distribution programs moved into higher gear, they remain unacceptably high.

Although it may seem an obvious point, it is worth noting that Africans have been dealing with diseases like malaria for a very long time, perhaps upward of fifty thousand years. Although malaria, no doubt, has exacted a heavy cost in deaths of family members and lost productive hours, the peoples of sub-Saharan Africa have nevertheless learned to live with it and do not seem to be alarmed by it. Indeed, if you asked average Africans what the continent's most pressing health issue is, they would probably say HIV/AIDS—not least because it is a new disease in comparison with malaria, and many people are dying of it. Even in the slums that are all too common in African cities, where people live packed tightly together, surrounded by the pools of stagnant water that are ideal habitats for mosquitoes to breed, more individuals are likely to consider unemployment, poverty, or HIV/AIDS greater problems than malaria. They wouldn't necessarily be wrong: HIV/AIDS remains the leading cause of death in sub-Saharan Africa, claiming the lives of 1.6 million adults and children in 2007.[8] But they may not know how deadly malaria also is—and that, perhaps worse, it may even increase the progression of the HIV virus.[9]

Just as it is essential that the people be engaged in the development process, so governments need to take the lead. In the context of aid, there is a big difference between asking donor agencies, philanthropic foundations, or individuals for help— for instance, to prevent and treat malaria—and only being persuaded to do so when funds are available from the outside. Africa's leaders cannot continue to wait for the international community to provide financing before doing the right thing. Half a century after independence, it is incumbent upon African governments to work for the good of their people without the need for "carrots" coming from donors to persuade them to do it.

In the long run, of course, Africa needs to move beyond aid and the culture of dependency it has helped create in Africa's leaders and her people. While I applaud the motives of the international community in providing technical and financial assistance to developing countries, including those in Africa, I do question how much good aid does versus how much damage it may do to the capacity of the African peoples to engineer their own solutions to their many problems.

GOALS FOR DEVELOPMENT

In a nod to the five species white hunters wanted to "bag" while on safari in Africa (a rhino, a leopard, a lion, a buffalo, and an elephant) in the reserves they set aside for this purpose, economist Jeffrey Sachs, director of the Earth Institute at Columbia University in New York City, has identified what he terms the "Big Five," a set of multipronged investments in development that can help communities climb the ladder out of extreme poverty. They are agricultural inputs; investments in basic health; improvements in education; more efficient and regular power, transport, and communication services; and the provision of clean drinking water and proper sanitation.

Professor Sachs is heading a group that includes the Earth Institute, the United Nations Development Programme

(UNDP), and the Millennium Promise in establishing a number of what are called "millennium villages" in ten African countries as part of an effort to realize the Millennium Development Goals.[10] Eleven of the villages are in Kenya, in the Sauri district of Nyanza Province, not far from Kisumu on the shores of Lake Victoria in the west of the country. Progress in the Sauri millennium villages on key development indicators, including those within the Millennium Development Goals, has been made since the initiative began there in 2004. Incidents of malaria in Sauri, for instance, have dropped by 50 percent. Students came in second rather than 108th out of 253 in district school examinations.[11] And corn production has, on average, tripled, enabling farmers to sell some of their harvest in the market and retain some for their families.[12]

These are significant achievements. The people in Sauri and the other millennium villages are, like those I have worked closely with through the Green Belt Movement, poor, largely outside of the mainstream development agenda, and stuck in a cycle of powerlessness and marginalization. The immediate results from the millennium villages indicate that when financial resources, including aid, are properly targeted and well spent, they have the potential to transform the lives of the world's poorest people.

Even as I welcome this progress, however, the very fact that the Big Five are needed raises a number of questions, some of which are uncomfortable, and several that touch on the same problems as the situation with malaria and bed nets. All of these questions lead to issues of leadership and governance, which may be defined as the way a country establishes its priorities, holds its officials accountable for their actions, makes decisions, empowers its citizens to feel invested in and engaged with their government and civil service, and communicates its vision to the people.

What was being done—or not being done—by African governments in Sauri and the other seventy-odd millennium villages throughout Africa before the team of international professionals conceived of helping the local people through these interventions? In the case of Kenya, the member of parliament who represents the region where Sauri is located is a professor of political science and economics, and was a minister for economic planning and development in Kenya's ninth parliament (2002–07). Given Sauri's low development status, one could conclude that either the MP didn't understand the policy prescriptions and economic conditions that the millennium village project identifies, or he didn't have the funds to implement a program like the Big Five, or, perhaps, he wasn't serious about dedicating funds to such purposes or implementing a holistic development plan.

One could also ask, given the demonstrable successes documented in Sauri, and the elementary nature of many of the interventions—ensuring that farmers have fertilizers, decent seeds, and markets, that villagers have access to clean drinking water, and that children receive good nutrition to support, in part, their academic studies—why the government hadn't made them a priority for *all* Kenyans. Why did implementation of the Big Five require the coordination of a range of international organizations and considerable infusions of donor aid? (In Kenya, to provide the Big Five to all those who, in Sachs's analysis, need them would cost about $1.5 billion a year.)

It is not because the Kenyan administration and other African governments are unaware of the validity of the components of the Big Five. Kenya, for instance, has a minister of agriculture, a minister of health, a minister of education, a minister of energy, a minister of roads and public works, a minister of information and communication, and a minister of water, all of whom are mandated to tackle the myriad development deficits facing Kenyans, including the Big Five. Rarely, however, does one find African governments genuinely emphasizing these ministries. In general, they are more concerned with funding and staffing ministries of defense, provincial administration, finance, and security. Nonetheless, one can still legitimately question why it is necessary for a raft of international agencies to inform African governments that the Big Five are important to combating the poverty that is killing their people, and why, in turn, the international experts are establishing mechanisms to deliver the interventions—a function that surely should fall to the governments themselves.

One measure that could be immediately undertaken, for instance, is in the provision of latrines. Three hundred million Africans—a third of the continent's population—do not have access to clean water and sound sanitation.[13] If the governments of Africa individually and collectively made it their mission to provide a latrine in every household and teach basic hygiene, particularly in schools and churches, countless lives would be saved, especially those of children, many of whom die from diarrhea and parasitical infections. In addition, this would provide all Africans with a degree of dignity that millions currently do not have. This would not have to be exorbitantly expensive, and the people themselves could provide the labor. The only reason I suspect this has yet to be done is because the elites who make these decisions have lived for many years with modern toilet facilities, and this level of privation is now outside their realm of experience. Nevertheless, they cannot say they do not know. If such a situation is unacceptable to donors, why should it not be for the elites?

It is true that the budgets of many African governments are stretched thin because substantial portions are being used to service their international debts (a topic I discuss in more detail in the next chapter). But it is also the case that for at least a century, Africa has been told that it is poor, and too many Africans have come to accept this as an unchangeable truth—even though the continent remains richly endowed with natural resources, despite decades of ecological degradation. Africa is also wealthy in human resources. The challenge for its leaders, both governmental and nongovernmental, is to acknowledge and then channel Africans' capabilities and energies into effective action for development.

Unfortunately, too many African governments have used their budgets, and their natural resources, not to invest in their people, but in precisely the opposite manner. Most likely, the millennium villages' initiative has instituted management systems that ensure that the funds budgeted for Sauri and the other villages throughout Africa are used efficiently, accountably, and responsibly—making sure the monies are not stolen or data deliberately falsified. This recognition leads to further questions about the prospects for devolving programs such as those being piloted in Sauri to national and local governments—which must, surely, be the ultimate goal.

How are the governments of Malawi, Ethiopia, Nigeria, Senegal, and Kenya—to name a few of the countries in which millennium villages have been established—to be persuaded to continue to support these development investments when the aid flow ends or is insufficient in future years? The International Monetary Fund reports that the commitments made by the G-8 nations in 2005 to increase bilateral development assistance for Africa by $22 billion, for a total by 2010 of nearly $38 billion each year, are "unlikely to materialize." As of June 2008, the nongovernmental organization DATA—Debt AIDS Trade Africa—founded by Bono reported that only 14 percent of the additional funds pledged by the G-8 nations had been provided.[14] Only a handful of industrialized nations have reached the benchmark they set in 1992 to provide 0.7 percent of their gross national products as development assistance.

Given this scenario, what kind of financial and logistical

commitment will the African governments make to ensure that the millennium village models are self-sustaining and also templates for future development without requiring yet more donor aid to continue? And if the funds to support millennium village–like interventions are used efficiently, accountably, and responsibly but are still not enough to reach all who could benefit, are the long-term prospects for such development approaches realistic?

While it is necessary to challenge the governments, the citizens of African countries also have a role to play in demanding development that discourages dependency. Why didn't *they* prioritize investments like the Big Five? Or if similar programs were in place, such as an effective agricultural extension service that advised farmers on preventing soil erosion and capturing rainwater, why did they allow them to collapse? Why was the emphasis on development lost?

Certainly, after independence, most Africans had the expectation that their societies, and they themselves, would become wealthier. Instead, Africa as a whole became poorer and more dependent on an infusion of aid from the very regions that had colonized and exploited the continent. Such assistance was welcomed with little skepticism and, in my view, helped further internalize Africans' sense of their inferiority when compared to the rest of the world. If postindependence aid had been provided to Africa in a manner designed to empower the economies and institutions of the continent and not to instill a long-term dependency, the future of Africa might have been very different, and the Big Five initiative unnecessary.

As it is, Africa is like a person who's fallen into a hole. Someone is telling her, "I'll throw you a rope so you can get out." While the rope provided is never quite long enough for her to grab on to it, it's long enough so she has a hope of reaching it. At the same time, the person holding the rope has thrown down a spade, and is encouraging the person in the hole to dig herself in deeper. While aid can be a very useful tool for development, it may also be achieving a completely opposite outcome, undermining its stated objectives and leaving a majority of Africans dependent rather than empowered. For instance, donor nations ship or fly in food aid rather than helping to implement sound food and agricultural policies that would allow African countries to feed themselves when harvests fail and global food prices rise. Instead of encouraging and fostering capacities and skills in countries themselves, foreign experts continue to manage many essential tasks. Many aid programs still treat symptoms and manage emergencies rather than supporting investments for the long term so that crises either do not occur or can be handled and resolved with limited or no international assistance.

Nevertheless, the culture of aid is hard to change. The international community often expects fast returns from its development investments, but the problems of underdevelopment, marginalization, lack of self-esteem, fear, and cynicism didn't afflict Africa's peoples yesterday—indeed, they have accumulated over centuries. This is a reality the international community understands but doesn't always acknowledge. At the same time, it is harder to raise funds to address environmental sustainability and preventative measures that would have long-term impacts than it is to raise money for famine relief, refugees, children, HIV/AIDS, and bed nets. One reason why the culture of aid is difficult to change is because of the images used to depict Africa.

THE IMAGE OF AFRICA

Although in recent years the state of development in Africa has risen on the global agenda, the voices of Africans speaking to these challenges are muted in comparison with those of the industrialized world speaking about the needs of Africa.

Unfortunately, this situation only reinforces the perception that African solutions for African problems don't exist, and that Africans are not equally equipped to propose a vision for Africa's development or provide concrete actions to bring it about.

Too often, Africa is still presented as a helpless victim of her own making. A representative image I saw a long time ago and that has stayed with me is that of an emaciated young girl with a distended belly on the cover of a UNICEF magazine. All of us have seen such horrific pictures. They prick our consciences, and may move many of us, including those with money or power, to try to help. Indeed, it was pictures of this kind beamed by the BBC from Ethiopia in 1984 that so disturbed the singers Bob Geldof and Midge Ure that they wrote the pop single "Do They Know It's Christmas?" to support Ethiopian famine relief. Their efforts grew into the fund-raising concerts Live Aid and, twenty years later, Live 8. It also inspired the launch of UK-based Comic Relief, a charity dedicated to eradicating poverty in Africa and elsewhere, and with whom the Green Belt Movement works in Africa.

A set of images has dominated the world's view of Africa for centuries, some intended to excuse injustice against the peoples of the continent, others to elicit compassion and wonder. The continent south of the Sahara has been seen as a land of unparalleled riches, startling beauty, and extraordinary wildlife; as a place of strange and at times primitive tribal customs, civil disorder, and armed militias; of child labor and child soldiers, mud huts, open sewers, and shantytowns; of corruption, dictatorship, and genocide. These and other perceptions have framed the world's response to Africa.

As someone who raises funds to support work in Africa, I understand the importance of images, and recognize that pictures of Africans in dire circumstances can, ultimately, lead to positive actions from those who are moved to want to help. However, on balance, I find these representations—and the associations they bring with them—demonstrably negative, perhaps even shameful, since they risk stereotyping all countries south of the Sahara as places of famine, death, and hopelessness. Because the children or adults pictured are rarely named, the people remain abstract, symbolic, and no longer individuals. That starving toddler or weeping mother or child soldier is "Africa." This projection only makes the task more difficult for those of us on the ground trying to help Africans to help themselves.

In addition, Africans themselves see these images of suffering and dysfunction on television, in newspapers, on websites, and in fund-raising appeals, and begin to internalize them. A dangerous and unfortunate psychological process ensues that subtly and perhaps unconsciously affirms to Africans their inability to be agents of their own destiny. Eventually, it may destroy the sense of confidence they should and must have to make progress.

Moreover, these depictions fail to capture another reality, which is that every day, tens of millions of African women and men go about their business, live their lives responsibly and industriously, and look after their immediate and extended families, even if they lack certain material possessions, higher education, or access to the range of opportunities and goods available to the wealthy in other countries, or even their own. These are the real African heroes, and it is these images the world should see more of.

I don't believe that charities or celebrities are buying into the stereotypical images of African helplessness and suffering in an effort to undermine Africans; the photos do, after all, represent a reality. Too many children *are* hungry in Africa or being forced to commit atrocities as child soldiers; or they are misusing drugs or sniffing glue on the streets of the continent's cities or are abused and raped and unable to go to school. And certainly, African governments have not paid enough attention to the continent's myriad problems, in part because in Africa they aren't viewed with the same gravity as elsewhere, or because communities have become used to them (as may be the case with malaria and other preventable diseases), or because Africans are surrounded by so many challenges that the particular condition being highlighted doesn't seem as problematic to them as it does to those in the developed world. To a degree, these governments may need to be shamed into taking on these problems.

An example of this was when Bob Geldof visited Ethiopia in 1985 to see for himself the effects of the famine devastating these proud and confident people. It was only because a Kenyan cameraman, Mohamed Amin, traveled with Geldof that we Kenyans learned about the tragedy unfolding in the country next door. Why weren't we told that our fellow Africans were suffering? Why didn't the Kenyan government mobilize its citizens with the means or skills to assist the victims of the famine, which had been greatly exacerbated by a dictatorship and a devastating civil war that had uprooted the underpinnings of Ethiopia's agricultural economy?

The challenge, therefore, is not only for the international community to use more positive depictions of Africa, but for Africans themselves to stop providing so many images of dysfunction in the first place. No one in Africa can be happy that a child with a belly distended from malnutrition comes to represent a particular country or the continent at large. Clearly, it's incumbent upon Africans to project themselves better and more affirmatively, without pretending that underdevelopment isn't real. They must recognize that these challenges exist, and then decide that they will work toward resolving them.

The governments must ask themselves what policies they can adopt and what commitments they can make, notwithstanding the availability of aid, so that the images of African children express a new reality: one not of malnutrition, but of health; not child soldiers or street children addicted to drugs, but hardworking students and intact families. This should not be because the hungry have been hidden away, or the street children thrown in jail, but because Africa has more achievements to display than famines to be covered up.

At the same time, development agencies need to present a vision of the Africa they wish to see rather than using images that undercut the very mission they are trying to accomplish. It should be possible for potential donors to respond to images of a functioning Africa that deserves support and not only give in response to those images that inspire pity and condescension.

That morning in Davos, as I listened to Sharon Stone urging other individuals to join her in raising money for bed nets, I couldn't help but notice the rather strained smile on President Mkapa's face. He was in an awkward situation. No doubt on one level he was grateful that someone cared enough about the toll of malaria on his country's children to help raise funds for bed nets there and then. But I also sensed in his demeanor a degree of discomfort—or maybe as an African myself, I was projecting such a sentiment onto him—that he was getting personal help from wealthy individuals to fund a basic intervention that, as a head of state and a proud African, he would want to provide for the Tanzanian people himself.

Indeed, at the end of his speech, President Mkapa had gotten to the heart of the need for Africa's leaders to commit to serving their peoples and to practicing better governance for their peoples' benefit:

Now for our own, let me say: I don't want to be putting the developed countries on the dock. We [Africans] also have a task, we also have a challenge; because we also have a capacity to some extent of funding the war on poverty ourselves: organizing our economies, organizing our revenue collection systems, organizing our own budgeting, being more accountable and transparent. Those we can undertake. A combination of those reforms I think would see a tremendous, truly predictable advance in the war against poverty.

President Mkapa knew what the right actions were. For me, however, the question still remains: If African leaders know what they ought to do, why aren't more of them doing it?

Five

DEFICITS: INDEBTEDNESS
AND UNFAIR TRADE

IN 1982, I visited Luanda, the capital of Angola, as part of research I was conducting for the United Nations Economic Commission of Africa. At that time, Angola was in the throes of a ruinous civil war that had begun shortly after the country became independent from Portugal in 1975.

When I'm in a foreign city, I like to go to the markets—preferably not those set aside for tourists, but ones used by the locals. In this way, I can get a feeling for the lives and conditions of the ordinary people. Even though a war was taking place, when I visited the market in Luanda I was surprised to find it as empty as it was of both people and goods for sale. The only vegetables seemed to be wild and green, the sort farmers collect from the field after the harvest or rains. The only meat appeared to be lungfish, which can grow up to two feet long and are as thin as eels. These lungfish were frozen, which indicated to me that they were imported. When I asked a stallholder about the fish, he told me that they'd come from the Soviet Union. The civil war was one of many conflicts between the two superpowers on the continent. It was clear which one had the upper hand in Angola.

The hotel I was staying in overlooked Luanda's harbor, which despite the war still retained a degree of elegance from the colonial-era houses that lined it. Very early each morning, I noticed that, at the ebb tide, hundreds of people would be on the beach collecting crabs. While some may have taken the crabs to the market, given that I didn't see any on my visits there, I assumed the vast majority of crabs went straight into the pots on people's stoves in their homes. What I found extraordinary, however, was that, in the afternoon as the tide came in, enormous shoals of flying fish would chase the waves to the shore.

Now, I am no fisherman, but it seemed to me that it would have been easy to put a net into the waters and catch vast numbers of these fish. When I inquired about this, though, I was told that because of the war, the fishing industry had become virtually moribund and only a few individuals entered the waters to see what they could catch. The people I spoke to said that while the Angolan fishing industry was no longer functioning, Soviet trawlers off Angola and up and down the west coast of Africa were busy fishing. They took their catch, including lungfish, back to the Soviet Union, from where they would be exported—including to countries such as Angola.

What struck me as particularly ironic was that, in spite of the demonstrable poverty of the people and the city and the lack of foodstuffs available in the market, the sea continually offered its bounty every morning and afternoon. And yet the citizens of Luanda were unable to use these resources to sustain their own fishing industry and provide themselves with food and an income. Here, in essence, were the twin tragedies of Africa: that on a continent of such abundance, there was such poverty; and that in a conflict that had very little to do with them, ordinary Angolans had become the playthings of outside forces and various militias, which often were backed by those same outside forces. Both had destroyed the political and economic structures of the state to such an extent that they had free rein to take the natural resources from under the noses of the people.

The proxy war that raged in Angola and that at various stages involved the Soviet Union, China, Cuba, and Mozambique, as well as the United States, Zaire, and South Africa, ended in 2002, having taken between five hundred thousand and a million lives, displaced more than four million people, exiled a further four hundred thousand, and left the country littered with more than fifteen million land mines.[1]

Since the conclusion of the conflict, Angola's economy has experienced rapid growth. In 2007, increased demand and a high price for Angola's daily production of 1.5 million barrels of oil meant that the country's GDP expanded by 21 percent that year alone. Angola's fiscal surplus in 2006 and 2007 was a healthy 14.8 percent and 6.1 percent of GDP, respectively, while the inflation rate decreased from 325.5 percent in 2000 to 12.6 percent in 2007.[2] Luanda itself is undergoing a construction boom, and hotel occupancy rates are near 100 percent. Throughout the country, the Angolan government has rebuilt 2,400 miles of road and 400 miles of railroad track and renovated the major airports.[3]

Nevertheless, peace and a growing economy have not yet brought prosperity for more than a small minority of Angola's long-suffering people. Two-thirds of Angolans still live on two dollars a day or less, and in 2006 the United Nations Human Development Report ranked Angola as the seventeenth least-developed country in the world. A third of adults remain illiterate, life expectancy is forty years, and a third of Angola's children are underweight for their age.[4] And according to a report from the U.S.-based group Human Rights Watch, Luanda's building spree has led to the forced evictions of twenty thousand poor people from their homes.[5]

In 1982, it was the Soviet Union that exploited the Angolan government's dependency on its aid and weaponry to extract Angola's natural resources (in that case, fish) and then sell them back. In 2008, it is now trawlers from Russia, joined by those from Europe and East Asia, that ply the coasts of Africa, depleting the continent's waters of fish from already-threatened stocks.[6]

Like Angola, Mauritania to the north has a long coast and potentially large revenues from its fishing industry. However, Mauritania processes only 12 percent of its fish stock, and its bilateral fishing agreements with other African countries as well as Russia, Japan, and the European Union have not markedly increased its capacity to capitalize on its resources. In fact, they often have the opposite outcome. One of these agreements led to Mauritania's octopus stock being overexploited by 25 to 40 percent.[7]

While much of this fishing is legal, made possible by formal arrangements between the fishing countries and African governments, including Angola's, there is also a large illegal trade. A report published by the South Africa–based Institute for Security Studies in 2007 found that each year revenues from illegal fishing of sardines and mackerel off the coast of Angola amounted to $49 million, or more than a fifth of the value of all Angolan fish exports.[8] Continent-wide, an estimated $1 billion each year is lost to illegal and unregulated fishing.[9]

The industrialized nations pay African governments for access to their fish stocks, not least because they have almost exhausted their own. One might have hoped that the ending of the Cold War would have meant a rebounding of Africa's fishing industries, and the reemergence of indigenous markets—such as one in flying fish, for instance, which in the eastern Atlantic range from Angola in the south to Mauritania in the north and beyond into the seas off western Europe. However, the effect of huge demand for diminished fish stocks, as well as cheap imports of foodstuffs and other products, has been to decimate the mainly small-scale fishing communities, and other business opportunities, along Africa's coasts. Indeed, the increase in piracy off the coast of Somalia has been blamed on reduced opportunities for local fishermen due to the lack of fish and increased competition from foreign trawlers.

Such realities have been implicated in malnutrition and

food insecurity. According to the United Nations Food and Agriculture Organization, although two hundred million sub-Saharan Africans eat fish, and it is a source of almost a quarter of the region's protein, they actually consume the least amount of fish in the world per capita.[10] Anemia caused by a deficiency in iron takes the lives of twenty thousand sub-Saharan African women each year, and half a million children die because of an inadequate supply of vitamin A. Both nutrients are found in fish. In several West African nations, some species of fish are now so scarce that their prices have risen beyond the reach of many local peoples.

The lack of fish protein in the diets of some sub-Saharan Africans is also one of the drivers in the trade and consumption of bushmeat—the capture and killing of wild animals, such as small mammals, antelope, and primates, and occasionally larger species as well. A 2004 study found that in Ghana consumption of bushmeat increases when supplies of fish fall; more bushmeat is seen in markets and more poaching occurs in game reserves when fish catches have been low.[11] People researching the bushmeat trade believe that this link exists in other countries along the coast of West Africa, including Liberia, Guinea-Bissau, Equatorial Guinea, and Senegal.

The policies now guiding the management of Africa's fisheries have even broader implications for Africa's economic development. In a 2008 survey of Senegalese, more than half of the respondents said they would leave their country permanently if they were able to.[12] Senegal once had a thriving, small-scale fishing industry. But its fish stocks have declined dramatically in recent decades. Senegal's government estimates that the fish catch fell from 95,000 tons to less than half that (45,000 tons) between 1994 and 2005. In 2006, the country did not renew fishing agreements with the European Commission. But this measure to protect its fishing industry is undercut by ships from Europe and other regions violating agreed quotas. Senegal, like most African nations, does not have an effective coast guard to patrol its waters.[13] As of the middle of 2008, Mozambique had only one patrol boat for its 1,500 miles of coastline.[14]

Senegalese fishermen, unable to compete with the foreign trawlers and seeing no prospects for other livelihoods, are, along with young men from Mauritania, Guinea-Bissau, and the Gambia, risking their lives every day by climbing into leaky boats and crossing treacherous seas to gain a foothold in Europe.[15] In 2007, an estimated six thousand Africans died trying to reach the Canary Islands.[16] Those who survive the crossing attempt to make their way to mainland Europe—as if following the fish—where they believe they have a better chance of earning a living. (Many who are caught are repatriated.) A few get through—to the continent that is, in part through its fishing policies, involved in making their lives in Africa that much harder in the first place.

The decline of much of Africa's fishing industry provides an unhappy glimpse into an economic order that continues to place commodities first and communities last, in which a problem like overfishing in the northern Atlantic and other regions of the world is exported to Africa, where it has led to African fish stocks and livelihoods being decimated. It is an example of how the world's interactions with Africa are not necessarily motivated by altruism, but by the self-interest of states seeking to maximize their opportunities and minimize their costs, often at the expense of those who are not in a position to do either.

Even though awareness of some of these inequities is greater than it was in the 1980s or '90s, the situation has not changed significantly—not least because African governments are still acceding to them. African countries remain caught in a web of relationships with international lending and aid agencies, the

World Trade Organization, and leading and emerging global powers in which a premium is put on the extraction and export of raw materials, with only minimal benefits for the majority of Africa's peoples.

INDEBTEDNESS

Despite the best efforts of the global Jubilee 2000 Campaign, which I cochaired in Kenya, and subsequent good-faith citizen- and celebrity-led initiatives, many African countries continue to be burdened by huge and unfair debts that inhibit government action to meet their people's pressing needs for the Big Five and other development investments.

From 1970 to 2002, Africa received over half a trillion dollars in loans from the World Bank, the IMF, and individual wealthy nations, and paid back roughly the same amount. However, because of the interest on that debt, by 2002 $300 billion was still outstanding.[17] Throughout this period, the international community continued to provide more loans to African states so they could pay back the old ones. More recently some of these loans came with economic "conditionalities"— requirements to curtail government spending, to open markets to foreign goods, and to restrict the money supply. These restrictions forced governments to slash budgets for health, education, and other essential services for their citizens.

The issue of debt relief encapsulates the differences in per- spective that challenge both Africans and the international community. Any individual who goes to a bank to take out a loan would expect the bank to ask for their credentials so that the individual can be assessed for creditworthiness. Likewise, the banker would expect the person to whom money is being lent to be responsible enough to know whether or not they can pay the loan back. If that individual's creditworthiness is an issue, it is appropriate for the lender to impose conditions on the recipient to encourage them to spend their money wisely and restrict their ability to misspend it.

From the 1970s onward, however, the donor community was aware that it was dealing with governments that, once freed from the constraints of accountability, could act completely irresponsibly. The banks and governments that loaned African leaders huge sums are, therefore, as culpable as those to whom they gave the money. They knew very well that the recipients were not creditworthy. Yet capital was extended over and over again, either to prop up "friendly" leaders during the Cold War or to encourage favorable business arrangements between the governments and the donor countries.

The supply or withholding of international aid provided a useful means of controlling Africa's leaders to the advantage of the industrialized world. Another outcome was that African leaders relied so much on the regular supply of foreign loans that they were more accountable to the international donors than they were to their own people, a situation made easier because most African citizens were living under repressive regimes. Not only were the people unaware of what was happening, but neither they nor civil society had the capacity to protest or hold anyone accountable, precisely because the regimes were so repressive. All issues dealing with the government were shrouded in secrecy. Indeed, one word for "government" in Kiswahili is *sirikali*, which means "a big secret." This practice of sealing deals "under the table" was a leftover from the colonial administrations. Even if civil society or the people themselves weren't struggling under autocratic rule, it would have been difficult for them to know what was taking place. But the lenders knew. In this and other ways, the normal relationship between lender and creditor was suspended when it came to African governments and the international community.

In addition, significant portions of loans and aid grants were appropriated by the leaders themselves, making a mockery of the fact that the funds were given in the name of and for their citizens. Much of the money never reached the people; instead, it was privatized by autocratic rulers. The amounts removed from the continent and the personal fortunes amassed by some of Africa's past leaders are astonishing. A French newspaper estimated that from 1989 to 1998, the back-to-back Nigerian leaders Ibrahim Babangida and Sani Abacha accumulated $8 billion between them. Samuel Doe and Charles Taylor of Liberia netted a total of $5 billion over the course of sixteen years. President Félix Houphouët-Boigny of Côte d'Ivoire is said to have amassed $6 billion over his thirty-three-year rule, while the late Zairian president Mobutu Sese Seko is thought to have appropriated to himself $5 billion. It is reported that between 1968 and 2004, in tiny Equatorial Guinea, with a population of five hundred thousand (in 2005), Francisco Macías Nguema and his successor, Teodoro Obiang Nguema Mbasogo, collected a total of $8 billion between them. In 2004, former Nigerian president Olusegun Obasanjo estimated that $140 billion had been stolen from Africa, through the privatizing of loans and aid to the state and kickbacks to corrupt officials since the main wave of independence.[18] Such figures only confirm what everyone knows: that Africa is not poor, but that she has yet to learn to protect her wealth for herself.

The monies stolen from the African people and deposited in foreign accounts were then available for further lending or investment by bankers from the donor nations. The consequences of such theft are still being felt by millions of ordinary Africans on whose shoulders those debts have been placed. Even today, foreign banks operating in Africa can make larger profits than they do in their home countries by charging significantly higher fees and interest rates on loans. One has to wonder why African leaders allow foreign banks and investors to make so much profit at the expense of their own people. (One way foreign businesses ensure their profits is by co-opting the African leaders, making them directors or giving them shares. This means everyone but the people are happy when financial statements are presented to shareholders.)

In 1996, pressure from activists in the rich, industrialized and non-industrialized countries forced the World Bank and the IMF to set up the Heavily Indebted Poor Countries (HIPC) Initiative to reduce developing countries' debts. Because of this and other campaigns, some African countries, and countries in other poor regions, have seen their debt reduced or canceled. As of 2005, the Malawian government paid $95 million annually on its $3.2 billion debt; in 2006, the payment was reduced to $5 million. Sierra Leone's debt of $1.6 billion shrank to $100 million. Overall, as of 2008, about $88 billion of debt owed by developing countries has been canceled, although for each $1 in aid poor countries receive, they continue to return an average of $5 in debt service.[19] In spite of having only 5 percent of the developing world's income, Africa still has about two-thirds of the world's debt. As of 2005, sub-Saharan Africa spent $14.5 billion annually repaying its debts.[20] According to the United Nations, in 2007, Africa's debt burden stood at $255 billion.[21]

In 1998, the Jubilee 2000 Campaign encouraged leaders of the world's richest countries not merely to extend the relief but to cancel all debts, and not only to some African countries but to all of them. At the time of writing, comprehensive cancellation has not yet been agreed upon, and some countries on the continent still labor under heavy or significant debt burdens.

After years of conflict under the rapacious warlord-presidents Samuel Doe and Charles Taylor, in November 2005 Liberians elected economist Ellen Johnson-Sirleaf as their president. She inherited a ravaged country. Not only is Liberia's physical infrastructure shattered, but it carries a $3.5 billion debt burden. "It's not fair for our young children to inherit this debt from which they've received very little benefits," Johnson-Sirleaf has rightly pointed out.[22]

Liberia is now on track for HIPC debt relief. But Kenya, like Nigeria, is currently considered rich enough to be able to service its debt. As of 2004, Kenya still owed $6.8 billion, and sends back to the rich nations who loaned the money a million dollars a day in debt payments. Like Nigeria and Liberia, much of the debt that Kenya is being forced to repay was accrued many years ago by a dictatorial leadership that mismanaged the economy and probably allowed much of the money to be stolen.

It is clear that the relationship between debt, poverty, and aid needs to be rectified. It makes no sense for African governments to receive aid on the one hand, while on the other paying back debts acquired in the past by discredited regimes for projects that in the main did not benefit the African people. These illegitimate debts must be canceled, for as much as one might wish otherwise, they dilute the impact of philanthropists and donors who care about Africa and its peoples. As much as Africans are being assisted in practical ways by their efforts, some of the philanthropists' and donors' governments, as well as international lenders, are draining Africa's resources. This makes it much harder for Africa's institutions to fulfill the basic functions for which the funds that were given were intended.

Thankfully, in the last few years, civil society's success in persuading international lenders to recognize that Africans should not be held responsible for the sins of governments and lenders they had no control over is being paralleled, not only by aid being given and received more transparently and accountably, but by countries in Africa beginning to open up to democratic governance and civil society participation—conditions that make governments more accountable to their people. Although many governments are still secretive and provide little information to the public about how they operate, greater possibilities now exist for citizens, in Africa and in the industrialized countries, to know how much money the government has received, how much debt relief has been provided, and what conditionalities apply.

Of course, after the relief of their debts, it will be up to the governments to behave responsibly, by not taking the opportunity either to divert the newly available funds away from development and antipoverty efforts or to accumulate more debt. African parliaments and civil society have important roles in ensuring that governments spend such funds appropriately.

Slowly, millions of dollars in donor funds or kickbacks on deals with multinational corporations that African leaders across the continent stole from their people are being recovered. For instance, as of 2008, $500 million from Sani Abacha's Swiss bank accounts had been returned to Nigeria.[23] This is not an insignificant amount—which is why, if the international donor community is serious about helping Africa, it should compel its banks to do a full accounting of the ill-gotten gains deposited in them over the decades.

It is also incumbent upon the nations from whom the money was stolen to demand its return. However, given that a country's government must request this action, the process may take some time. In some cases, because of the longevity of many of the politicians and their tenacious hold on office, the very individuals who should be asking for the repatriation of the funds are those whose money is in question. In other instances, politicians are unwilling to launch an investigation into siphoned funds because they know they will be scrutinizing friends and colleagues, some of whom, they may hope, will protect them from potential prosecution when they lose power.

THE IMBALANCE OF TRADE

In his critique of Africa's development policies since independence, the Ethiopian economist Fantu Cheru examines why Africa has failed to capitalize successfully on the natural resources that have always been so evident to the rich world. He points a finger at a number of problems: lack of political will, weak institutions, a shortage of skills, too many ties to former colonial powers, and inadequate infrastructure, transport, and communication networks. Moreover, African economies have had an overreliance on commodities[24]—raw materials, usually from agriculture or mining, the prices for which are set in the world market and that are qualitatively undifferentiated (that is, oil is oil, copper is copper, and sugarcane is sugarcane, no matter where they originate). Cheru and the Ghanaian economist George Ayittey argue that the continent's growth has been stymied because African governments have failed to diversify their economies. They have not strengthened their agricultural sectors, broadened their range of exports, developed mechanisms and industries to add value to the commodities they produce, or supported the entrepreneurial impulses and market heritage of the African people.

At the same time, despite the priority placed on fair trade for Africa and other developing regions by international civil society, considerable obstacles remain. The African peoples' ability to engage in economic activities and creative initiatives that generate wealth are inhibited by mass-produced, imported consumer goods. These are often sold at prices cheaper than those of local goods, marginalizing homegrown businesses that cannot compete with giant transnational corporations and large sums of foreign capital. What also has been missing is access to, and the ability to capitalize on, information and knowledge;

both of these problems stem from a lack of education and, in combination, constrain creativity.

Africa is still overwhelmingly a producer of commodities such as petroleum, minerals, and metals. In 1960, nine commodities—including coffee, cocoa, cotton, and sugar—made up 70 percent of sub-Saharan Africa's agricultural exports. By the 1980s, they constituted almost the same amount—76 percent—even as countries in other regions expanded their range of exports and their share of other markets.

Today, much of Africa's economic activity still rests on an unstable mix of aid, tourism, the export of natural resources, and the sale of cash crops—such as coffee, tea, sugarcane, nuts, and other foodstuffs—which has characterized the continent since independence and, in some cases, as far back as the colonial period. Newly independent African countries were encouraged by international financial institutions, some donor governments, and some development agencies to expand their economies by focusing on cash crops, which could be sold in the global market, with the proceeds used to grow other essential products. As a consequence, peasant farmers (who are largely uninformed) in much of Africa have become almost completely dependent on income from producing these cash crops to meet all the household's needs, such as food to eat, clothes, school fees, and transportation.

In the late 1970s and '80s, prices for commodities collapsed, further impoverishing many African nations. Africa's share of developing-country exports went from 12 percent in 1961 to just under 6 percent in 1980. The dramatic lowering of commodity prices cost Africa $50 billion in lost earnings between 1986 and 1990, more than twice the amount the region received in aid during the same time. There were several reasons for this steep decline: stiffer competition appeared from emerging Asian economies along with new markets in synthetic or alternate materials; the collapse of the Soviet

Union closed off one avenue for some African countries' products; and, as prices fell, Africans also overproduced, which in turn depressed prices further. Between 1970 and 2005, sub-Saharan Africa's share of global trade fell from 4 to 2 percent.[25]

Like most Africans, Kenyans are producers of raw materials, for which little is paid, and excellent consumers of imported products—clothing, food, and other essentials—for which we have paid quite a lot. Our hairpins and plastic combs come from China, and the oil to produce goods both comes from the Middle East; our soap, toothpaste, and shampoo are imported from England; our body creams are from Germany; and our clothes and shoes, both old and new, are brought in from outside Kenya. Even the buttons that we sew on with Chinese needles threading Indian cotton are foreign. When I was young, we used to go to shops where you would literally place your foot on a piece of paper and the cobbler would make you shoes, from local leather. Or a local tailor would take your measurements and make you a dress. There were no secondhand clothes or plastic shoes. We used to sew socks by hand; now they too are imported from China. While life has been made easier, it has also become very expensive and heavily dependent on imported goods.

Our food might be produced in Kenya—either chickens or rice, as well as some greens—but the income received from it generally flows in one direction: out. Consequently, the money brought to rural areas through the sale of commodities such as cash crops is then siphoned back to the towns where the consumer goods are transported from, and eventually repatriated to the countries that produce them. Even most of the industries that are located in Kenya—tourism, and the growing of flowers, coffee, and tea—are largely owned by foreign companies.

Because commodities depend on availability as much as demand, they are subject to sometimes volatile price variations. In recent years, the world price of oil and certain minerals has gone up, which has meant that some of Africa's economies have been prospering. According to the United Nations Economic Report on Africa for 2008, Africa's GDP has increased from just under 4 percent annually in 2001 to just over 6 percent in 2008. Inflation is down over the same period, from just over 10 percent to 5 percent.[26]

While this news is welcome for those countries that have large deposits of desirable commodities, their economies are still overly dependent on too few industries for them to ride the inevitable ups and downs of the market. At the same time, not enough African countries have diversified their economic base, nor made progress toward self-sufficiency in essential sectors such as food production. For instance, between 2002 and 2005, Zambia's total exports more than doubled, from just under a billion dollars to nearly $2.1 billion; however, this increase was mainly because of a rise in the price of copper, which amounted to 50 percent of total exports in 2005.[27] Ever since its independence from Britain, Nigeria's economy has been almost wholly reliant on oil, accounting for over 95 percent of total exports since the mid-1980s.[28] The International Monetary Fund anticipates further divergence in growth rates between oil-exporting and oil-importing nations in sub-Saharan Africa.[29]

The overreliance on a natural resource to the detriment of creating other industries and diversifying a country's economy is called by development specialists the "resource curse."[30] It is especially problematic when the country does not have the technological know-how to use those resources, and is instead dependent on others to exploit and share the end products. One of the challenges for Africa's newly growing, oil-exporting nations will be to overcome the continent's dispiriting pattern of the citizens of resource-rich states remaining mired in poverty, even as a small elite and the international speculators and multinational corporations reap huge benefits. To that end, former World Bank economist Paul Collier has proposed an internationally agreed-upon charter for natural resource revenues that would ensure transparency in awarding contracts and payments to exploit resources; assure some stability in prices (avoiding cycles of boom and bust); make visible public expenditures; and better manage public spending when resource revenues aren't consistent from year to year. Civil society, particularly within countries dealing with the "resource curse," would be central to getting such a charter adopted.[31]

The economic dominance of one natural resource, however, need not always be a curse. Norway, for instance, has half of Europe's oil and gas reserves and in 2004 became the third-largest exporter of oil in the world.[32] In the nineteenth and early twentieth centuries, Norway was so poor that 15 percent of its population emigrated, in search of more opportunities and better lives. However, by 2007, it had the third-highest GDP per capita in the world, average life expectancy at birth was eighty years, and it ranked second in the United Nations' Human Development Index.[33] Norway maintains high rates of taxation, and costs of living are also high, which together mean that disparities in wealth are relatively small and within the society an egalitarian ethos predominates.

Since 1990, Norway has been saving some of the money it receives from its oil exports in a sovereign wealth fund. As of June 2007, this fund was worth $300 billion, or $62,000 for every Norwegian citizen. The oil industry is largely controlled by the Norwegian government, a fact that suggests that a state-run enterprise need be neither inefficient nor a locus of corruption. The Norwegian economy's low inflation rate and the government's emphasis on research and development in non-oil sectors demonstrate its recognition that today's vast oil income should not be squandered. It also shows that Norway is preparing for when its oil runs out and so avoiding the "trap" that many African states that are heavily dependent on natural resources have fallen into.[34]

The rulers of the United Arab Emirates—seven small city-states that have integrated economically and politically, thus raising their international profiles—are using their oil and natural gas reserves to diversify their economies through service industries and leisure resorts. When I visited in 2007, I was impressed by how much the UAE has invested in higher education, particularly to develop a generation of men and women able to capitalize on future innovations in science and information technology. UAE ministers made it clear to me that they were preparing for a time without oil. The governance structures of Norway and the UAE could not be more different, yet leaders in both countries recognize that the long-term stability and sustainability of their economies depend on sound management of their resources.

Nigeria, on the other hand, offers a classic example of how poor leadership can facilitate the exploitation of a commodity, in this case oil, at the expense of the vast majority of a country's people. Partly because of the competition for oil revenues within a small elite, Nigeria has experienced political violence, social unrest, long periods of military rule, massive corruption, a continuing lack of basic services, and extreme poverty. Disparities between rich and poor are still vast, and decent basic infrastructure and health and education remain, in the eyes of most Nigerians, beyond reach. By some accounts, Nigeria has earned $400 billion in oil revenues since independence, of which perhaps $380 billion has been mismanaged.[35] In 1998, Nigeria returned to a system of democratic governance; however, it is reported that many Nigerians are losing their conviction that democracy will lead to development, greater equality and equity, and a more farsighted use of Nigeria's oil income.

An additional, crucial element in the difficulties Africa has had in accessing the benefits of the global economy has been the policies of the World Bank, the IMF, and developed-country governments. In the 1980s, the Common Agricultural Policy of the European Union restricted access to Africa's agricultural products, while the World Bank and IMF's structural adjustment policies emphasized commodity development over diversification. One of the conditionalities imposed through structural adjustment programs and, more recently, debt relief initiatives is that poor countries further open their markets to goods from the developed world, as a way to bring in foreign currency and stimulate foreign investment.

But this call for open markets has not been reciprocated. The European Union, the United States, and some East Asian countries still protect their own producers of cotton, wheat, sugar, and other products either by subsidizing their industries or by placing tariffs on such products and others from outside. The unwillingness of the industrialized nations to remove these subsidies, coupled with developing countries' growing concerns about food security in the wake of high prices for oil and staple grains, led to the collapse of global trade talks in 2008.

Sometimes what seems like a breakthrough in trade is actually a further impediment in disguise. For instance, the 2000 African Growth and Opportunity Act, passed by the U.S. Congress, gave Kenya and other African nations a chance to manufacture cotton products and sell them into the American market. One of the catches, however, was that Kenyans had to use American yarn, even though Kenya also grows cotton. This means that Kenya was, in effect, subsidizing U.S. cotton growers and cutting off a market for its own producers. In this way, less powerful states can be flattered by the international community or individual nations to feel they're more important than they are, or they can be bullied into providing advantageous trade terms to wealthier countries.

Despite this difficult environment, it would not be in Africa's best interests to shut up shop; Africa cannot avoid the fact of globalization. Indeed, the exponential growth in the telecommunications industry in such countries as Kenya,

South Africa, Ghana, Namibia, and even war-torn Somalia is just one example of the enormous potential of emerging markets in sub-Saharan Africa.[36] These present Africans with opportunities to increase their standard of living, expand intra- and inter-African trade, and develop their economies beyond the extraction of natural resources and the export of commodities. Indeed, Africa has an opportunity to add value to those commodities by generating finished products. The cocoa of West Africa could be turned into chocolates in that part of the world rather than in Belgium; the coltan of Congo could be added to capacitors in the same country it is mined from; or the abundant sunshine of many parts of Africa could be harvested by solar panels built on the continent.

One of the ways in which the friends of Africa can help is by making education in science and technology, as well as the required technical assistance, available and affordable to African countries. African governments have a responsibility, too. Unless they nurture an environment that encourages creativity and innovation and supports the same, their countries will remain backward in a world where technology dominates— despite the huge amount of resources at their disposal. Achieving this will involve increasing the capacities of Africa's young people through education, in particular in the areas of science and technology. Investing in people and in relevant education can lead to the refining of gold or oil—something understood by the Asian economic "tigers," who made education in science and technology a national priority while too many African nations invested in "security" and wars.

Nevertheless, the recent expansion of some African economies is a hopeful sign that Africa can move beyond aid toward self-reliance, and perhaps in so doing realign the imbalances in the international trading system. In 2007, domestic investment was a record 22 percent of GDP, while in 2006, according to the OECD's Development Assistance Committee, the $48 billion of private capital that flowed to sub-Saharan Africa—four times what it was in 2000—surpassed official development aid ($40 billion) for the first time.[37]

Greater private investment and capital flows, however, are not panaceas for underdevelopment. While Africans are using cellular technology productively to help facilitate business and transfer money,[38] and a few African entrepreneurs are becoming very wealthy by establishing cell phone connections, even in remote areas, Africans as a whole are still only talking on cell phones and not making them; likewise, they are watching televisions rather than generating content for them or manufacturing the sets themselves. One way to ensure that African countries are more self-reliant and competitive is for industrialized nations to transfer technology—with a priority on green technologies—to those nations that are technologically less advanced. But African countries themselves should also invest in science and technology.

The clear need for capital investments to generate wealth for citizens and promote development does not obviate the equally clear need that the wealth created be produced and distributed in a manner that is fair and just. Investors must work closely with governments to promote businesses that benefit the people, and not take advantage of the weaknesses or corruption of those governments, or their laws and regulations, to exploit citizens.

Of course, one of the reasons politicians allow their people and the nation's resources to be exploited is because they have been co-opted—made directors of investors' businesses, offered opportunities to invest themselves, or given lucrative kickbacks. What more governments in Africa need to appreciate is that the inequities that characterize their societies, which are perpetuated by governance and economic systems that are inherently unjust, will only fuel violence and conflict. Sooner or later, the grievances of the local populations will come to the fore, whether encouraged by politicians during elections or when the politicians themselves are aggrieved; injustices can be contained only for so long.

The repayment of debts, the realignment of trade, and the capitalization of African economies all depend on a rebalancing of globalization. One of its main arbiters, the World Trade Organization (WTO), doesn't operate on a level playing field: developed countries demand that developing nations open their markets, but they do not reciprocate sufficiently by opening their own. In the WTO, all countries sit as equals, even though it's self-evident that all countries are *not* equal.[39] Each representative is, of course, trying to get the best deal for his or her country, but given that the combined GDPs of the East African nations of Kenya, Tanzania, and Uganda (with a total population of one hundred million) are less than that of the small American state of Delaware, with a population of fewer than one million, it's clear that African states, with limited bargaining power, can continue to be taken advantage of.

One of the ways for Africa to get a better deal at the WTO or in other arenas where trading rules are being negotiated is to band together, as a continent or in regions. President Kwame Nkrumah of Ghana foresaw this need fifty years ago, when he called for a united Africa to offset the political power of Europe, the United States, and the Soviet Union. Today, the axes have altered slightly. Outside the leverage supplied by the oil-producing states, it is now the European Union, the United States, and East and South Asian economies that exert the most influence over international trade.

During the Cold War, Africa tried to respond to Nkrumah's call through the Organization of African Unity. Various regional associations were also created. In 1967, Kenya, Tanzania, and Uganda formulated arrangements to create a stronger political and economic union, the East African Community. It lasted for a decade before geopolitical interests and internal political conflict led to its collapse. If it had been nurtured, the East African Community could have taken the region very far by removing the artificial economic and political barriers created by the colonial powers and continued by the postcolonial African leadership.

In 2002, to meet the needs and opportunities of Africa in a rapidly globalizing world, the OAU joined with the African Economic Community to become the African Union (AU). Numerous regional trading blocs have also been created in recent years, such as the Common Market for Eastern and Southern Africa (COMESA), the Southern African Development Community (SADC), the Economic Community of West African States (ECOWAS), the Customs and Economic Union of Central Africa (UDEAC), and, in 2002, the New Partnership for Africa's Development (NEPAD).[40] Unfortunately, these have not performed as well as they should have, and many ordinary Africans are not even aware of them.

New efforts are being made to re-create the East African Community, this time including the original three members plus Burundi and Rwanda, with the objectives of expanding and strengthening cooperation between the nations. Regrettably, such efforts are, as they have been for years, riddled with suspicion and mistrust between both governments and citizens of the countries concerned, so movement toward the unity and development the community envisions is very slow. As a consequence, the imbalances in trade between Africa and the industrialized world remain.

Outside of Africa, other political-economic blocs have fared better. In the same year that Ghana became independent, the European Economic Community was founded, with France, Italy, West Germany, Belgium, the Netherlands, and Luxembourg as member states. Today, its successor, the European

Union (EU), has twenty-seven members, with a total population nearing five hundred million, a GDP in 2007 of nearly
$15 trillion, and a per capita GDP of around $32,000.[41] As it has
expanded, the EU has helped once relatively poor countries
like Ireland, Spain, Greece, and nations in eastern Europe
develop and stabilize. Although the political and economic
integration of the EU has not been without its difficulties, it
does demonstrate that with political will, and if leaders put
their people first, much can be achieved.

For too long, Africans have been falsely divided and weakened by Cold War politics, Great Power rivalries, greed, petty
squabbles, and conflicts trumped up by demagogues and
tyrants. By raising their voices in unison at a regional and
continent-wide level, Africans can both demand and achieve
more in the negotiating rooms and halls of power. It is not too
much to say that unless African leaders embrace their common goals and work together to make their individual nations
and the whole continent stronger, Africa will remain a victim
of globalization and unfair global trade rules, not a beneficiary.

The world is not going to wait for Africa. History suggests that it will move forward without her, and exploit her
resources for as long as they are exploitable. Africa can no
longer stand still; like the Angolan people with the flying fish
of Luanda, she must grasp the opportunities that are right
before her eyes.

THE IMPACT OF THE EAST

In recent years, China and other Asian nations have been
assuming a larger role in African affairs. Drawing upon common experiences with Africa as victims of imperialism, countries like China have begun to form bilateral arrangements,
offering African nations development aid and construction
assistance on the one hand, and seeking access to oil and

mineral deposits to fund its own exponential growth on the other. For instance, currently China gets nearly a third of its oil from Africa. Chinese development assistance to African nations is around $2 billion, while trade between Africa and China increased from $10 billion in 2000 to $70 billion in 2007. China's direct investment was $2.5 billion in 2006, a nearly fivefold increase since 2003.[42] China considers herself a friend of Africa and works closely with the Group of 77, the largest intergovernmental organization of developing states in the United Nations, comprised of 130 countries, many of them former colonies of European powers. China, as one of only five countries with veto power on the UN Security Council, can, and indeed has, used this power to protect the interests of African states.

Some governments and civil society groups in the West, including human rights advocates, have been dismayed by the growing presence of China in Africa. They have accused China of doing business with African governments that turn a blind eye to human rights and environmental destruction. This is partly because civil society has largely succeeded in persuading the West not to support oppressive governments. In tandem with some Africans, they complain that China is not only flooding Africa with cheap, poorly made goods that threaten to extinguish local African businesses, but that the Chinese government and private companies are bringing in Chinese labor to finish projects.

It can be argued that Africa benefits from these new sources of investment; that along with its trade agreements, countries like China are building much-needed hospitals, roads, and even soccer stadiums in communities that haven't had such services provided by their own governments. Further, they are able to do so at competitive rates. So perhaps what really worries other trading partners of Africa is that the East, especially China, is entering their traditional sphere of influence and that their

long-standing economic power over African countries is being
threatened.[43]

In the past, people entered Africa by force. These days, they
come with similarly lethal packages, but they are camouflaged
attractively to persuade Africa's leaders and peoples to cooperate. Of course, such packages are eye-catching to many African
governments, not least because they may be free of "conditionalities," such as respect for human rights, protection of the
environment, and promotion of equity.

Some Africans are asking themselves whether the continent
is being exposed to a new wave of colonialism. It was certainly
a signifier that the African leadership considers China a great
friend when no fewer than forty African heads of state traveled
to Beijing in November 2006 for a China-Africa forum.[44] It was
perhaps also representative of the relative power of Africa in
the world that so many presidents and prime ministers felt it
was necessary to be there.

Like any would-be Great Power—and, indeed, like many
other powerful nations today—China, South Korea, Iran, and
others are seeking to advance their interests, acquire needed
resources, find new markets for their products, and exert their
influence in regional and global policymaking. Also, as with
any Great Power, China's interests may be pursued at the
expense of human rights—by, for instance, placing access to oil
above protecting the population of Darfur by blocking moves
to sanction Sudan in the United Nations; allying itself with
Russia to stop more forceful action against the government of
Zimbabwe by the Security Council;[45] and conducting business
with African leaders who still abuse their citizens or constrain
democratic space. In this regard, China really is no different
from the United States, the Soviet Union, and the colonizing
European nations, which facilitated the rise of African strong-
men in the postcolonial period and protected them, despite

knowing of their corruption and cruelty, and continued to extract Africa's resources unhindered.

The sale of arms to Africa illustrates how varied, and occasionally destructive, some of Africa's trading partners are. China, Israel, former republics of the Soviet Union, and more than twenty members of the Organization for Security and Cooperation in Europe supply illicit small firearms to Africa.[46] The legal trade also thrives. The United Kingdom sold more than £125 million ($200 million) worth of weaponry to Africa in 2000. Between 1998 and 2005, the United States sold more than $157 million worth of arms to Africa, with China accounting for $600 million, Russia $700 million, and western European countries (excluding France) accounting for $1.2 billion. France's arms sales alone were worth $900 million.[47]

As with so many of Africa's challenges, it is up to the African leadership to stop internal conflicts powered by greed and to ensure that it no longer continues its inequitable arrangements with other regions. There is also opportunity for leadership at other levels—for instance, Africa's civil society reaching out to China's nascent civil society to share information and to try to hold each other's governments accountable for their actions, particularly as they affect human rights.

A good example of the possibilities for Africans to recognize common interests and act in concert arose in April 2008 when unionized dockworkers in Durban, South Africa, refused to unload a shipment of Chinese arms bound for Zimbabwe at a time when Zimbabwe was embroiled in a major political and humanitarian crisis. They had been alerted to the shipment by civil society activists in Zimbabwe, who were fearful that the reported cargo of some 3 million rounds of ammunition for AK-47s, 1,500 rocket-propelled grenades, and 3,000 mortar rounds and tubes might be used in the lead-up to a highly contested runoff election.[48] The late Zambian president Levy

Mwanawasa, then the presiding officer of the Southern African Development Community, asked the fourteen states that belong to SADC not to allow the ship to dock and unload, fearing that delivery of the weapons would further destabilize Zimbabwe.[49]

However, the ship did not turn around to head back to China; instead, it sailed around the Cape of Good Hope, bound for Namibia. At that point, news of the ship's whereabouts became harder to come by. Even though the Chinese government indicated that it would have the ship return to China, in May reports began to emerge that the cargo had not only been brought to land, but indeed had made it to Zimbabwe. Some journalists suggested that the ship had unloaded its lethal cargo at Pointe-Noire in the Republic of the Congo (Congo-Brazzaville), while others claimed that the ship was seen docked at another port along the West African coast.

As I followed this story, I was reminded that this port was the same one where a quarter of a century earlier I had seen the deprivations caused by conflict and the pernicious effects of irresponsible interference with an African state. Peace may have returned to Angola, but the legacy of internal conflicts and arms sales are still plaguing the region. It appears that Zimbabwean officials had flown to Angola to arrange delivery of the shipment, and the port where the cargo came ashore was Luanda.

Six

LEADERSHIP

I FIRMLY BELIEVE that unless Africans from *all* levels of society recognize and embrace the challenge of leadership, Africa will not move forward. In chapter 2 I discussed the historical, cultural, and economic roots of the failure of African leadership, and how it neglected to give the African people reason to hope. In this chapter I will examine in more detail what good leadership—and its correlative, good governance—might look like.

Leadership is not simply a matter of filling the top positions in a government, institution, or private business. Nor is it a quality restricted to the ambitious, the elite, the politically gifted, or the highly educated. In fact, leadership can be demonstrated by those who are marginalized and poor as much as by those who have had all the privileges that society has been able to bestow on them. Indeed, not every person in a leadership position is truly a leader.

Many aid and development scholars and practitioners have pointed to Africa's leadership deficit and wondered why it has been so hard to overcome. Some have suggested that the issue of poor governance has been overemphasized as a factor in development failures; in this view, poor countries generally produce poor governance, not vice versa. Some scholars have also pointed to Africa's geography—few navigable rivers, many landlocked nations, debilitating diseases like malaria—as inhibiting economic growth. They also note Africa's climate—many arid and semi-arid regions; tropical forests, with fragile soils; too little or too much rain—which makes agriculture more difficult than it is in temperate regions.

As a biologist, I agree that the environment underlies all human activities. However, I don't believe that Africa's geography and climate have to be permanent obstacles to its development. Switzerland and Austria are both small and landlocked countries; Japan does not possess many natural resources; all three have mountainous landscapes that make farming difficult. Every country has geographical and climatic challenges that require management and adaptation. While some African countries do have a climate and geography that places them at a disadvantage, what deficits they have could be overcome or mitigated through effective leadership that utilizes the resources available—both natural and human—responsibly. However, in the absence of such leadership, development for the common good will be held in check, even in the most fertile and resource-rich countries.

One might ask: What does it take to produce leaders with such values, whose lives become their message and who humble themselves and sacrifice for the common good? It should not be impossible to find leaders in Africa willing to raise the standard of leadership and to nurture them so that they become beacons for the continent. To be sure, some leaders tried, often at great personal sacrifice, to give that hope to their people and to the African people at large—men such as Nelson Mandela in South Africa, Julius Nyerere in Tanzania, Seretse Khama in Botswana, Léopold Senghor in Senegal, Ahmed Ben Bella in Algeria, and even Kwame Nkrumah of Ghana in his early years. Will their example ever be followed by leaders and would-be leaders in Africa today and in coming decades?

The exercise of good leadership would end government violations of human rights and restrictions on freedoms such as the right to move, assemble, access information, and organize. Good leadership could decide, for instance, not to sell off

Africa's natural resources for such low prices, and then to invest the additional revenue to accelerate human and economic development. Good leadership could curtail corruption, one of the most corrosive aspects of poor leadership that has been rife in postindependence Africa. Good leadership would provide the milieu in which citizens can be creative, productive, and build wealth and opportunity.

It may be true that who the person leading the country is becomes less of a concern when you do not have enough to eat, or money with which to purchase necessities, or a roof over your head. But, despite the poverty that afflicts so many in Africa, I do not believe that Africans are more intrinsically incapable of organizing their lives and asserting their rights, or more willing to accept bad leadership, than peoples from other parts of the world. Furthermore, I am convinced there isn't a single person in Africa who genuinely prefers to live in a corrupt, broken society that has poor infrastructure, stifles innovation and achievement, fails to reward merit and capabilities, cannot provide basic services, and doesn't offer democratic space or ensure peace and security. All people desire a system that works.

The realization of good leadership could start with an African president or prime minister stepping forward and declaring: "We have a problem in our country and as a people. We are cheating and undermining ourselves, and we need to change. For whether it is a policeman bribing a bus driver, or a government minister receiving a kickback in order to license a business, or someone stealing someone else's crops to make a quick penny—we are failing ourselves, our country, those who came before us, and, indeed, future generations. I want us as a country to work on it. And it will start with me, and I will do my best to fight greed and corruption. I will value honesty in whatever I do. I will genuinely put the people first."

Then it could extend to the people themselves. It is also up to a critical mass of Africans to recognize that there *is* a problem of leadership, which in itself would be a step away from stasis. They could ask themselves: *Do we feel marginalized? Are we capable of acting in concert to make sure that our resources are used equitably? Do we recognize the value of belonging to a state? When we are entrusted with positions of leadership, are we committed to enhancing the welfare of our fellow citizens?* These are the questions that make a society work, and their answers express themselves through a system of governance, which can evolve and change to meet the needs of the people over time.

FROM TRAPPINGS TO TRAPS

The pathology of power only intensifies the longer a leader remains in office, even to the extent that leaders find themselves prisoners of the lieutenants and associates who helped them achieve that office in the first place—whether through patronage, a coup, or solely with the support (armed or otherwise) of their ethnic group. There have been many cases where it is the leader's lieutenants who do not allow the head of state to leave office, because they fear prosecution by a new government for their involvement in gross violations of human rights or crimes against humanity committed by the regime they serve. In a winner-take-all presidential system, which is the case in many African countries, these men and women have a great deal to lose if the head of state relinquishes power. They will no longer have easy access to the wealth and resources of the nation, and those replacing them will have the levers of the state to hold them accountable for the actions they took while in power, if they choose to do so.

As long as African politicians are pressured by their constituencies—parliamentary or ethnic—to remain in the government whether they win elections or not, because the people believe the politicians will provide them with patronage, and as long as politicians continue to supply these gifts, handouts, and favors, then any system of governance will be broken. When this toxic combination means that leaders cling to power at all costs—when some of the best and brightest Africans demonstrate that it matters more to be a minister, prime minister, or president than it does to promote the welfare of the country or protect its citizens—then neither development nor peace will be sustainable; the three-legged stool will remain unstable.

It is a truism, but it is very difficult to fight a dictator using democratic means, as any pro-democracy campaigner or organization will attest. How, then, do people remove themselves from underneath the boot of those who control them and their resources, who violate their rights and destroy their livelihoods or even take their lives? In Kenya, for instance, civil society and the opposition sought for years to remove a dictatorial regime from power through elections, flawed though they might have been, but they were unable to; even a coup attempt didn't dislodge it. This is not to say that Africans have accepted their fate where tragic failures of leadership have occurred. They have not, and the struggle continues.

In Africa, as elsewhere, democratic space can be created and sustained only when a critical mass of people is aware of the situation and willing to speak out, protest, monitor government actions, and risk harassment, arrest, or even death. That courage, however, also requires a leader (or his backers) who will acknowledge the rights of the people to self-determination and prosperity, and as a result demonstrate leadership that avoids bloodshed or further violence. So although the people of eastern Europe brought down the Berlin Wall, they needed Soviet leader Mikhail Gorbachev not to send in the tanks. While Nelson Mandela's principled stance led to sanctions against South Africa that brought unbearable pressure upon er THE CHALLENGE FOR AFRICA

the apartheid regime, F. W. de Klerk had to concede that the era of apartheid had to come to an end.

One of the reasons why success in securing democratic space continues to elude the populace in many African countries is that politicians tend to change with the tide. For instance, they become "democrats" when democracy is seen as the route to power. But when another route appears that is shorter, they are often willing to take it, even if it means joining a rival group or faction. Indeed, many of Africa's civil wars have been fought by former colleagues who broke ranks or linked up with opposing camps if doing so would allow them to reach the leadership position they coveted more quickly.

In recognition of the need to develop good leadership in Africa and encourage the peaceful transfer of power, in 2007 the Sudanese telecom billionaire Mo Ibrahim established the Mo Ibrahim Prize for Achievement in African Leadership. (His foundation is dedicated to promoting good governance in Africa.) In creating the prize, which provides the winner with $5 million over ten years and $200,000 each year for the rest of the winner's life, Mr. Ibrahim pointed out that many African leaders are reluctant to leave power because they no longer have access to the perks of office:

> Suddenly all the mansions, cars, food, wine is withdrawn. Some find it difficult to rent a house in the capital. That incites corruption; it incites people to cling to power. The prize will offer essentially good people, who may be wavering, the chance to opt for the good life after office.[1]

The first winner of the prize was Joaquim Chissano, the former president of Mozambique, who stepped down from power at the end of his second term in 2005. In his acceptance speech, Mr. Chissano emphasized two of the three pillars of the African stool:

We need to develop and root in our societies a culture of peace. We need to promote regional integration. We need to encourage public-private partnerships and give a more robust role to our private sector. We must fight corruption and promote integrity and good governance. And we need to establish a sustained process of national dialogue and reconciliation in all the countries emerging from conflict. In short, we need to work towards building capable states in Africa.[2]

On the face of it, it may seem scandalous that a leader has to be enticed by a potential award *not* to be corrupt or to cling to power, and a damning indictment of the failure of Africa over the last half century to cultivate genuine leadership on a continental scale. But, curiously, the award reflects a reality for African leaders, which is that, unlike prime ministers, presidents, or senior politicians in the industrialized world—who will receive a sizeable pension from the state once they retire and can earn substantial income from speaking engagements, book deals, consulting fees, lobbying positions, and chairmanships of various boards of directors, and enjoy respect and a place of honor in society—African leaders have many fewer opportunities to live a decent lifestyle and retain respect and honor once out of office. Indeed, many civil servants and MPs in Africa are still struggling to secure a reasonable pension once their government service is over. This naturally makes them even less likely to want to leave their positions, and much less the heads of state they may well support. What is needed are institutions, like those in other regions, that would provide pensions and other support to former heads of state, civil servants, and veterans who have earned them. The lack of such institutions is another facet of the leadership deficit.

What might be an even more powerful incentive than the Mo Ibrahim Prize would be an award bestowed by the African Union to a head of state when the AU felt that he or she had practiced good governance and visionary leadership. It would be very interesting to see leaders competing to win *that* prize, as well as the one established by Mo Ibrahim.

UNDUE DEFERENCE

Many observers have wondered why it is that Africans have seemed to tolerate poor leadership over many decades. Is it passivity, or apparent deference to their leaders—even when the latter have proven so disastrous to their countries? Some believe that these attitudes are the result of Africans' natural tendency to venerate elders, a misconception that may persist because many of Africa's precolonial systems of governance were based on age groups. However, as the following case from my micro-nation indicates, the relationship between leaders and their people is perhaps more complex and subtle.

Precolonial Kikuyu society developed its social and leadership structures from birth. While the methods wouldn't be considered scientific by today's standards, midwives observed the infant at birth and could apparently tell whether the child was likely to be a warrior or a medicine man, a priest or a smith, an information gatherer (whom today we'd call a spy) or a counselor. Because there were no formal schools or seminaries, the community watched the children closely as they grew, to see whether they were developing the talents expected of them and that would qualify them for the profession they'd been marked for. If they were, they would become apprentices. Sometimes, the child, having been born to a family that traditionally worked in one area, such as metallurgy, would continue that lineage as an apprentice.

The community had developed these ways of ensuring that talents were cultivated and leadership nurtured as children grew into adulthood and assumed their responsibilities. Leadership took many different forms. If someone was a smith, he was considered a leader in his own right, because he had specialized knowledge important for the community's welfare, which could be passed from one generation to the next. Another group of leaders was the medicine men—whom today we would call psychiatrists and healers—who were deeply respected by all members of society. I recall that one of my uncles had the paraphernalia of a medicine man or healer, but he abandoned his position during the course of my childhood because he could no longer practice freely. As nearly everyone in the Kikuyu community became a Christian, the clientele for medicine men declined dramatically; to consult one was to risk the accusation of being "anti-Christian." They and their powers were demystified, and they came to be seen by communities as signifiers of backwardness.

If an individual in the society clearly expressed a talent for something other than what the midwife had marked them for, or the counselor had directed them toward, or if they were acting inappropriately, the community would steer them toward the new talent and away from wrongdoing long before they inherited a position for which they were temperamentally or practically unsuited. Indeed, by the time anyone reached a position of authority, they would have gone through an initiation ceremony and rituals, in which both genders had a role to play. After each of these, the individual would have been entrusted with more responsibility. In addition, as he or she graduated from one level to another, there were always older authorities, both men and women, ahead to make sure the younger person understood their responsibilities. This meant that by the time the individual became a counselor or a priest, they would have been in their sixties or seventies, and well seasoned and well judged by the community. This is why old age in Africa is associated with wisdom and respect, even though the cultural context of creating just and seasoned leaders has been lost.

In communities where governance and leadership resided in one age group, after a period of time in power the entire age group retired in favor of the next generation. In the Kikuyu tradition, this was a formal procedure that took several years to complete and was known as *ituika*, literally translated as "the severance." These ceremonies served as de facto "term limits," and acted as a guarantee to all generations that their time to guide the destiny of their people would come, and that they needed to be both patient and prepared to take on their responsibilities. It also meant that there were checks and balances to guard against corruption. Each generation of leaders understood that they were being watched closely by the next, just as they observed those who'd gone before them, to make sure they were not squandering the resources—whether privately owned or held in common—that they had under their control. This ensured that common resources like forests, rivers, and land were protected and handed on to the next generation to continue managing.

The last such *ituika* in the Kikuyu community was to take place between 1925 and 1928, but it remains incomplete. The British colonial authorities, fearing the gathering of a large group of people in one place, cut it short and banned it. Since the symbols of power were never handed over to the next generation, this signaled the end of the Kikuyu system of self-governance. In similar fashion, throughout the continent the European powers ended (sometimes unknowingly) or severely eroded other precolonial systems of governance. Three generations of Kikuyus later, that mode of self-government, or even the knowledge that the community once ruled itself using an indigenous form of democratic space, has been virtually forgotten. Even today, and even among the most sophisticated of contemporary Kikuyus, many are unaware of this and the multiple governance structures that existed in Africa before the Europeans came.

The Kikuyu system is one of the many such structures that could offer insight into how Africans practiced justice and protected individual and property rights. People may argue that such systems were not "democratic" in the way that we would understand the word today. What this system did, however, was provide a methodology by which good leadership could be cultivated and nurtured, and also be held accountable. By the time they reached the apogee of responsibility in the society, every individual had been tested for years. At each stage of their progression through the age-sets, the community had an opportunity to guide that person's use (or abuse) of power through the presence of an older authority, and the careful observation of the generation below. Such systems were also in certain ways more protective of property, women, children, and even life than some modern governance structures.

This heritage has by and large been lost. For instance, Kenya is currently debating whether it should adopt American, British, or German constitutions in redrafting its own; as in many modern African nations, no mention or use is made of the experiences of governance bequeathed to us by our ancestors. African constitutions were in the main written by the colonial powers, drawing on European traditions and not those of the indigenous populations. In Kenya's current form of governance, for instance, modeled on the British parliamentary system, individuals can stay in power for thirty or even forty years, or, indeed, for life. Although young people can be, and are, voted into office in each election, the attractions of incumbency and the undesirability of leaving office are such that many in the older generation are reluctant to relinquish power. At the same time, younger generations chafe at not being able to take their turn.

This is a pattern we see repeated in many countries in Africa. Unfortunately, there is no guarantee that the new political leadership will outstrip the old in its ethics, performance, or commitment to service. Instead, the path to power today in modern African states is often much easier than it was for precolonial Kikuyus. What talks loudest generally is not honesty, commitment, or vision, but money. If you are willing to use enough of it, not only for yourself but also for those who will wield power, you can buy a leadership position. It is not unlikely that if you are elected as an MP, you will be given a post in the government commensurate with the level of financial support you provided to the person distributing power. The more that was spent, the better the position. You may have all the titles befitting a leader, but none of the serious examination, experience, or ethical beliefs that befit someone who has been entrusted with leadership.

It is true that many Africans still trust their leaders and want to believe in them. Certainly, Africa's leaders have relied on that trust, and the fact that the majority of their citizens are still uneducated, uninformed, unexposed, and poor—and therefore very dependent—to exploit them. This entrenched legacy is a vestige of the colonial era, when many citizens viewed their founders—the individuals who helped them gain independence—as almost superhuman.

The presidents who retained power for decades, and those who continue to this day, are not in control because of any intrinsic deference due to age or position of power. Some post-independence leaders genuinely earned the respect and trust of their people. Most, however, maintained power because either they were protected during the Cold War by one of the two blocs, or the leader ensured that enough of his supporters received the benefits of his patronage to assent to his continued hold on power.

In such a situation, this apparent passivity or fatalism does not emerge because of a natural tendency to accept one's lot. Rather, it is a bitter recognition that, until recently, in most independent African states all avenues for the nonviolent removal of political leaders were blocked, not least because of the behind-the-scenes support of the colonial and emerging global powers. After all, during the colonial period those same "fatalistic" Africans carried out acts of resistance and waged wars of liberation. Even though they were—literally—outgunned, and the reprisals were often brutal and disproportionate, they forced some of the most powerful nations and empires the world has seen to leave their continent. Indeed, in some ways, the numerous violent or undemocratic changes in power in Africa since independence suggest a distinctive lack of deference. At the same time, most of these coups have led only to further repression and the substitution of one dictator for another. Rarely have they resulted in the flourishing of democracy.

Perhaps it is African leaders' sense that their hold on power is actually quite tenuous that explains why so many flaunt the trappings of power so ostentatiously. Of course, to some degree, all leaders need to show they're more important than others, and to invest their office with dignity and authority. In Europe and Asia, nineteenth- and twentieth-century kings and emperors didn't dress like commoners either, for instance. Today in older countries, leaders have tended to reduce their preoccupation with excessive showiness, while in Africa they've done the opposite. Around the continent, heads of state, prime ministers, and sometimes even senior politicians travel with huge retinues and a large security detail—complete with stretch limousines, a convoy of cars, and outriders—that swoop down like eagles whenever the motorcade reaches its destination.

This rarely has anything to do with actual security; rather, it is an exhibition of the illusion of importance. Jokes are often made about the political elites' preoccupation with displays of power, privilege, and importance. Ministers are called *wabenzi*, a Kiswahili term meaning "the people of the Mercedes-Benz"; the term has become shorthand for a member of the new

African ruling class—generally a government official or member of his or her family—who loves to show off the prerogatives of power and wealth. Critics of the privileged may laugh, but in the countryside the poor masses are impressed and regard such displays with adulation. They can only dream of such wealth and comfort or of holding such a position themselves.

Nevertheless, the insecurity evident within such a leader's show of power is almost palpable. An illustration of this is how quickly new leaders ensure that the previous incumbents of high government offices are immediately stripped of any status the minute they leave their position. This expresses the chronic paranoia and desperation that hang around the offices of so many of the presidents and prime ministers of Africa—a disorder that, as was witnessed during the deeply flawed elections in Zimbabwe and Kenya, can have terrible consequences for the state and its people.

The outside world has been at once horrified and astonished by the self-aggrandizement of African heads of state like Jean-Bédel Bokassa of the Central African Republic, Idi Amin of Uganda, and Mobutu Sese Seko of Zaire. However, the message conveyed to these men by the industrialized world has not been consistent. In my experience, foreign diplomats and businessmen speak politely when African leaders are present. In the quiet of their boardrooms and embassies, however, I'm sure they know all too well when the leaders with whom they conduct business are not doing right by their people. If their own leaders were doing the same things, they would be chastising them.

Ultimately, even today, twenty years after the end of the Cold War, the rules of realpolitik apply. Actual or potential business opportunities that await the foreign powers depend on maintaining a relationship with African leaders; in the end, these opportunities are often more significant to both sides than seemingly abstract notions such as practicing good governance or protecting human rights. After all, if that country is not the one doing business with an African government, then there may be other nations eager to step in. At times, it suits both non-African and African leaders to claim that the African people have, in some measure, accepted the form of governance they live with. Then they can cynically ask the question: Who are the foreign powers to dictate to sovereign nations how they should govern themselves? This attitude serves only the leaders on both sides of the divide; the victims, as always, are the African people.

A NEW CENTURY, A NEW GENERATION?

As the first and second generations of postindependence African presidents leave the scene, and the third takes power, most Africans have cause to reflect on the fact that they are still waiting for a genuine say in how their countries are governed. In a 2008 study, the U.S.-based organization Freedom House listed only eleven of sub-Saharan Africa's forty-eight nations as "free"—meaning that they had more than one political party, a free press, and protections for civil rights. This situation, while grim, was in fact an improvement over a similar survey conducted thirty years previously, when just three sub-Saharan African states were considered free. In Freedom House's analysis, the number of such nations defined in 2008 as "not free" was fourteen, down from twenty-five in 1977.[3] Most African states were judged in the middle: "partly free." This is not a record to be proud of.

In *Africa Unchained,* George Ayittey draws a distinction between those Africans whom he terms "the cheetahs" and those he calls "the hippos." The cheetahs are the young Africans, who, as this designation suggests, are agile and dynamic, ready to move Africa ahead. They are confronted, however, by the hippos—sturdy members of the older generation who cling to power and protect their territory fiercely when they perceive they are being attacked.[4] (Indeed, hippos are reputed to kill the most people in Africa of any wild animal!)

Like Ayittey, I would like to hope that the challenge of African leadership could be solved simply by persuading the hippos to leave the watering hole and retire to the shade. Unfortunately, many of the hippos were once cheetahs; and while I might wish I could be as confident as Ayittey that the cheetahs he places his hopes in won't become hippos, I am not so sure. The new generation of African leaders, drivers of a potential African Renaissance, have in some cases provided their countries with much-needed economic growth, political stability, and a measure of national reconciliation after years of devastating civil conflict and mismanagement. But a number of them have now been in power for quite a few years. Like previous African heads of state, some of them have also initiated conflicts with their neighbors, compromised elections, and sought to contain political dissent.

It is too early to say whether a new generation of cheetahs will remain cheetahs and truly open up a new chapter in Africa. A bright spot in 2005 was the election of Ellen Johnson-Sirleaf in Liberia. It is admirable that even though she hadn't won the presidency in an earlier vote, she tried again. It was also especially empowering for African women to see her succeed. Indeed, every time someone from a "disadvantaged" group makes a big leap like this, it is an inspiration to others in that group, who can now think, *Maybe I can do it too.* It also clearly challenged men, who until then had assumed that only they could be elected African presidents or prime ministers.

The expectations are very high for Johnson-Sirleaf to deliver for her people. After nearly a decade of civil war, Liberians have multiple needs. In 2006, about a year after Johnson-Sirleaf had taken the oath of office, I was part of a small group that met with her in New York. In our discussions, she mentioned that

Liberia's market women needed her special attention because of the important role they were playing in restoring Liberia's spirit after years of devastation. She is aiming to reconstruct the markets that were destroyed during the war and thereby grow a literally market-based economy.[5] This work with local women to stimulate self-reliance reminded me how essential it is that political leaders, no matter what is happening at international or national levels, recognize the importance of improving conditions in people's daily lives.

Johnson-Sirleaf has been in power for only a short time and has yet to meet all of the challenges and temptations her presidential colleagues encounter once in office. But if she decides to raise the bar, both because she is the first African woman to be elected head of state of a modern African nation and also because she seeks to embody a new form of leadership, she will be in the company of such other African heads of state as Presidents Chissano and Mandela. They elevated the standard of leadership and set an example that can, and should, be emulated.

Moreover, throughout the continent a genuine and deliberate effort has begun to provide a different kind of leadership from the past. Democratic space is significantly broader in many countries, while free elections are far more common, and coups far less so, than at any time since the continent's independence.

In recent years, I have been privileged to attend summits of the African Union, where generally I have been encouraged. The leadership is very different in values and principles from that which characterized the OAU, and the desire for change is reflected in the progressive development of demands for democratization, responsibility, and accountability within the African Union itself. Of course, I know that what I hear is partly rhetoric and not always accompanied by commitment to action. Furthermore, it is surprising to see the transformation

that apparently democratic, responsible, and even revolutionary leaders undergo once they are in power. Who can know
what power does to leaders? While there are many areas of
hope in Africa, there are also areas where the sense of hopelessness runs deep. Events in Sudan and Chad, the August 2008
overthrow of the first democratically elected president of Mauritania since independence, and the December 2008 military
coup in Guinea are all discouraging.

Nonetheless, I remain optimistic about the prospects for
improved leadership and governance in Africa because I see
some positive signs: the prompt response of the AU, under the
chairmanship of John Kufuor, then president of Ghana, to the
postelectoral violence in Kenya in 2008; the peaceful transition
of power in 2005 in Tanzania from President Mkapa to President Jakaya Kikwete; and the fact that the AU has not embraced
leaders who assume power undemocratically. These are all
indications of an Africa that may be embracing a new form of
leadership, one that will put the African people first, whether
in parliament or the treasury or the judiciary, and will make
them feel, and be, respected and valued.

Seven

MOVING THE SOCIAL MACHINE

ALMOST HALF the population of sub-Saharan Africa lives on less than one dollar a day, the highest level of poverty in the world. While poverty is at the root of many of the pressing problems Africa faces, so is the poor's apparent powerlessness. During the course of the last forty to fifty years, most Africans, in large measure because of their leaders' attitudes and policies, have come to believe that they cannot act on their own behalf. Self-determination and personal and collective uplift, values embraced by the great majority of Africans in the period just after independence, have been eroded.

Disempowerment—whether through a lack of self-confidence, apathy, fear, or an inability to take charge of one's own life—is perhaps the most unrecognized problem in Africa today. To the disempowered, it seems much easier or even more acceptable to leave one's life in the hands of third parties, whether governments, elected leaders, or, in some cases, aid agencies and faith-based organizations. Ultimately, they may believe that whatever happens is God's will, predetermined and inevitable. To try to convince such people that one can alleviate one's circumstances through one's own effort is hard. Whether the poor's self-reliance and motivation have been destroyed by decades of embedded state corruption or if there is a pathology of willed helplessness—indeed, a stubborn refusal to help oneself—is perhaps a discussion for social scientists, although I suspect that the loss of cultural bearings has contributed.

This "dependency syndrome" is a substantial bottleneck to

development, as challenging as corruption and poor governance. It has added an extra weight to the work of those who
want to enable individuals and communities to better their
circumstances.

Poor people need to be engaged in their own development,
and, by extension, in expanding the democratic space that
many African societies desperately need. Just as communities
should be mobilized to combat malaria, or HIV/AIDS, for
instance, so they must work together to fight the scourges of
failed leadership, corruption, and moral blindness. However,
because the poor are more likely to be uneducated, illiterate, and ignored, and feel powerless, this requires both political
and economic commitment, as well as patience and persistence, since change does not occur overnight.

Societies are like machines. When everything is working
smoothly, society can move forward. Because modern societies
are so complex and multilayered, most of us have little idea
how the societal machine operates beyond the parts that most
immediately affect us. However, although we may not see the
entire mechanism, it's clear that for a society to function,
everyone needs to do his or her part. If pieces of the machine
are not working properly, not only does the machine not move
forward, but it begins to grind. The broken cogs jam other
areas, even though they may not be immediately connected to
the nonworking parts. Before the machine comes to a complete
stop, that grinding can be excruciating.

In societies that are in the process of breaking down, people
become frustrated by their part of the system that isn't functioning. They then try to work around that broken area, which
only further damages the societal machine, further angering
the people. The irony is that if everybody performed their tasks
to the best of their ability, the machine would move. But if
individuals are more inclined to do things that bring the

machine to a halt or a crawl, eventually everybody becomes a victim. This is called "underdevelopment." What it means is that even the smallest move forward appears to take forever, and the societal machine is under constant threat of stopping altogether.

In Kenya in 2002, a coalition of political parties finally laid to rest the presidency of Daniel arap Moi, and the first new administration in twenty-four years came into power. A new-found spirit of enthusiasm pervaded the country; in fact, there was so much goodwill when the new government was formed that something extraordinary happened: across Kenya, the "social machine" began to move again.

Here is just one example. For years, policemen had cadged bribes from the drivers of *matatus,* the cheap, private minivans that, given the generally poor state of public transit, are the main means of transportation for millions of Kenyans. To the drivers, the bribes were an accepted cost of doing business— allowing them and not another driver to ply a certain route, or ensuring that police officers would ignore any infractions in the vehicle's condition or running. *Matatus* had become extremely unsafe; high-speed accidents were common, and thousands of lives were being lost every year. And yet, people had few other alternatives but to continue riding in them.

After the 2002 election, *matatu* passengers began to challenge any policeman who demanded a bribe from the driver. Inspired by the new government, which had vowed to make fighting the corruption that riddled society from top to bottom a priority, ordinary citizens stood up and demanded that nei-ther the police nor the drivers conduct business as usual. This reached a point where policemen stopped asking for the bribes, either because they feared the reaction of the *matatu* passengers, or, possibly, because even *they* embraced the new spirit and did their part to facilitate the service without demanding a kickback.

Matatu drivers also began obeying speed restrictions and agreed to abide by the new government's directive to install seatbelts, a practical safety measure that also limits the number of passengers. (Previously, drivers would pick up as many people as they could, even when riders were literally hanging out of the doors.) This was evidence of the "new Kenya" that citizens wanted to work for and believed was possible, after decades of a government devaluing their aspirations for a more honest and just society.

But as soon as it was clear that individuals in the new government were not honest and refused to honor the promises they'd made to each other during the campaign, this spirit was suddenly lost; and unfortunately, before too long many people went back to the bad old habits.

In 2002, I, too, joined the new government, as a member of parliament for the constituency of Tetu, the region in which I had grown up. Increasingly, I had begun to feel that in order to bring about the change I was working to achieve at the grassroots, and what I believed needed to happen in the country as a whole, it was worth trying to enter parliament—either to alter existing legislation or to draft or pass new laws. The fact that the regime that had been in power for decades had come to an end provided a greater opportunity than previously had existed for me and other members of civil society to join the government.

If elected, we could also actively involve ourselves in shaping policy and the future of the country. As a member of civil society, one can have the most brilliant ideas in the world and still be ignored if one is not in a position to influence the leadership in power and the leaders aren't generating good ideas of their own. If, however, one has access to the leadership or if the leaders are pursuing policies that are beneficial to the country, then one's good ideas can be very quickly adopted on a larger scale.

I was also keen to see how I could apply in a parliamentary constituency the Green Belt Movement's approach to development: working from the bottom up to reach those who plan and execute the large-scale development models whose benefits rarely trickle down to the poor. I also hoped to empower communities to undertake their own development and learn to assume responsibilities as well as assert their rights. In theory there is no better way to address poverty than to go to the people themselves and ask them to name their priorities for local-level projects. I was pleased, therefore, when in 2003 the new Kenyan government took an important, indeed revolutionary, step and offered all MPs and their constituents an opportunity to try a similar approach.

Through an act of parliament, the government established the Constituency Development Fund, or CDF. The CDF would provide direct funding for local development initiatives, particularly targeting those that would combat poverty, to be decided on by the citizens themselves. The total amount dispensed was 2.5 percent of the tax revenues the government collected. The act stated that each of the 210 parliamentary constituencies would receive an equal portion of 75 percent of the funds, while the remaining 25 percent was allocated according to the poverty levels in each constituency, with those with higher poverty levels receiving more. The act also mandated that up to 10 percent of the CDF be allotted to bursaries—grants—for education. It was, indeed, an effort toward the equitable distribution of resources in all communities.

For years, Kenyans had complained about their taxes being misused by the ruling elite so that few of those funds, in the form of services, trickled down to the people—especially the rural poor; here, the government, for the first time, was attempting to ensure that some of the revenues it collected went directly to those who needed them most. The top was reaching out to the bottom. Finally, the approach that civil society had been advocating had been accepted by the government. An additional benefit of the act was that it encouraged Kenyans to pay their taxes, in the belief that the money would be used more transparently and accountably than in the past. The public knew that the more revenue the government received, the more funds would flow to the CDF. These revenues did indeed rise under the new government because more citizens were willing to pay their taxes. In 2004, the CDF was allotted 1.26 billion Kenyan shillings (nearly $20 million). By 2008, this had grown to 10.1 billion shillings (almost $155 million).[1]

In my judgment, the CDF presented a perfect opportunity to put into action a long-held belief of mine that for Africa to develop, it would be necessary to reach local people at the most elementary representative level and encourage them to both make decisions about projects and oversee their implementation for their community's benefit. Because Kenya, along with many other African countries, has a highly centralized governmental system—a legacy of colonialism—that over the years has tended to marginalize rural populations, it was necessary to devolve decision making to counter the dependency culture that had been created. The CDF opened up the possibility of converting talk into action by letting the people, for the first time, determine their development priorities themselves.

The CDF Act passed through parliament without a hitch, because it was to replace the practice of *harambees*, which had become a scourge in parliamentary constituencies. *Harambee* is the Kiswahili word for "pulling together." President Jomo Kenyatta introduced the term in Kenya in 1963 to instill a community spirit and sense of self-reliance and hard work in promoting small-scale local development. It had since come to mean something like a fund-raiser, or a donation, having been hijacked by politicians, who recognized it as an important forum for influencing potential voters. Members of parliament were constantly being asked to participate in *harambees,* both formal and informal—to build a new church hall, help parents pay for their children's school fees, assist in getting someone buried or married, or make possible a trip to the doctor or surgery. Although MPs in Kenya are now relatively well paid, much of one's salary, and more, could be consumed in various *harambees.*

By 2002, *harambees* had become almost a form of extortion: a means for constituents, church organizations, or women's groups to ask for, and receive, a donation from their MP. They had also become a way for the MPs, particularly at election time, to, in effect, buy votes to ensure their reelection. This problem is not confined to Kenya; it is not uncommon for politicians to give enticements—for instance, food, clothing, or cash—to citizens, especially those who are poor, to assure their support at the polls. Citizens are usually not interested in knowing whether the money and gifts came from the MP's pocket or were siphoned from the national treasury.

The CDF offered an opportunity to end some of this form of graft, and to use national funds not simply to dole out sacks of grain that might feed a family for a week, but to build health centers or ensure that children finished secondary school, the benefits of which would accrue to the whole community and, in theory, would lead to longer-term positive changes. The CDF also could be an important model on which to base anti-poverty, pro-development efforts in other African countries, and even other regions. Of course, if corruption set in, the CDF would be judged a failed experiment.

My constituency, Tetu, is in the Highlands of Central Kenya, near the provincial capital of Nyeri. The landscape is marked by hills and the mountain range of the Aberdares to the west and, in the distance, Mount Kenya to the north. The area has relatively high annual rainfall, and many rivers and streams. The economy is primarily agricultural, dominated by livestock farming and cash crops of coffee, tea, and maize. All agriculture in Tetu is small-scale; there are no large-scale farms except on the forested slopes of the Aberdares; very few industries operate here, apart from one tea factory. Per capita GDP is $400 a year, or $1.11 a day.

Through the CDF, Tetu was given 134 million shillings (about $2 million) over the five years I was an MP—the amount at the end being six times that at the beginning. Each MP was charged with the responsibility of making sure that the funds allocated to the CDF were actually used to benefit the people; the people themselves, the press, and a national-level CDF committee impaneled by the government would act as watchdogs. The government stipulated that each constituency create a committee of fifteen individuals to determine which projects would be funded. They would be paid a small stipend for their work.

I found this an unsatisfactory way to approach the allocation of CDF funds; I felt the CDF effort should be as participatory as possible. I'm someone who likes to experiment with ideas: if they work, I pursue them; if they don't, I drop them. I couldn't see how fifteen committee members would be sufficiently representative or able to identify the needs of the whole constituency, which numbered about ninety thousand people. So I went to the sub-locations—the smallest administrative units in Kenya, governing (in my constituency's case) around 2,500 people—and encouraged each of them to form a committee of fifteen people.

What I was trying to do was to ensure that the members of the committee were elected by the people. In establishing itself, each sub-locational committee had to follow criteria for representation of women and youth. There are thirty-seven sub-locations in Tetu, which meant that 555 people were involved directly in the CDF's operation. The committees would meet and decide on the priorities of their sub-location: Should they repair their social hall or a school classroom? Did they want to have pipes laid or extended, or have water flowing to a particular spot? Did they wish to build or complete a health center? Or hire a teacher for a school? This bottom-up approach helped people take ownership and feel like the projects were theirs.

The chair and vice-chair of each sub-locational committee met and formed locational committees, also with fifteen members, to discuss what they'd prioritized in their sub-locations: What was most strategic? What would serve people the best? What would most effectively alleviate poverty? Then each locational committee would choose two representatives to serve on the constituency-level committee. This committee of fifteen at the constituency level received five proposals from every location and then agreed on which projects to fund. Most of our decisions were unanimous. Only very rarely did we have to take a vote.

At each committee level, the government was also represented through local officials. However, it was made clear to them that while they were welcome to participate in the committee's deliberations, they had no role in choosing the members of any of the committees, or in determining the committee's priorities for the use of CDF funds. While the government representatives could vote, it was the people themselves who identified the projects, prioritized them, and implemented them. (In the classical governance structure, the government's representatives would have imposed their views on the people and, for the most part, people would have remained passive and endorsed what the government's representatives decreed.)

Every project also had an elected project committee: again, a means of encouraging local participation. I wanted people not only to choose projects, but also to see them through to completion. Whether it was a new classroom, the renovation of a health dispensary, or the installation of water pipes, it was the local project committee members who paid out the funds and ensured that the work progressed. As much as possible, the actual work was done by members of the community. Why look for high-level artisans and builders from Nairobi when they existed in the villages of the constituency, especially when many of them didn't have jobs or were underemployed? By having these individuals participate in the CDF projects, employment opportunities were created, money stayed in the community, and even more local people got involved.

This administrative structure kept corruption to a minimum and maximized efficiency, since the supervisors and workers all lived in the community and would be harshly judged by their peers if the project was mismanaged. Such grassroots responsibility has been lacking in most governance structures in Kenya and throughout Africa. Just about everything has been left to "officialdom," so when officialdom disappears, the project collapses. The CDF model developed in Tetu made this far less likely.

The committees were also charged with determining how to use the money allotted to educational grants. Since the Kenyan government was now providing free primary education, the decision was made to allocate money for students in secondary schools and encourage them to stay in school until they reached eighteen and graduated. As in the community projects, each sub-locational committee set to work and identified ten students in high schools—370 in all, both boys and girls—who would benefit from a grant.

Here, too, the community was empowered to make its own choices. The decision as to which child would get the grants no longer rested with an individual at the district or provincial level who might have thought that the son of the local chief or the daughter of the headmaster at his local school should receive the funds. Instead, the committee members at the sub-locational level, who knew the children well and lived in the community, made these decisions. Significantly, it was often children from the poorest families, or orphans, or children with HIV/AIDS, who were prioritized.

Unfortunately, the large number of children on the list meant that the communities didn't have enough money to fund grants in full for every student. However, the committees felt strongly that each sub-location should have the maximum representation. They therefore decided to provide a minimum of 40 percent of the grant for each child. They asked the principals of each school in the constituency, "If we give you 40 percent of the costs of these children's education, will you keep these children in school until the parents are able to find the remaining 60 percent?" Thankfully, the principals agreed to this plan—and in so doing became part of the decision making process. This allowed the communities not only to ensure that the children could stay in school, but to have all of the students who needed the grants receive them.

In devolving power in this manner, we were trying to create a bottom-up model of development. The process was transparent and accountable; it promoted equity and fairness; it also showed that "democratic space" could be opened up at the grassroots level in such a way that the phrase actually meant something. This way of working, I believe, strengthens the pillars of the three-legged stool, and has the potential to empower poor people and give them a sense of participating in government and decision making, and of being a part of the whole—rather than acting as passive observers of what happens far away in the capital city. I was gratified to discover that the Parliamentary Monitoring Committee, a bipartisan group that examined the performance of MPs in their constituencies, particularly regarding the management of projects such as the CDF, determined that some aspects of the method we had developed should be emulated by others.

My strategy was not without its problems. The whole process of creating the sub-locational and locational committees, and the deliberations about the projects, took a considerable amount of time, which slowed initial implementation—so much so that some people in Tetu complained that the constituency took too long to distribute CDF funds. I told myself that while it might take longer to establish the multilayered committee structure, once it was in place it would work well and my constituents would appreciate the expanded opportunities to exercise leadership. It did.

Another challenge was that the budget for the CDF allowed a comfortable travel and expense allowance only for committee members at the constituency level; members at the other levels wondered why they couldn't be similarly compensated. It was a challenge for me to explain the situation, and many were still unhappy about the disparity. Although I believe strongly in the value of service and of individuals not always having to be paid to work for the common good, most people in Tetu are poor. Leaving their fields, putting aside work on their small business, or finding someone to look after their children in order to attend a committee meeting was a sacrifice. Several expressed their dissatisfaction, and I heard the mutterings of others.

In my view, the people of Tetu did get the best benefit for the money the government provided through the CDF. By seeking a small allowance for travel and expenses, those committee members were, in a way, putting their own immediate interest ahead of the greater good of the community and the benefits all those in Tetu could receive, by making sure that the funds provided by the government were not being wasted. Moreover, if I hadn't set up additional committees at the locational and sub-locational levels, those people would have had very little say over how the CDF funds were allocated. The decisions would have been left to the fifteen members of the constituency committee alone. It is almost as if some of my constituents wanted to be compensated to help themselves, as if they were owed assistance.

Nonetheless, if I had to do it again, I would try to find a way to compensate those who served on the locational and sub-locational committees for their time, even if it were only a small amount. Indeed, the government later decided that those participating at the sub-locational level would receive an allowance for travel and expenses.

Nationally, the CDF encountered other difficulties. Most MPs decided to work with only the committee of fifteen people the CDF required at the constituency level, and in a number of cases they appointed friends or political cronies as members. Kenyan journalists began reporting on CDF shortcomings: some MPs had shown nepotism in managing the CDF and had used funds for pet projects and in parts of the constituency they preferred, without giving the citizens a real voice. Indeed, the new Tetu MP who replaced me after I lost the election in 2007 abandoned my methodology. He picked his own committee of fifteen for the constituency as a whole; the locational and sub-locational committees are no more. I received reports that my constituents were not happy about this; they had appreciated the devolved power and had owned the process. Regrettably, they do not seem to have had the courage to demand its continued application and to push their leaders to embrace good governance.

By the time I left office, the CDF had resulted in a number of concrete projects that will have a positive impact on my former constituents' development prospects. Nearly half of the funds were directed to education—to secondary school scholarships for more than six hundred students, and support for the building or refurbishment of classrooms, science laboratories, and dormitories at schools, as well as at local vocational schools. The communities also chose to invest CDF funds in repairing and expanding health centers and dispensaries, as well as providing them with upgraded equipment, throughout the constituencies.

An irrigation project was also initiated and a number of miles of pipes were laid. Electricity was provided to more than a hundred homesteads, as well as to schools, churches, a dispensary, and a tea-trading center. Funds also supported the repair and maintenance of roads, the construction of a community hall, and improved facilities for police and local officials, designed to enhance the services communities received from them. In addition, storage and collection capacities at local coffee factories were expanded, and funds were apportioned for youth projects, including the development of microenterprises and environmental conservation initiatives.

What was particularly pleasing in the implementation of the CDF in Tetu was that the multilayered structure helped minimize the risk of corruption. At a moment when I was feeling disappointed by the number of people who were willing to cheat and take advantage of others, a colleague encouraged me by sharing information to the effect that in any society, a quarter of the population is honest, a quarter is dishonest, and the remaining half can be persuaded either way. For corruption to be curtailed, open and transparent systems are essential. The better the systems and the better the institutions in place, the more likely it is that the 50 percent of the population will join the 25 percent who are honest.

In Tetu's case, the constituency committee routinely monitored and evaluated the progress of the committees at the locational and sub-locational levels, and would submit written progress reports to my constituency office, which had a full-time coordinator on staff. That said, I cannot be sure that nothing untoward took place. Opportunities for price gouging on supplies for projects, such as water pipes, existed, and in one case the price paid for a certain grade of pipe seemed high.

What I wanted to create was a system for use of the CDF funds that was transparent, accountable, and highly participatory. In forming the multilayered approach, I tried to establish a structure that would enshrine the constituency priorities, no matter who represented Tetu in parliament. Before the end of my term as MP, I gathered together the fifteen members of the constituency-level committee with the fifteen people who represented each of the thirty-seven sub-locations—nearly six hundred people in all—to produce a strategic plan for Tetu for the next five years. Under the guidance of a trained facilitator, the assembly developed a set of concrete priorities for education, agriculture, health, water, electricity, tourism, and the environment. With the plan completed, no one would have to ask the people of Tetu: *What do you want?* Although I don't have my parliamentary seat, my former constituents do have the strategic plan, and it's a good one. It is my hope that they—the people who created it—will implement it.

Other countries, including South Africa and Nigeria, are now looking at adopting the CDF model. When Uganda introduced it in 2005, no system was put in place to provide for stringent oversight of the funds. Most MPs didn't account for their spending, much to the dismay of the national government and the MPs' constituents. Such safeguards are vital to ensure that MPs who misuse money are exposed, that citizens have a means to report corruption, and that implementation of all CDF-funded projects is monitored closely.

In spite of the teething problems and shortcomings of the various CDF models, I hope that the idea spreads, and that efforts are made to improve upon it. The CDF is truly an

African solution to an African problem, dependent on the budget of the government and not an international agency, and on the active participation and leadership of local communities rather than international experts. Essentially, the CDF represents a partnership that has been all too rare in Africa: between the people and their leadership against poverty and passivity.

HIV/AIDS: EMERGING FROM THE SHADOWS

The CDF process aside, there were other encouraging signs of the development of grassroots leadership: for instance, in the fight against the devastation of HIV/AIDS and the stigma that so often clings to people who are HIV positive. While serving as an MP, I tried to respond to the needs of people living with HIV/AIDS in Tetu and also promoted voluntary testing for my constituents.

MPs are encouraged in their constituency work to partner with local government ministries as well as local NGOs. Therefore, I requested that the Green Belt Movement, which had many groups active in the Nyeri area, provide the financial resources to rehabilitate an existing building next to my constituency office to create the first Voluntary Counseling and Testing (VCT) center in Tetu. As with the CDF projects, the actual construction was completed by local artisans. The ministry of health and the NGO People Living with HIV/AIDS (PLWHA) supplemented these efforts: the ministry of health provided a staff person to provide counseling and testing; the Green Belt Movement employed an assistant for him; and PLWHA organized counselors to come and speak to people in the constituency about how to live positively and responsibly with HIV/AIDS, and how to protect their partners from infection. Once the center was established, it was vital to encourage people in Tetu to be tested.

It was during these efforts that I met a young woman who had lost her husband to AIDS. Although her two children were HIV free, she herself was HIV positive, but she refused to live in the self-imposed exile that many of those living with HIV/AIDS adopt. Each constituency in Kenya had a government-mandated Constituency AIDS Control Committee; this woman became a very frequent attendee at meetings of the committee, and eventually I learned her story. She proved to be very creative, innovative, and motivated, and she needed a job.

So the Green Belt Movement employed her as a support person for people living with HIV/AIDS. With the assistance of my local constituency office, this woman played a major role in organizing other HIV-positive men, women, and children to come out of the isolation of their homes, to which many had retreated after receiving a positive diagnosis. Due in large measure to her work, many of these people are now caring for and encouraging themselves and others.

Once the VCT was established, a monthly assembly was organized there to support those living with HIV/AIDS. They prayed and sang together, gave personal testimonies—descriptions of experiences of rejection or acceptance—and talked about how they were living responsibly, or not. They learned to open up to the pain, anger, and frustration they were experiencing. Sometimes a priest would come to offer spiritual encouragement to those who felt they were living in the shadow of death. Gatherings of children and youth—some of whom were orphans, some of whom were HIV positive, and some of whom were both—were also organized at the center. Constituents felt it was important for young people to learn how to protect themselves, live positively, and look forward.

The soils in the Central Highlands are highly suited to growing vegetables. The Green Belt Movement introduced a campaign to encourage people living with HIV/AIDS to establish kitchen gardens, so they could include more health-promoting foods, especially green vegetables, in their diets. Since Tetu's economy is heavily dependent on cash crops, most people no longer grow food, but, rather, buy it in the market. For those who are poor and are weakened by HIV/AIDS, a vicious cycle can develop, in which they don't have food but can't go to the market, either because they are too sick or because they cannot afford to buy the food, since they are no longer working.

GBM provided an extension service to assist people in doing this, using a method that produced, organically, a good amount of produce within a small area right near their homes. Individuals were provided with seeds and training, and, given the increase in the supply of nutritious food, many of them improved in health. Even though a number of those participating were in a weakened state, it was encouraging to see them growing their own food—since before the campaign, people had locked themselves inside their houses, waiting to die. Now they were outside in the fresh air, talking with neighbors, and feeling more confident about the future: living positively.

CORRUPTED INSTITUTIONS

In other ways, however, the old culture of underdevelopment, corruption, and modes of inadequate leadership remained a challenge. How much so was brought home by the plight of small-scale coffee growers in my constituency. Shortly after the end of the Vietnam War, the Vietnamese government sent emissaries to Kenya to study how to expand its coffee industry. Kenya, in addition to having some of the best coffee in the world, conducts research in developing high-yield and disease-resistant varieties of coffee. The Vietnamese not only bought different strains of Kenyan coffee, but they invited some Kenyan coffee experts to Vietnam. In the twenty years since it began in earnest, the Vietnamese coffee industry has grown so large that it not only has outstripped many traditional coffee-producing countries, such as Indonesia, Colombia, and Ethiopia, but also has overtaken Kenya to become, after Brazil, the world's second-largest exporter of coffee.

Because coffee is a commodity, it is subject to speculation on international markets, and thus growing or selling it is a very risky business. If the market for the product collapses, whether due to political instability or overproduction, farmers can end up with nothing. On a large scale, the whole country suffers; on a local level, entire communities and families go hungry because the farmers are growing either crops to feed people and animals in other countries or commodities such as coffee. Some are not growing food crops at all (as is the case with many coffee farmers). Since the developed world has stacked current international trade rules against developing countries by levying large duties on their exports while flooding their markets with cheap imports, poorer societies are at a major disadvantage when it comes to commodity crops like coffee.

Despite my considerable reservations about the wisdom of pursuing a cash-crop-based economy, I nevertheless felt it was incumbent upon me as an MP to do what I could to enable local businesses to survive, especially as my constituency had many coffee growers and it was clear that a market for Kenyan coffee existed. To that end, I encouraged some German businessmen to take an interest in Tetu's coffee. It was they who told me about the thriving coffee industry in Vietnam, and that the average Vietnamese coffee farmer regularly returns a considerable profit on his crop. Naturally, with high margins, the farmer works very hard! In addition, the Vietnamese government supports the coffee industry and ensures not only that coffee producers find international buyers for their product, but also that the farmers are able to keep their commitments and maintain the quality and quantity buyers are looking for. This consistency means that the farmers both retain and expand their customer base.

Coffee and tea are the base of the economy in the Central Highlands, and therefore were supposed to be the major income earners for most people in Tetu. However, as I discovered, Kenya's small-scale coffee farmers, who form the great majority of the industry, had numerous obstacles confronting them, in addition to relying on an uncertain crop for their primary means of income. I learned that a great deal of corruption existed at the factories, where the farmers delivered the coffee and where the beans were partly processed. This corruption pervaded the management, the procurement of inputs such as fertilizers, and the loans and advances the factories made to the farmers against expected earnings. The farmer could neither negotiate the price for the inputs nor, of course, determine the price his coffee would be sold at in local and international markets.

Further up the levels of management, overheads and processing and marketing fees were extremely high, while there was corruption in the cooperative movement itself. Income from the sale of the coffee was received and processed in the centralized bureaucracies of the Coffee Board of Kenya and the Kenya Planters Cooperative Union (PCU), and then distributed to the farmers without their involvement.

This left the farmer with no possibility of negotiating how much should be deducted from the sale price by the bureaucracy, whether for research, or payments to and allowances of the board members of both bodies. In some cases, management had the audacity to inform farmers that they *owed* the factories money and should borrow funds to clear their loans! The farmer, with the government's sanction, had been turned into a virtual serf; even though he owned the land, he received a pittance for his labor. And he didn't even own the coffee; indeed, as a cash crop, the coffee bushes were considered the property of the government. Due to a colonial-era law, still in place, farmers who dared to cut coffee or tea bushes risked being arrested and charged with an offense.

The income of many coffee and tea farmers is extremely low: many cannot pay school fees for their children, or afford to go to the hospital when they or members of their family are sick; the clothes they wear and the food they eat are both of poor quality. They might even need help burying their dead.

Unlike the small-scale farmers, the large-scale coffee farmers, of which there are a number in Kenya, can, like the white settlers before them, deal directly with the government and negotiate a fair price for their product. Cooperatives were recommended to small farmers to allow them to benefit, even as small landowners, from the economies of scale that operate in the marketplace. But the cooperative movement has become so riddled with corruption that far from rescuing the small farmers, it has become the monster within. As much as it behooves the governing elites to be more fair and just to the small farmers, it is also up to the farmers to liberate themselves by demanding better governance from their leaders.

What I found frustrating, alongside the entrenched corruption in the parastatals that had been established with the aim of protecting rather than working against the interests of the Kenyan coffee growers, were the attitudes of some of the farmers themselves. They often didn't give the crop the attention it needed, and instead of working collaboratively to further their collective aims—by, for instance, applying pressure on the Kenyan government to reform the parastatals to ensure a better price from international buyers and reduce the expenses and deductions they were charged; or raise their standards and encourage consistency; or promote the whole region as a prime coffee-growing area—the farmers competed against each other.

Some were unreliable and indeed corrupt themselves, cheating other farmers by inflating the weight of their beans or the amount of coffee or tea they'd delivered to the factory. Others trusted the factory managers blindly because the latter were educated, and thus—so the farmers thought—inclined to be more honest.

Of course, people at the bottom of the economic ladder, like the coffee farmers, have limited power and capacity to negotiate a better deal. That's why it's up to the government to protect them from an inherently exploitative system that preys upon a vulnerable population. When it doesn't, I ask myself: *Is it that the government doesn't see what's happening to the farmers, or that it just refuses to acknowledge their struggle, because elites benefit from the current system governing cash crops like coffee, tea, and sugarcane?*

Another example of how the poor can be their own worst enemy concerned macadamia nut farmers in my parliamentary constituency. Macadamia nuts were introduced into Kenya in 1944, but were not extensively farmed until the late 1960s, when the government became aware of their potential to generate income. Not only can the nuts be eaten whole or used in confectionary and snacks, but the oil is useful in salads, the cake for livestock feed, and the shells for fuel and charcoal making. The wood from the macadamia trees is durable, and the tree itself is suitable for planting among other crops, a practice that is called agroforestry.[2] Because of the wide variety of its applications, the macadamia nut fetches a good price in the market. If a macadamia nut farmer's trees are already planted and producing nuts to harvest, there is no reason why the farmer shouldn't succeed and become wealthy by rural standards.

One day, a group of macadamia nut farmers approached me. These particular farmers reported that they sold their nuts into the Japanese market through a Kenyan processor and exporter, who did not appear to be corrupt. The nuts garnered a very good price per kilogram, and the farmers should have been earning a decent income. They were, however, unhappy. They explained that because there was so much potential money to be made in macadamia nuts, the farmers' neighbors, who were also farmers, had begun to steal them.

Macadamia nuts need to be fully ripe to be ready for processing, so farmers wait until they fall to the ground. However, the farmers told me, some people had started shaking the trees before the nuts were ripe. Then others had begun climbing the trees and picking the nuts before they were ripe enough even to be shaken from the tree. Finally, the greed had become so enormous that some individuals had simply crept onto the farmers' land at night, cut down the trees, and hauled them away, so they could harvest every single nut for themselves. Of course, because the nuts were not ready, the thieves needed to find ways to make the nuts look ripe. I was told they would boil the nuts with tea leaves to change their color. But when the nuts arrived at quality control in the market outside the country, they were discovered to have rotted, and the middleman told the farmers he didn't want any more macadamia nuts from them in the future.

When these farmers came to me with their story, they were desperate. When they told me why they had lost their lucrative market, I was astonished at the avarice and shortsightedness of some members of the community. I told them I would try to find another market for the nuts, although I didn't hold out much hope. "We can work on it," I said, "but you have already killed the goose that was laying the golden eggs." It was clear, I continued, that it was going to take much more effort to convince a new market of these farmers' reliability.

What needs to be realized is that the individuals who came to me were not what the industrialized world may think of as farmers, with an understanding of agricultural inputs, international markets, and commodity prices. Indeed, like the individuals on the hillside in Yaoundé, these farmers were in fact little different from their neighbors who stole the nuts, since nearly everyone who lives in rural areas grows one crop or another on their land. They have little or no information about the product they grow; they have little or no formal education and therefore may be functionally or actually illiterate. If they *are* able to read or write, they do not have access to written materials or the Internet in order to inform themselves about the crops that are their primary source of income; and, in the case of the coffee and macadamia nut growers, they may never eat or drink what they harvest, since they do not process what they're selling.

This is why, even though the nut farmers may organize themselves, there is still a need for strong national leadership to make sure that they receive their due if they are willing to work hard, act responsibly, and not cheat the system.

In the cases of the macadamia nut and coffee farmers, however, the Kenyan government had made little effort to put in place an extension service to educate the growers, or to empower them to advocate for themselves, through a collective, in the international marketplace. I advised the macadamia nut farmers to form their own cooperative and work together to find out who owned trees before they were cut down, register them, and then determine who was selling macadamia nuts even though they didn't have the trees growing on their land. I also urged them to start again and instill discipline among the growers; this way, they would produce nuts of sufficient quality that they might ultimately be able to find another vendor who would process the nuts in their own region. This would in turn add value to their product before they gave the nuts to the middleman to sell to the exporter.

Unfortunately, I was voted out of parliament before I had a chance to help the macadamia nut and coffee farmers further. However, I was an MP long enough to see quite clearly that there was another problem that affected these farmers in addition to their ignorance about their own products, their lack of education, and the government's failure to support them in the way the Vietnamese government had apparently done with Vietnam's coffee farmers. What kept both coffee and macadamia growers in poverty, amid the manifold riches of the best coffee in the world and a valuable nut, was not only the failure of the government to protect them from local exploiters, but also their own failure to understand the consequences of their self-destructive actions. Instead of working together to further the common good of their communities, they pursued their individual interests, allowing greed and selfishness to thrive among them.

Since the macadamia nuts were already getting an excellent price on the market, the farmers could have pooled some of their earnings and made them available so more people in their communities could buy trees with a low-interest loan. This would mean more macadamia trees for the community to share in the wealth. It would, of course, have had to be a long-term strategy, since macadamia trees require time to grow, but it would have reaped dividends within a few years. However, the thieves wanted the money first, and they wanted it quick. Intoxicated with the expectation of selling the nuts, they not only were willing to ruin their prospects for further wealth by cutting down the trees, but also thought nothing of impoverishing their neighbors in doing so. Their actions made sure not only that no more nuts would come from those particular trees, but also that it would be many more years before they would be able to make money from macadamia nuts—if they could even find a market again.

I consider actions like these a form of corruption. It is no different from a minister demanding a kickback before he gives out a license to harvest trees in the forest. It expresses the same unwillingness to work for what one earns and the same willingness to cheat the system. It flies in the face of common sense and collective will. It also helps to create a stereotype that discourages those who are genuine and compassionate in committing their money or expertise to helping Africa. The result is that communities end up dealing with governments or companies that are mainly interested in taking advantage of this vacuum created by the culture of corruption to extract as many resources as possible. By exposing their own greed and selfishness, the people are easily bought, exploited, and victimized, thereby working against their own interests.

LOOKING BACK TO MOVE FORWARD

When all these forms of corruption, along with the more usual graft and theft, become embedded, the societal machine grinds to a halt. I'm not so naive as to believe that personal and collective corruption can ever be wholly eliminated; it will exist as long as there are selfish people and money to be made. But there are concrete measures that governments could take to bring about the needed revolution in ethics, if they were committed to it. An important element would be for Africans to understand collectively that the current situation wasn't always so perilous—that the majority of their forebears were honest, fair, and just, and that their societies were functional and people's basic needs were met—and challenge themselves to emulate some of these values. Part of the tragedy of Africa is that ordinary Africans don't, for the most part, remember and take pride in this history. But this history is part of who they are, and it needs to be taught and celebrated. If they did this, they could celebrate themselves, too, and not trust so much in those who mean them harm.

Another component in this revolution is for Africans to recognize that, while they may think they are "better" than their ancestors by being educated and literate, and living in an age with motorized transportation, computers, and some modern amenities, if those ancestors were to rise from the dead, they would look at them and wonder why so many contemporary Africans apparently have scorned justice, abandoned fairness, stolen from each other so freely, and let those among them who are cheats and rogues not only go unpunished but indeed be rewarded, while the weak and vulnerable are left unprotected.

While Africans cannot change the past, they can try to mold the future. One measure to which I would give priority is for children throughout Africa, from the first grade of primary school through the last year of secondary school, to be taught the values of hard work, honesty, justice, fairness, and accountability as part of the normal curriculum, so they might grow into the leaders and citizens that Africa needs. A number of leadership initiatives already exist for Africans primarily in their early twenties to mid-thirties, both within African countries and abroad; it is my hope that each of them includes as a core matter the issue of ethics.

The aim here is not education, per se: it is not as if the leadership in Africa hasn't had its share of highly educated individuals. The point is to recognize that, just as one develops new technologies and expands the potential for breakthroughs in computer science and engineering through technical colleges, so advances in leadership and the application of values must receive similar impetus.

I don't believe that the peoples of Africa are more accepting of corruption than those in other nations. As the *matatu* pas-

sengers confronting the policemen showed, people can sponta-
neously rise up and demand an end to inappropriate behavior.
However, they will want to know that if they stand up or speak
out, everybody else will do the same—especially their leaders,
who should be at the forefront of this revolution in ethics.

Civil society also has a vital role to play. On the one hand, it
should ensure that the government is held accountable to the
needs of the people. On the other, it can also communicate to
the people when the government is adopting beneficial policies. This is especially important in a developing country
where people at the grassroots, because of their lack of education or exposure, can be very localized in their way of thinking.

Civil society in Africa is still not fully developed, although
regional differences exist in strength and organization. In most
countries, civil society remains relatively small and comprised
of individuals and groups, not the mass of the people. If it were
the latter, more African capitals would see protestors in their
streets rallying against governmental injustices and inequities
and demanding greater accountability and responsibility. But
in many African countries today, governments can still ignore
civil society fairly easily.

A challenge to strengthening civil society in Africa lies in
the fact that since the majority of African leaders have at least
accepted the concept of democracy, the international community is more interested now in fostering the government and its
institutions than in fostering civil society. This is understandable: what could take years for a voluntary organization to
accomplish can be done by a government in months; indeed,
that is why I wanted to enter parliament. Once the government
demonstrates its commitment to a policy, it's easy to move
that policy through the system. Nevertheless, what the international community would do well to appreciate is that issues
of values and leadership are subtle—leaders either may not be

willing to admit there are problems (because they are part of them!) or may consider them a waste of time. Therefore, a strong civil society is necessary to advance them.

Civil society and government needn't always be at logger-heads. In the 1960s and '70s, for example, the Kenyan government helped fund civil society organizations, many of which were carryovers from the colonial administration: women's organizations, including the National Council of Women of Kenya and Maendeleo ya Wanawake; Kenya Red Cross; the YWCA; St. John's Ambulance; and the Scouts, among others. While it would be essential to ensure transparency in any government's financial support for civil society groups today, because of widespread corruption and favoritism, it would nonetheless be beneficial for African governments to acknowledge, as others around the world have, that there are certain things they cannot do or that civil society can do better.

Moreover, in funding civil society organizations, the government would also be supporting volunteerism and, in so doing, encouraging the creation of a much-needed culture of service. Talent could also be fostered: many civil society groups are staffed by young people, who accept that not every task needs to have financial compensation and that service can be its own reward. In addition, the government could, if it were willing, learn from these organizations.

As long as governments regard civil society with suspicion and hostility, however, and civil society remains weak, fractured, or able to be co-opted, real development will be difficult to achieve—not least because a vast gap quite often exists between what leaders agree on in the cabinet or parliament and what is actually occurring at the community level. The CDF is one attempt to bridge this gap. On a continent-wide level, this is the special value of the Economic, Social and Cultural Council (ECOSOCC) of the African Union.

THE CHALLENGE FOR ECOSOCC

In 2005, the African Union took an important step toward acknowledging—and, perhaps, in the future, embracing—civil society, by establishing ECOSOCC. As an arm of the AU, with a mandate to report directly to the union's heads of state and government, ECOSOCC's task is threefold: to bring the voices of the African peoples into the AU's decision making processes; to educate the peoples of Africa on all aspects of African affairs (politics, economics, culture, and health); and to encourage civil society throughout the continent to work for the welfare of the African peoples. The assembly is comprised of two civil society delegates from fifty-two of Africa's fifty-three countries, with a planned role for the African diaspora across the world. ECOSOCC has the potential to contribute continent-wide solutions to Africa's problems.

In 2005, I was asked by the AU to serve as the presiding officer for the formation of ECOSOCC, a position I was pleased to accept. In this role, I oversaw elections for these representatives and the launch of ECOSOCC as a fully constituted body in September 2008. In the past, civil society tried, often fruitlessly, to reach out to Africa's heads of state to urge them to respond to the myriad needs of their people, and to involve ordinary Africans in making decisions about what happened in their countries. In turn, some leaders dismissed members of civil society as ignorant and unpatriotic, funded by the West to destabilize African governments. The creation of ECOSOCC recognizes, albeit perhaps only partially, the need for civil society and governments to work together.

Like all institutions, ECOSOCC will be only as effective in meeting its mandate as the commitment of those who participate in it. While I'm sure that people in every African country would like to see a strong civil society, some of their leaders may not want it to flourish. Others seek to appoint those who will serve in civil society organizations, thus maintaining a degree of control over them. Indeed, this has been a problem in establishing ECOSOCC itself. However, it is the duty of those of us in Africa, both government officials and civil society representatives, to make the partnership that ECOSOCC represents work. If this effort is successful, it has the potential to help the continent rebuild the much-splintered and twisted three-legged stool.

Eight

CULTURE: THE MISSING LINK?

THE IMPORTANCE of Africans' cultural heritage to their sense of who they are still isn't recognized sufficiently by them, or others. Culture is the means by which a people expresses itself, through language, traditional wisdom, politics, religion, architecture, music, tools, greetings, symbols, festivals, ethics, values, and collective identity. Agriculture, systems of governance, heritage, and ecology are all dimensions and functions of culture—for instance, "agri-culture" is the way we deal with seeds, crops, harvesting, processing, and eating. Whether written or oral, the political, historical, and spiritual heritage of a community forms its cultural record, passed from one generation to another, with each generation building on the experience of the previous one. Such a collective self-understanding directs a community in times of peace and insecurity; it celebrates and soothes it during the passages of birth, adolescence, marriage, and death; and it enables it to survive during transitions from one generation of leaders to another.

Culture gives a people self-identity and character. It allows them to be in harmony with their physical and spiritual environment, to form the basis for their sense of self-fulfillment and personal peace. It enhances their ability to guide themselves, make their own decisions, and protect their interests. It's their reference point to the past and their antennae to the future. Conversely, without culture, a community loses self-awareness and guidance, and grows weak and vulnerable. It disintegrates from within as it suffers a lack of identity, dignity, self-respect, and a sense of destiny. People without culture feel insecure and are obsessed with the acquisition of material things and public displays, which give them a temporary security that itself is a delusional bulwark against future insecurity. We see this in many places in Africa today. An example of the destruction to African cultures wrought by the imposition of arbitrary imperial boundaries can be seen in the fact that, while most of us know what might constitute a French, Russian, Chinese, Japanese, or Indian culture, it is impossible to speak meaningfully of a South African, Congolese, Kenyan, or Zambian culture.

My long-standing attempt to understand the impact of the destruction of culture on Africa's current challenges has partly been a personal journey to discover who I really am. It began on my first day of primary school, when I was too young to appreciate the deliberate trivialization of my culture and the political, economic, and social impact of the colonial administration's imposition of their culture on ours.

I absorbed a beautifully prepackaged set of beliefs intended to indoctrinate and prepare my community for a long colonial rule without any resistance: once Africans accepted our second-class position, we would be safe and taken care of— happy slaves in our own land. It was not until I went to the United States in 1960 to begin my university education that I started to become interested in my cultural roots. Recalling what my grandparents told me of the history of our community, I began to realize that, unlike what I had been taught, much of what occurred in Africa before colonialism was good. As with the ritual through which power changed, the *ituika,* the leaders were accountable to their people, who were able to feed, clothe, and house themselves. People carried their cultural practices, stories, and sense of the world around them in their oral traditions, which were rich and meaningful. They lived in harmony with the other species and the natural environment, and they protected that world.

My grandparents and others of their generation measured their happiness, their material and spiritual well-being, in ways far different from today. Their medium of exchange was goats. They kept domestic animals, which they used carefully for survival and treated humanely, and cultivated a variety of food crops on their lands. Because most of their basic needs were met, they didn't consider themselves poor. They lived within a community full of rituals, ceremonies, and expressions of their connection to the land and their culture; they didn't feel alienated or adrift in a meaningless, highly materialistic world that assigns value only in dollars and cents, because their world was animated by the spirit of God. They took what they needed for their own quality of life, but didn't accumulate and destroy in the process—and they did all this so that future generations would survive and thrive. By the time my mother died, in 2000, everything could be sacrificed for money: forests, land, goats, values, and even people. In a cash economy, it became necessary to destroy the environment, own part of it, and deny others access to it—including those whose families had lived on it for many generations.

It is my search into this heritage I have in common with millions of others in Africa and elsewhere that convinces me that the tenets of modernity—with its belief that material goods, greater technology, and innovation at any cost will solve all our problems and meet all our needs—are insufficient to provide an ethical direction for our lives. Ultimately, I began to accept, and even yearn for, the part of me that had been concealed for so long, the part found in the culture into which I was born and within which I'd partly been raised. It was impatiently waiting for me to explore and understand. I suspect this is an experience shared by Africans across the continent and in the diaspora, and by many others whose cultures have been threatened with extinction.

One way I felt this dislocation between who I was and what I was educated to be was through my name, which reflected the imposition of a "foreign" identity upon my own. When I was born, as was traditional in Kikuyu culture I was given the name Wangari, after my paternal grandmother, and Muta, my father's first name. But, as the child of Christians, I was baptized and given a biblical name, Miriam, which is how my parents, friends, and teachers addressed me while I was growing up. Miriam became my first name and Wangari my last, a practice encouraged by the colonial administration to downplay African surnames, so that only the British would be called by their formal last names. (Clearly, this process served to facilitate the local peoples' acceptance of their inferior status and colonized identity.) When I came under the influence of the nuns at the schools I attended, I embraced the Catholic faith and was encouraged to take a new name, because Miriam was perceived as more akin to Protestantism. To honor the Holy Family of the New Testament, I chose to be renamed for Mary and Joseph, feminized to Josephine, upon being received into the Catholic Church as a teenager. Josephine was shortened to the nickname Jo, and from then on I was known as Mary Jo Wangari. It was at college in the United States that I recognized the strangeness of being called Miss Wangari, which is the equivalent of being called the daughter of myself. Eventually, I reclaimed my birth name—and with it some measure of my origins.

Even today, although Africans living in Africa will more likely use their Christian names, they often very quickly reclaim their African names once they go beyond the continent. Through a process of self-liberation, they appreciate the satisfaction of owning aspects of their culture. Through my own journey, I know that it takes effort and will to recognize that one is not backward, inferior, out of touch, or a "tribalist" if one accepts one's cultural heritage and defines oneself by it— that, indeed, only *that* culture can provide self-knowledge and self-identity.

To be sure, culture is a double-edged sword that can be used as a weapon to strike a blow for empowerment or to threaten those who would assert their own self-expression or self-identity. In many communities in Africa and other regions, women are discriminated against, exploited, and controlled through prevailing cultures, which demand that they act a certain way. They are denied power, access to wealth and services, and even control of their bodies through practices such as female genital mutilation, early or child marriage, and rules of disinheritance. Some cultures demand that men be warriors and learn to kill, or to treat women a certain way, or to repress emotions, such as affection, pain, and compassion. Those who break away from the norm are punished or ostracized. These are some of the negative aspects of culture. We cannot shy away from these realities.

When I first began to engage with Kenyan civil society in the early 1970s and joined the National Council of Women of Kenya, it was on behalf of the Kenya Association of University Women. Although I'd returned to Kenya as Wangari Muta, committed to playing my part in advancing my newly independent country, I wore Western clothing and spoke fluent English, including at home with my family. I moved into the privileged setting of the university, where I achieved a doctorate, available then only to the tiniest minority of people in Africa, and an even smaller minority of African women. Although opportunities have expanded since, the number of African PhDs, and in particular women PhDs, is still comparatively small.

It was, therefore, as a member of an exclusive, Westernized

elite common then to many societies in postindependence Africa that I began to listen to rural women speak of their difficulties in obtaining firewood to cook nutritious foods and providing clean drinking water and fodder for their animals—the beginnings of the Green Belt Movement.

It was through my contact with these women that I began to seek the linkages between poverty and environmental degradation and the loss of culture. When I began to build the Green Belt Movement, I thought that all that was needed to encourage people to conserve their ecosystem and restore food security was to teach them how to plant trees and to make connections between their degraded environment and their difficulties. However, over the years I began to recognize that the rediscovery of culture was not something simply personal, but a political and social necessity, and that a reengagement with one's roots meant attempting to embrace all of its richness, contradictions, and challenges in fitting into the modern world.

I started to understand why communities were not only culturally uprooted, but were also literally pulling up the few remaining trees available to them, on which they and their children and grandchildren depended. When communities were told that their culture was demonic and primitive, they lost their sense of collective power and responsibility and succumbed, not to the god of love and compassion they knew, but to the gods of commercialism, materialism, and individualism. The result was an expanding impoverishment, with the peoples' granaries and stomachs as empty as their souls.

When I began to become active on environmental issues, people were curious about why I was helping women plant trees. *Was it because of where I was born or raised, or how and where I was educated? Was it because of my parents or grandparents? Was it something in my cultural heritage that partic-*

ularly cherished the natural world? Was I doing it to advance my career, become rich, achieve fame, or gain political power? Why, they continued, *did I persist in pursuing environmental conservation when so many odds were stacked against me?* After all, I had a flourishing academic career at the pinnacle of learning in postindependence Kenya, the University of Nairobi.

Their incomprehension was understandable. During the 1980s, the regime in Kenya regularly accused people who challenged the government's policies or practices that subverted rural populations of being "antigovernment." When I was accused of both, it wasn't because I was planting trees. Rather, it had more to do with the journey I had embarked upon.

While I could understand to some extent the government's paranoia about holding on to power, what I couldn't fathom was why the environment was not as important to my fellow Africans, or Kenyans, or even Kikuyus, who were in the government or in positions of authority in society, as it was to me. Why were political leaders behaving as if they had colonized their own country—and, in so doing, had facilitated the exploitation of natural resources like indigenous forests and land by handing them over to their political supporters or making them available to corporate interests? Why were they disinheriting their own people and future generations?

I realized then that it was not just the poor who had been culturally uprooted. Even those with power and wealth were not only unwilling but also unable to protect their environment from immediate destruction or preserve it for future generations. Since they, too, had been culturally disinherited, they did not seem to recognize that they had something to pass on. Although they were the people expected to protect their countries' wealth, they perceived themselves as passersby, and so took whatever they could on their way through. This also explained to me why many Africans, both leaders and ordinary citizens, facilitated the exploitation of their countries and peoples. Without culture, they'd lost their knowledge of who they were and what their destiny should be.

Of course, this problem isn't only an African one: people all over the world, rich and poor, are shortsightedly stripping the Earth of her bounty in favor of acquiring wealth today, at the expense of the survival of future generations, whether theirs or other peoples'. And yet, I feel the problem acutely as an African, precisely because I am within a generation or two of those who had a culture that, albeit unknowingly, contributed to the conservation rather than the destruction of their environment. By making these linkages, the full dimensions and impact of the loss of cultural connection to the environment became clear to me.

THE WRONG BUS SYNDROME

Through this analysis of the intersections of culture, the degradation of the environment, and political corruption, I realized it was necessary to enlarge the Green Belt Movement's conception of conservation to include a recognition of cultural heritage and the consequences of its loss, how and why culture was important, and how its neglect manifested itself in the ways the public reacts to the environment, and even to life itself. We came to understand that we had to allow people to see that the system in which they were living was fundamentally flawed. Until it was corrected, and people could feel empowered and hold their government accountable, the Green Belt Movement's work would not be fully realized. This is how the Civic and Environmental Education seminars gradually became an essential part of the Green Belt Movement's approach to development.

One part of the seminar is an exercise we named "The Wrong Bus Syndrome." Traveling by bus is a very common experience in Kenya, as it is in many African countries. Since most Africans can identify with a traveler in a bus, it's easy for seminar participants to visualize what happens if a traveler makes the wrong decision and gets onto the wrong bus: she or he will arrive at the wrong destination and will, without a doubt, encounter unexpected problems. These may include sleeping out in the cold, going hungry, or experiencing something dispiriting or dangerous (such as harassment by the police or attacks by thugs). If the traveler gets on the right bus, he or she should have a relatively easy journey, because all has gone according to plan.

Throughout the many seminars the Green Belt Movement has held over the years, people have offered the following main reasons why a traveler could get on the wrong bus: he or she fails to ask for directions and does not seek all the necessary information; someone accidentally or deliberately misinforms the traveler; the traveler is incapacitated through mental illness, drug abuse, alcoholism, a state of distress and confusion, or genetic impairment of the mind; the traveler has a misplaced sense of arrogance and adopts a know-it-all attitude; the traveler cheats him- or herself and trivializes the implications of making the wrong decision; the traveler is fearful, intimidated, cowed, and lacks confidence and self-assurance; or the traveler is simply ignorant.

As part of this exercise, seminar participants are asked to enumerate the problems they're facing in their communities. The answers are issues familiar to poor people, and those concerned with development, all over the world—and they are legion. A group of a hundred once enumerated no fewer than 150 problems! Among the most common are hunger, poverty, unemployment, collapsed institutions, a lack of security, violations of human rights, and religious differences that split communities and divide friends and neighbors. Other problems relate to the immediate environment: loss of local biological diversity, especially forests; soil erosion; pollution; the disappearance of indigenous food crops; and the drying up of marshlands, streams, and springs.

In light of all these challenges, when asked if they're moving in the right or wrong direction, or traveling on the right or wrong bus, individuals in the seminars are usually unanimous in their opinions: they *are* on the wrong bus. They recognize that they haven't asked questions of their leaders—from the local chief to their MP to the head of state. They've been over-trusting, and haven't paid adequate attention to the information available to them. They haven't had the courage to stand up to these leaders and challenge the direction they have been taking the people in, or they have relied too much on their leaders' assurances that all the people have to do is to trust them. Or they have assumed that politics is beyond their understanding. Some may have allowed themselves to be misled by alcohol, drugs, or misinformation, making them easy victims for exploitation. All of these choices mean they are less capable of reaching the destination they want.

Interestingly, in every seminar, participants point to the loss of traditional culture as one of the major causes of troubles such as the misuse of alcohol and drugs, irresponsible behavior toward women and girl children, high secondary school dropout rates (especially for girls), prostitution, theft, the breakup of family relationships, and the commercialization of religion. They express distress at the phenomenon of street children, and the spread of HIV/AIDS. As they analyze further the causes of their problems, many people come to the conclusion that their society has lost its accepted values and taboos and has, therefore, become both vulnerable and susceptible to any leader who promises them the immediate satisfaction of their felt needs.

In turn, the seminars aim to allow individuals to deepen their sense of self-knowledge and realize that to care for the environment is to take care of themselves and their children—that in healing the earth they are healing themselves. The Green Belt Movement's tree-planting program and Civic and Environmental Education seminars seek not only to empower the poor economically and politically, but also to encourage them to internalize a sense of working beyond self-interest and make a greater commitment to service for the common good.

In the course of the seminar, after participants have concluded that they are moving in the wrong direction, the question is put to them: "What do you do now?" It is at that point that attendees reach the state where they decide that they must take charge—not to continue going the wrong way, but to get off that bus, board the appropriate one, and start moving in the right direction.

Getting on the right bus will help them deal eventually with the long set of problems they have listed. At this point in the process, participants gain what in Kikuyu is called *kwimenya*, or *kujijua* in Kiswahili, or in English, "self-knowledge." When they experience *kwimenya*, participants can confront the choices they made that led them to take the wrong bus. They can also begin to choose differently.

Attendees recognize that they cannot be fatalistic, but must acknowledge their own agency. They comprehend that they need not only to choose wisely which bus to take, but to exercise *kwimenya* on issues as significant as how they are governed, how they govern themselves, how they manage their resources, how they expand democratic space, whether they respect or violate each other's rights, and whether they create or destroy peace. They see that if they are going to get better governance, they have to participate in elections, and determine which leaders they want.

Exercising *kwimenya* entails being responsible oneself, but holding leaders responsible as well—in other words, not only protecting the soil on your own land and conserving nearby forests, but also demanding that the government protect the country's soil and forests from degradation and exploitation. The recognition of the need for both personal and political responsibility and accountability leads people to the realization of the central importance of democratic governance.

In my own personal journey, I realized that not only was I on the wrong bus, but everyone else was, too—and that one of the main reasons why we had gotten on the wrong bus was because we had lost our cultures. My analysis led me to conclude that if people are denied their culture, they are vulnerable to being exploited by their leaders and to being exploiters themselves.

The reawakening of *kwimenya* can provide individuals with deep psychological and spiritual clarity. There is enormous relief, as well as anger and sadness, when people realize that without a culture one not only is a slave, but also has in effect collaborated with the slave trader, and that the consequences have been long-lasting and devastating, extending back through generations. A new appreciation of culture gives traditional communities a chance, quite literally, to rediscover themselves, revalue and reclaim who they are, and get on the right bus.

RECLAIMING CULTURE

The challenge for the many parts of Africa that were decultured is to rediscover their cultural heritages, and use them to both reconnect with the past and help direct them in their political, spiritual, economic, and social development. Despite their apparent simplicity to outsiders, who might consider their own culture more complex and sophisticated as well as more relevant and practical, the expressions of one's own culture are much more meaningful and constructive to those who claim them than alien (and supposedly superior) holy scriptures, or masterpieces of literature and music produced by an occupying power. As wonderful and enriching to human experience as foreign heritages are to those who subscribe to and value them, they are nevertheless aspects of other peoples' experiences and heritage.

Indeed, through their strong power of suggestion, foreign cultures may reinforce a sense of inadequacy and nurture an inferiority complex in those constantly exposed to them and urged to perceive them as "better." This is partly why foreign cultures play an important role in power politics, and in economic and social control. Once people have been conquered and are persuaded to accept that they not only are inherently inferior but also should gratefully receive the wisdom of the "superior" culture, their society is undermined, disempowered, and becomes willing to accept outside guidance and direction. This experience has been repeated throughout human history.

Citizens of former colonial powers are often baffled as to why indigenous or colonized peoples seem to suffer disproportionately from alcoholism, homelessness, mental illness, disease, lethargy, fatalism, or dependency. They cannot fathom why many of these peoples seem unable to relate to the modern world, why many of their children cannot stay in school, or why many do not thrive in the contemporary, industrialized world of big cities and corporate capitalism. They are surprised that their development programs don't produce the desired results and their attempts to alleviate the conditions under which so many indigenous or colonized peoples suffer may meet with passivity, indifference, resistance, or sometimes hostility.

What these well-meaning development specialists, philanthropists, politicians, and others perhaps don't fully appreciate is that indigenous or colonized people have been living a split life for centuries. In the colonial era and the decades following

African independence, the cultures of the African peoples were trivialized and demonized by colonial administrators, missionaries, and local devotees. Then the pre- and postindependence leaders and the international community urged the peoples of Africa to modernize, move beyond their "tribal" inheritance, and embrace the newer cultures, readily available today in films and on television and the Internet.

African communities have been attempting to reconcile their traditional way of life with the foreign cultures that condemned their own and encouraged them to abandon it. What are people to do when everything they believe in—and everything that makes them who they are—has been called "Satanic" or "primitive" or "witchcraft" or "sorcery"? What do they turn to? What wisdom do they call upon? What can be done to resist? And when, as is usually the case, this heritage is solely oral, how can they rediscover and reclaim its positive aspects?

Before the arrival of the Europeans, Mount Kenya was called Kirinyaga, or "Place of Brightness," by the people who lived in its shadow. The Kikuyus believed that God dwelled on the mountain, and that the rains, clean drinking water, green vegetation, and crops, all of which had a central place in their lives, flowed from it. When Christian missionaries arrived in the area toward the end of the nineteenth century, they told the local people that God did not live on Mount Kenya, but rather in heaven, and that the mountain and its forests, previously considered sacred grounds, could be encroached upon and the reverence accorded to them abandoned. The people believed this and were persuaded to consider their relationship with the mountain and, indeed, nature itself as primitive, worthless, and an obstacle to development and progress in an age of modernity and advances in science and technology. This did not happen only, of course, to the people who lived around Mount Kenya.

Over the next generations, the reverence and spirit that had led the communities to preserve specific species of tree, like the wild fig, and the forests on Mount Kenya died away. When the white settlers and then the local communities themselves cut down the trees to plant coffee and tea and other agricultural products, encroaching farther and farther up the mountain, there was little resistance. From then on, they were seen as commodities only, to be privatized and exploited. The awe and sense of place that had allowed the communities around Mount Kenya to recognize, however unconsciously, that in order to safeguard their livelihoods they needed to protect the mountain's ecosystem, including its forests, were gone.

This is why culture is intimately linked with environmental conservation. Because communities that haven't yet undergone industrialization often retain a close, reverential connection with nature, and their lifestyle and natural resources are not yet commercialized, the areas where they live are rich in biological diversity. But these habitats are most in danger from globalization, privatization, and the piracy of biological materials, precisely because of the wealth of natural resources contained in the biodiversity. As a result, communities are losing their rights to the resources they have preserved throughout the ages as part of their cultural heritage. The belittling of indigenous culture continues for many minority groups. The source of the disdain these days, however, is more likely to be other Africans rather than people from other regions of the world.

The demonization of the indigenous cultures to which Africans were subjected for centuries extended into every facet of their lives, and left them vulnerable to diseases and social pathologies that dog them to this day. In the case of the Kikuyus, it led not only to the continuing deforestation of Mount Kenya and the degradation of the environment in the surrounding region, but also to the virtual disappearance of the cultivation of many indigenous foods like millet, sorghum, arrowroots, yams, and green vegetables, as well as the decimation of wildlife, all in favor of a small variety of cash crops. The colonizers and those who accepted their beliefs trivialized the old ways, including the owning of cattle as a sign of wealth, growing crops that evolved in the local environment for household consumption, and sourcing medicinals from local foods and plants. All of these were considered indicative of a "primitive" way of life. The loss of indigenous plants and the methods to grow them has contributed not only to food insecurity but also to malnutrition, hunger, and a reduction of local biological diversity.

In many African societies, traditional cuisine has also drastically changed, and for the worse. Instead of a largely meatless, saltless, and fatless diet, full of steamed or roasted vegetables, the colonized rich have adopted the perceived diet of the rich, with all the ailments that come with it, such as high blood pressure, diabetes, gout, and the loss of teeth. In the meantime, the poor have tried their best to catch up with the wealthier citizens, and soon suffer from malnutrition, hunger, and diseases associated with trying to chase an unsustainable lifestyle rather than maintaining a traditional, more nutritious diet.

The brewing and sale of alcohol during the colonial period provide another example of how cultural norms were subverted, introducing a new set of social problems that persist to this day. When the British came to Kenya, they banned the brewing of local beer and even initially forbade Africans to drink bottled (European) alcohol, lest they forget their place. However, once the British had built breweries and put the local ones out of business, they allowed, indeed *promoted*, the locals' consumption of foreign brands of alcohol, with ready cash the only constraint. Locals were given business licenses to open village bars for consumption of only the bottled brews from breweries owned by the colonialists. Before this, bars did not exist. People drank alcohol only at home or at community celebrations.

By this time, all the traditional strictures on the use of alcohol—such as allowing its consumption only in middle age and reserving its use for ceremonies or festivals—had been done away with by the colonial authorities. When the festivals and ceremonies themselves were also banned, a culture of drinking alcohol without a reason, age limits, or social controls was encouraged. Drinking halls sprouted in every shopping center and opened their doors to men, women, youth, and today, even children. When colonial laws gave Africans the freedom to drink alcohol in village bars without the restraint of cultural norms, many locals drank themselves to destruction. As elsewhere in Africa, the banning of indigenous practices had relatively little to do with maintaining purity, spreading civilization, or stimulating a love of Christ—or, for that matter, warding off the temptations of Satan. It had a lot to do with rubber, gold, diamonds, oil, slaves, and cash.

In Kenya now, alcohol and cigarettes appear to receive more attention from advertising agencies than food and medicine. The pursuit of profits is so aggressive that in small towns it is easier to identify the brands of beer and cigarettes than to know the names of the shops they're sold in or those of the centers where the shops are located. Even today, in some communities, the brewing of local alcohol is still prohibited by colonial legislation held over as part of national law. Partly because of poverty, many people often consume illegal and adulterated alcohol bought and sold in secret; many such brews have destroyed health and caused blindness and death, not to mention the breakdown of families.

TOWARD HEALING AND RECOGNITION

At long last, development agencies, religious leaders, academic institutions, and even some government officials are beginning to acknowledge the multiple facets of culture in Africa, and its role in the political, economic, and social life of African communities and nations. Environmentalists and international institutions are also coming to realize culture's centrality in the protection of biological diversity. For all human beings, wherever we were born or grew up, the environment fostered our values, nurtured our bodies, and developed our religions. It defined who we are and how we see ourselves. No one culture is applicable to all human beings; none can satisfy all communities. Just as we are finally starting to see the value of biological diversity, we are also belatedly recognizing that humanity needs to find beauty in its diversity of cultures and accept that there are many languages, religions, attires, dances, songs, symbols, festivals, and traditions, and that this cultural diversity should be seen as a natural heritage of humankind.

In addition, efforts are being made to undo some of the cultural and psychological damage inflicted on Africa by the many forces that have competed with themselves on her soil. For example, church leaders are facilitating what is being called the Africanization of the Church of Christ. African priests, for instance, will now accept indigenous names instead of demanding that an African take a European name at baptism. Performing African dances in churches (albeit with changed words and meaning) is now quite common. Farm produce and livestock rather than cash is now an acceptable part of the offertory.

New converts are not forced to discard their traditional clothing and adornments in favor of Western dress, and they can proudly accept Christian fraternity without the need to

look like a Westerner. All this would probably make the original missionaries and converts turn in their graves, but it is a
reflection of the new consciousness and tolerance for different
cultures that many Africans—including those in mainstream
Christian religions—are acknowledging.

This isn't to say that there aren't still difficulties. Even now,
some African religious leaders find it difficult to preach in
favor of their own culture when they have been preaching
against and distancing themselves from it for many years. It
takes courage to be in charge of one's own identity and recognize that one was deliberately misinformed.

Nonetheless, progressive religious leaders from Africa and
Europe have begun finding political and social space for African
cultures. Hence the significance of the message from the then
head of the Anglican Communion, Archbishop George Carey
of Canterbury, in December 1993, when he publicly apologized
in Nairobi on behalf of those missionaries who had condemned
all aspects of African spirituality and traditions. He conceded
that some facets of the culture were completely compatible
with the teachings of Christ, even though some of them may
have been incompatible with European culture, traditions, and
values. Dr. Carey said he hoped that this wrong would be put
right so that the confidence and self-respect of the African way
of life, including aspects of its spirituality, sense of justice,
respect for life, and basic human rights, might be restored for
Africa's benefit.

In September 1995, Pope John Paul II similarly apologized to
Africans for the sins committed by missionaries when he came
to Nairobi to present the report of the African Synod on the
Catholic Church in Africa. He also acknowledged that not all
African heritage was Satanic or incompatible with Christ's
teachings. Indeed, at an open mass at Uhuru Park in Nairobi,
the pope was treated to aspects of church liturgy that were bor-
rowed from African cultures and would have been unaccept-

able to the missionaries and the African priests who followed in their footsteps.

The pope encouraged Africa's religious leaders to recognize that a people's culture is dynamic and must be influenced by other cultures it interacts with. Therefore, African cultures will have been affected and influenced by the cultural traditions and practices from the Europeans, Indians, and Arabs who left their mark on the continent of Africa. Nevertheless, he concluded, Africans themselves had to decide what they wished to take from other cultures, to claim what is good and retain it, and decide what was worthless at this time in their development and needed to be abandoned. Others cannot do this for Africans, the pope emphasized, without perpetuating the culture of patronizing the African people.

Undoubtedly, the cultures that existed in the past had problems: an overdependence on an elite who determined what was acceptable and what wasn't; and an attitude that assigned every setback to God's will. Some of what occurred, and continues to this day, was and is cruel and ignorant. As we've seen in recent years in Kenya, Rwanda, Congo, Sudan, Sierra Leone, Côte d'Ivoire, Uganda, and other countries, Africans are still maiming and killing each other in senseless conflicts, as well as forcing vast numbers of people from their homes to live in misery in unsanitary and overcrowded encampments.

However, there is nothing particularly African about human beings preying upon one another, or people attacking each other because of their religious affiliation or ethnic or racial background, or women being discriminated against. Furthermore, I am inclined to believe that because the precolonial societies were mostly intact and had a robust cultural life, the African cultures that were demonized by the colonizers and the missionaries had some sense of *kwimenya* that allowed them to survive the vicissitudes of the weather, the occasional wars between other groups, and cultural upheavals. *Kwimenya* would have enabled them to open up to the progressive ideas of human rights and self-determination without the jettisoning of everything their culture valued. And, surely, one attribute these societies possessed was a recognition that there was no one else to whom they could turn to solve the problems that affected them—no international donors or agencies, no government beyond their own immediate council, no big brother to look after them—apart from the resources found within their own culture. Consequently, they were forced to embrace their challenges and seek solutions for themselves.

One resource for precolonial Africans that is sorely missed is the traditional healer or medicine man or woman, which in Western terms would be defined, at least in part, as a psychiatrist. Both provide a similar service, in that they attempt to plumb the psyche in ways that cannot ordinarily be reached by either surgery or drugs. They possess a natural ability to listen and empathize, and are skilled in responding to emotional trauma and suffering. As repositories of the wisdom gathered over generations, traditional healers served an important function in indigenous societies. If the colonial administrators had not demonized them—as they had their own traditional healers—they might have been introduced to reading and writing and thus been able to share, in written form, their knowledge as it evolved with the times.

Today, genuine medicine men and women could play an important role in helping contemporary Africans understand the problems they face as they straddle modernity and tradition, the West and their native cultures, and as they try to meet the challenges of determining their identity in relation to other communities. But, because Africa has few psychologists in the Western sense, the choices for Africans are stark: they are either mentally sound or in a mental hospital. Of course, people can seek counsel from their priests or imams, but because it is generally still believed in Africa that one cannot be either a good Christian or a good Muslim while being open to traditional healing, the individual's turmoil may not be fully acknowledged or addressed. It will take many years for African authorities to accept the presence of traditional healers again, just as it has taken many years for them to concede that traditional midwives can fill certain gaps in the nursing profession, so that all women are provided with basic hygiene and assistance when they give birth.

It is within this context that reports, for instance, of older women in Kenya being burned alive because they have been accused of practicing witchcraft, or of children in Angola and Congo who have been cast onto the streets because their families believed them to be possessed by the devil, should be interpreted. This persecution expresses a dichotomy common to many Africans caught between tradition and modernity.

Behind these phenomena lies a trauma sadly familiar to many of the world's poor. As in other regions, many African societies are in tumult, only just emerging from years of civil war and with economies, communities, and families fractured or decimated. When calamities follow one upon the other—disease, war, poverty, or famine—it is not surprising that the reactions can become outsized and extreme. In such circumstances, a desperate people may turn on their own, hoping they will have one fewer mouth to feed by demonizing a family member, or ridding themselves of what they perceive to be a "cursed" existence.

As I have suggested, the transition Africans underwent from indigenous practices and worldviews to imposed spiritual and cultural systems from elsewhere was rapid, and in many cases incomplete. Consequently, while many Africans want to say they don't believe in the traditional way of life, their understanding of, say, the Christian doctrine of suffering and redemption is often nonexistent or only skin deep. For many Africans, Christianity is as full of devils and good and bad angels as their "old" religions were. They believe they can hear and communicate with God, speak in tongues, and prophesy. These facets of religious expression remind them of the supernatural elements in their own traditions. As I see it, in both cases people are torn between belief systems they don't fully understand.

As Pope John Paul II also recognized, cultures are dynamic, changing with time and place, interacting with other cultures and evolving and adapting: people should not have to become walking museums. Progressive cultures help their peoples survive and pass their wisdom and a sense of destiny to the next generation. African cultures, of course, cannot return to where they were. Too much has been lost, and reverting to a precolonial mind-set—even if it were possible—would not serve contemporary African peoples well as they struggle to move forward. What Africans need to do, as much as they can, is recapture a feeling for their pasts that is not solely filtered through the prism of the colonialists. This will not be easy, because five hundred years is a long time to struggle against all forms of oppression. Nonetheless, just as Africans can honor sacredness beyond that contained in the Bible or the Koran, so they should not be embarrassed that, for instance, their languages were not written down or that their weapons against the colonial forces were spears. Even the British, who perfected stainless steel and the Gatling gun, once discovered themselves faced with an enemy—in this case, the Romans—who possessed greater technological skills and superior weaponry, and whose cultural achievements dominated their own.

Traditional technology and artifacts reflect the creativity inherent in those societies. When that sense of creative potential is lost, the innovative part of the brain is left dormant, making it more difficult to think in new or pioneering ways. The latent creativity lacks a medium for expression. This is why Africans should honor and record, in written form for current and future generations, the fact that their communities once knew how to make spears, and take the ingenuity and skill employed in forging these weapons and apply them to developing products that are more relevant to today's needs.

Culture could be the missing link to creativity, productivity, and confidence. Ultimately, it is critical that Africans dispense with what might be called the culture of forgetting that has enveloped Africa since colonialism and re-collect their history and culture, and the *kwimenya* that comes from both. Without them, Africans lack a foundation on which to build for the future.

Nine

THE CRISIS OF
NATIONAL IDENTITY

THE MODERN African state is a superficial creation: a loose collection of ethnic communities or micro-nations, brought together in a single entity, or macro-nation, by the colonial powers. Some countries include hundreds of micro-nations within their borders; others, only a few. Kenya has forty-two; Nigeria, two hundred and fifty; Cameroon, at least two hundred; Mozambique, more than ten; Gabon, more than forty; Zimbabwe, fewer than ten; and Burundi and Rwanda, three. The largest of the micro-nations can have populations in the millions; the smallest usually number only in the thousands. With a few exceptions, it is these numbers that determine political power.

Most Africans didn't understand or relate to the nation-states created for them by the colonial powers; they understood, related to, and remained attached to the physical and psychological boundaries of their micro-nations. Consequently, even today, for many African peoples, a threat to their micro-nation or those they consider their leaders within their micro-nation carries more weight than a threat to the nation-state. At the same time, each community hopes to have access to the resources of the nation-state should someone from their micro-nation assume political power (particularly the post of president or prime minister). In this way, the community will have, as is said in Kenya, its "time to eat."

In turn, the elites know that to acquire and maintain power they need the support of their micro-nation and therefore must demonstrate loyalty to it. The result has been a kind of political schizophrenia. While expressing allegiance to the nation-state, African leaders have repeatedly used their identification with a micro-nation to divide their citizens from each other and control them, to the detriment of the larger macro-nation. They have downplayed the role of micro-nations' traditional cultures in a modern society, even as they have used ethnicity to maintain their hold on power. In doing so, they have mirrored the colonial era's tactics of divide and rule with disastrous effects. Consequently, what the leaders and some politicians in the rest of the world call "tribal conflicts" have almost nothing at their root to do with "tribes."

(It is general practice in discussing micro-nations in developing countries to refer to them as "tribes," although this is not the case in developed regions of the world when ethnic communities are being described. In my view, the word "tribe" is not really a pejorative, but it has taken on negative connotations. "Tribes" are generally seen as primitive or backward, comprised of people who have not completely realized the concept of the nation. The use of the word "tribe" becomes a way of looking down on some communities, pushing them to the margins rather than seeing them as part of a larger whole. In the Yugoslav wars, by contrast, the term "tribe" was never used to describe the ethnic factions. Micro-nations may be very small, but they have all the characteristics that define nationhood, notably shared common customs, physical boundaries, origins, history, and language. Calling micro-nations "tribes" suggests, falsely, that they have not yet arrived at nationhood.)

When conflicts arise in Africa, they are almost exclusively over governance, corruption, poverty, and a perception that national resources are not distributed equitably. It is true, of course, that when a micro-nation is aggrieved, it naturally calls upon its own for support. This is probably no different from the conflicts in the former Yugoslavia, when Serb leaders rallied

Serbs, and Albanian, Croat, and Bosnian leaders did the same with their ethnic groups. For those who share the same ethnic heritage but need to differentiate themselves even further, there are smaller groupings, like clans, as in the case of Somalia.

Some scholars of modern Africa have suggested that keeping the ordinary people focused on the interests of their micronation, and fomenting suspicion and competition between them, prevents them from perceiving the stark class and wealth divides that characterize African societies, with a small elite at the top and large numbers of poor at the bottom. This reality is obscured from the people to the advantage of political leaders who incite hatred and violence between micro-nations and facilitate the violence through armaments and logistical support. Even if the conflicts temporarily give the members of the micro-nations some sense of power, in the long run they are marginalized, experiencing neither progress in development nor self-knowledge, as their leaders and their cronies bleed their nation dry.

What tends to happen is that one micro-nation judges itself worthier and therefore more entitled to power and the wealth that goes with it, and claims that the other micro-nations are less entitled to both. The colonial authorities are responsible for some of these self-perceptions by favoring one group over the other and, when they left, putting power in the preferred group's hands. In much of independent Africa, the leaders of micro-nations, who often form a ruling clique, are constantly competing for power and privileges. If they are not included in the sharing of these, conflicts can easily develop when they mobilize their often poorly informed communities in the name of their micro-nation and become, in effect, warlords. The mass media, both nationally and internationally, however, usually report such conflicts in Africa as arising from ancient

tribal animosities. Such misconceptions and misrepresenta-
tions obscure the real source of the violence.

Two examples that perhaps encapsulate the challenge of the
micro-nation within the nation-state, the complex relationship
between micro-nations and their leaders, and the possibility of
African solutions to African problems, are the ongoing conflicts in Chad and Sudan and what occurred in Kenya in the
run-up to, and immediately after, the 2007 general elections.

THE CASE OF CHAD AND SUDAN

In August 2008, I traveled to Ethiopia, Sudan, and Chad as part
of a delegation organized under the auspices of the Nobel
Women's Initiative, which I and five other women Nobel peace
laureates founded in 2006. Our mission was fivefold: to high-
light and bring further awareness to the massive violations of
women's human rights, especially with respect to displacement, rape, and destruction of homes; to reinforce efforts to
bring about participatory governance in Sudan; to give encouragement to women's groups working for peace, reconciliation,
and reconstruction in southern Sudan; to stand in solidarity
with all those working at the front lines to bring about peace
with justice in Sudan and the region; and to call upon citizens
throughout the world to take individual and collective action
to build a sustainable peace and to insist that the international
community implement existing commitments to peace and
justice in Sudan.

The delegation included 1997 U.S. Nobel peace laureate
Jody Williams and the American actress and activist Mia Far-
row, both of whom have been diligent in trying to bring the sit-
uation in Darfur and Chad to the world's attention; Gloria
White-Hammond, an American pastor and cofounder of an
NGO, My Sister's Keeper, which is supporting girls' education

THE CHALLENGE FOR AFRICA

initiatives in southern Sudan; Qing Zhang, a Chinese labor advocate; and a small group of other colleagues.

During the mission we met with government officials; the staffs of international relief and development organizations working on the ground in Sudan and Chad, including the office of the UN high commissioner for refugees and the World Food Programme, the staff of which are doing a heroic job in refugee camps under extremely harsh conditions with limited resources (including food) and at considerable risk to their own safety; local women's groups in Juba, southern Sudan; and refugees from Darfur, living in camps in Chad—some of them for years.

In Ethiopia, it was clear that senior leadership in the African Union was troubled by the political and humanitarian situation in Darfur, as well as the International Criminal Court's 2008 indictment for war crimes of Sudan's president, Omar al-Bashir. AU officials were concerned that the ICC was applying indictments only in Africa, because of the perceived weakness and vulnerability of its leadership. At the same time, an impasse had been reached over the composition of a larger, better-equipped, and more effective peacekeeping force for Darfur.

The African leadership wanted the force to be fully African in character, while the international community insisted that, if it offered logistical support, equipment had to be accompanied by personnel who could operate and maintain it. The standoff had left the force on the ground in Darfur ill-equipped and vulnerable to attack by armed militias. Civilians have suffered further, as villages and even camps for displaced people continue to be invaded by the Janjaweed, the militia on horseback, increasing the number of Darfurian refugees.

Here again, Africa faces a challenge in leadership. The ICC is not a "kangaroo court," so if President al-Bashir does not have anything to hide, he should not fear it. Even though the African leadership cannot itself provide the necessary logistical support, the AU is demanding that the peacekeeping force be 100 percent African. This could be interpreted to mean that the leadership in Khartoum does not wish to have the conflict in Darfur resolved, except on its own terms. Unfortunately, in all of this, the plight of the citizens in Darfur is seemingly ignored.

The Sudanese government has the primary responsibility to protect all of its peoples, including those in the Darfur region. If the government fails to do so, then the responsibility falls to the African leadership in general, through the AU. However, when such leadership falters or fails, the international community has a moral responsibility to assist Sudan and Africa to save lives. In recognition of such situations in Africa and elsewhere, in 2005 the United Nations General Assembly unanimously agreed that when governments anywhere in the world do not protect their own peoples from genocide, crimes against humanity, war crimes, or ethnic cleansing, then other nation-states have a responsibility to provide this protection. Unfortunately, the actions to make the words real have been insufficient, and a culture of impunity persists.

While some of the political and social problems in Sudan, Chad, and Africa in general are the legacies of colonialism—arbitrary borders or the favoring of one micro-nation, which then has access to more resources at the expense of other communities—after more than forty years of independence, none of these excuses justify poor governance or leaders committing crimes against their own people. It is inexcusable for African leadership to fail to protect its own citizens and then complain or respond defensively when these citizens seek help or redress elsewhere.

Military power will not resolve the crisis in Sudan, any more than it has in Somalia or elsewhere in Africa—especially if all parties continue to invest in arms, soldiers, and militias. Only dialogue and a willingness to share power and resources more equitably can produce lasting peace and the opportunity to utilize those resources (specifically oil, land, and water) for the benefit of all of Sudan's micro-nations.

For the sake of Sudan and its neighboring countries, which have also been destabilized, further deterioration of the situation must be avoided. To end the crisis in Darfur, mediation must focus on power and resource sharing between the parties now locked in conflict. Mediators must be trusted by both sides and, given all the suspicion and recrimination in evidence, not appear to be biased.

In Juba, southern Sudan, we saw encouraging signs of post-conflict restoration: the approximately thirty women's groups we met with were very active, although anxious for a resolution of the conflict in Darfur and worried that the 2005 comprehensive settlement between north and south that ended Sudan's long civil war wasn't being fully honored. While they were happy to have peace, they felt the political commitment by the government in Khartoum was shaky, particularly along the transitional border between the two parts of the country. If the peace agreement didn't hold, they indicated, the possibility existed that Sudan would once again be engulfed in a ruinous civil war; the soldiers and the weapons are still there.

Throughout southern Sudan urgent work is being undertaken to reestablish functioning systems of governance and to provide basic services and new opportunities for the southern Sudanese people. It is still a very poor region, struggling to move forward. However, the land around Juba is not a desert, but rather green and fertile. Possibilities exist for new agricultural initiatives as well as rehabilitation of degraded land. One government official stated that she would like to plant at least a million trees.

Our time in Chad provided a very different story. There we encountered desperation among the Darfurian women we met who had, with their children, fled attacks by the Janjaweed militia. When I inquired why they thought the Janjaweed would seek to kill them when they, too, were Muslims, they replied: "The Janjaweed are doing this because they are not practicing the correct Koran." When we asked why the government would attack them when they too were its citizens, they responded that it was because of their ethnicity. They may not have understood that it was water and land that were being fought over. None mentioned oil, which is also said to be in the ground in Darfur.

These women refugees were very unhappy with the AU, which they said was against them. The woman who served as spokesperson for the others said they wanted justice.

We discovered that complicating the situation in Sudan even further was a difficult history between the southern Sudanese and the Darfurians. During the north-south civil war, some Darfurians joined the government's forces in attacks on the southerners, who unlike most people in the north and west of Sudan are Christians. As a result, some in southern Sudan are ambivalent about the Darfurians' resistance to the central government, a resistance that has gotten more pronounced as the conflict has dragged on and the antigovernment factions in Darfur have splintered and, in some cases, begun fighting each other—another case of divide and rule.

Another challenge to peace in the region appeared to be that the Zaghawa micro-nation, which is dominant in Darfur and is the object of the Janjaweed attacks, is also present in Chad. The Chadian president, Idriss Déby, is a Zaghawa. We were told by various people during our trip that the rivalry between the leaders in the two neighboring countries was also fueling the conflict—with militias on both sides of the border being supported by the rivals. At stake in each country is access to oil, much coveted by the international community.

Our delegation expressed its concern about the practice of extracting resources from the region, and indeed all of Africa, in exchange for weapons (and the money to buy them) that fuel conflicts and are the cause of untold suffering. We called upon the international community—particularly those who do business directly with African governments and consider themselves friends of the continent—to cease supplying weapons and work instead to build sustainable peace, human security, and real development to benefit all the people of Africa. The mission made clear to me that to end these regional conflicts and create cultures of peace, leadership from African nations is essential, along with the full support of the international community. In addition, those countries that are truly friends of Africa will pursue a relationship that is less exploitative and that encourages respect for human rights and the protection of women and children.

The trip also showed me that bringing peace and reconciliation to areas of conflict in Africa will not be easy. When leaders are not only fighting among themselves, but are also undermining each other across borders, the challenges Africa is facing come into sharp relief. What the mission also brought home to me is that many of the continent's conflicts were, and appear still to be, based on political jealousies and competition between heads of states and micro-nations, and those trying to replace them. In so many cases, the antagonists were not willing to come together to share power, but instead would fight to the death, taking thousands of members of their micro-nation with them. I had already seen how volatile that mixture was closer to home in my own country of Kenya.

THE CASE OF THE 2007 KENYAN ELECTIONS

On December 27, 2007, millions of Kenyans lined up peacefully outside polling stations around the country to vote in the general election. These elections, coming five years after those held in 2002, were keenly anticipated throughout the country. Most observers and participants agreed that they would confirm that, after the 2002 elections had proven free and fair, Kenya was on the path of real democracy. The country had a government elected by and accountable to all Kenyans—and not to a small elite, particular ethnic group, specific class of businessperson, or landowner. While some sporadic violence had broken out in the run-up to the polling, on the day of voting itself the mood among the electorate was relatively upbeat.

Preelection opinion polls suggested a very close race between the incumbent president, Mwai Kibaki, and the main challenger, Raila Odinga. In 2002, Kibaki and Odinga had joined forces and, with other opposition leaders, had forged the National Rainbow Coalition (NARC), which won a momentous victory over the Kenya African National Union (KANU), the party of Kenya's longtime president, Daniel arap Moi. The fact that many of the country's different micro-nations had come together to bring an end to a discredited regime by democratic means, and that the elections themselves were conducted in a positive, even joyful, atmosphere, led me and others to anticipate the possibility that 2002 might finally be when Kenya turned a page on the negative, competitive politics between the micro-nations that supported those in power and those who sought a more democratic system of governance.

After the 2002 elections, many Kenyans looked forward to an honest and critical debate on reforming our constitution. We could finally provide ourselves with a truly representative government, with powers devolved from the president to a prime minister and sufficient checks and balances to make the abuse of authority less likely and governance more transparent. I was also eager to see Kenyans grapple seriously with the issues facing them—issues the Green Belt Movement and civil society had been working on for a quarter century.

Nevertheless, as I reflected at the end of my autobiography, *Unbowed*, I knew that the simple exercising of the vote would not provide the panacea for Kenya's ills. "Even as I savored the peaceful exchange of power," I wrote of December 30, 2002, the day the new government was inaugurated, "in the back of my mind lingered the knowledge of the many challenges that awaited Kenya. The years of misrule, corruption, violence, environmental mismanagement, and oppression had devastated our country. The economy was in ruins and many institutions needed rebuilding."

Unfortunately, much of what needed to be done in the years between 2002 and 2007 was left undone, and the political honeymoon for the new government lasted barely a year. The memorandum of understanding that Mr. Kibaki and Mr. Odinga and their parties had signed to share power—a prerequisite that had been necessary for the formation of the National Rainbow Coalition itself in 2002—was not honored. Efforts to stamp out corruption were pursued halfheartedly or curtailed; attempts to reach out to the people and bring them into the democratization process were thwarted.

The NARC government had undertaken to present a new constitution to the Kenyan people within a hundred days of the election. However, instead of focusing on the constitution (which had been drafted through an unprecedented process of public deliberation, but was not agreed upon), a fight ensued between personalities in the government and leaders of some of the micro-nations over the failure to honor the memorandum of understanding and devolve power. When the constitution was finally brought to the people in 2005, the referendum became, in effect, a vote on the government and the communities that supported it. In an ominous sign of things to come, the poll divided Kenyans along ethnic lines. Those in favor of the constitution (represented on the ballot paper with the symbol of a banana) were aligned with the supporters of the president. Those against the new constitution (signified by an orange) were represented by the coalition led by Raila Odinga. The "no" vote won by a wide margin.

The president responded to the loss by dismissing his entire cabinet and marginalizing those leaders who had opposed the constitution in the form in which it had been presented to the country. Out of the cabinet but still members of parliament, Raila Odinga and others established the Orange Democratic Movement (ODM), a political party that provided an umbrella for the opposition. Mwai Kibaki eventually would form his own coalition, the Party of National Unity (PNU), to contest the next elections.

Given this history, everyone expected the December 2007 elections to be close. The vote would elect local counselors, members of the Kenyan National Assembly (the parliament), and the president—both the head of state and of government and a position that, under the existing constitution, wielded a substantial amount of power. In the months preceding the vote, the PNU and ODM positions had hardened. Although each party drew the majority of its support from specific ethnic groups—in the case of PNU, the Kikuyus and the Merus; in the case of ODM, the Luos and the Kalenjins—the election was not only about supporting leaders of one's own ethnic bloc. It was also about the devolution of power and equitable distribution of national resources.

As it happened, the contest was the closest since Kenya gained its independence; it also became one of the most bitter. When parliamentary results began to come in to the Electoral Commission of Kenya (ECK) headquarters in Nairobi, they were quickly and publicly announced. The presidential vote, however, was another story. Surveys taken in the days before the contest indicated that Raila Odinga was likely to prevail, and indeed, initial vote tallies showed him leading the president by a substantial margin. Throughout the night, many stalwart supporters in parliament of Mwai Kibaki lost their seats, a sign that the PNU parliamentary coalition could be going down to defeat. The ECK, however, delayed declaring a winner in the presidential contest, which stoked unease and, not long after, suspicion of foul play among voters and the Kenyan press.

Finally, two full days after the election, on Sunday, December 30, the chair of the ECK dismissed from the room where he spoke all journalists except those from state-owned media, and announced that Mwai Kibaki had won the presidency by a margin of about 230,000 votes. Shortly after, Mr. Kibaki was sworn in for a second term at State House, the president's official residence. So hurried was the ceremony that, reportedly, those present forgot to sing the national anthem.

I had already digested the news of my own defeat at the polls two days before. I had sought reelection to my seat in parliament for Tetu. That fall, I had stood with others in the equivalent of a primary to determine who would be the official candidate of the PNU, which had formed relatively late in the run-up to the election. Many of us who lost suspected, however, that the primary election had been rigged. In the belief that the ECK would oversee a more fair and transparent process, and would prevent, for example, the bribing of voters, some of us decided to present ourselves to the voters again in the December general election, to be held shortly after the primary.

In my case, I ran under the banner of the Mazingira Green Party, which I'd helped found in Kenya in the early 1990s (*mazingira* means "environment" in Kiswahili). The reasons for the launching of Mazingira were to promote "green" values and greater environmental consciousness and also to introduce the country to the concept of having a political party with an ideology. In Kenya, as in much of Africa, the political culture is one in which parties generally don't have specific ideologies, even though they have manifestos (party platforms). Some parties are nothing but vehicles for particular individuals to participate in elections. I felt it was important to stick with Mazingira rather than do what was customary—to switch parties when politically expedient. Because of the lack of ideology governing most parties, changing parties is not generally considered an issue. However, as a Kikuyu, I was expected to follow the party of Mr. Kibaki, who was, along with being president, the leader of the Kikuyu micro-nation. Staying with the Mazingira Green Party was, therefore, viewed as unforgivable by my constituents.

There were other reasons why I was punished at the polls. Even though I felt I had served my constituents to the best of my ability, I had insisted that it would be dishonest for Mr. Kibaki not to honor the 2002 memorandum of understanding. Then, in 2005, when the constitution was put to a referendum, I again urged the president not to hold the vote. It seemed to me bad policy to impose a constitution on the people, and I thought that, far from uniting Kenyans, the referendum would split the country down the middle along ethnic lines. However, as far as the Kikuyus I represented in my constituency were concerned, it was important that the president, a favorite son, be supported, right or wrong.

Some of my constituents were also unhappy because, when the president named the new cabinet following the constitutional referendum, and I was reappointed as assistant minister for the environment and natural resources, a position I had held since 2003, I declined to take up the post. All the cabinet ministers who opposed the constitution during the referendum had been dismissed, and I had urged that the president talk with the opposition members rather than exile them from the government. It was obvious that they represented a large public voice, and they deserved to be listened to. I indicated that I would take up the position when such a dialogue had been undertaken, and warned that failure to do this would increase divisions in the country that were already getting wider. All of these breaches of trust, and what I considered faulty policies, were, in my opinion, driving the country toward a conflict.

In making these decisions I was seeking to promote both dialogue and good governance that would be inclusive and embrace the country's diversity. However, in doing so I disappointed my constituents, who would have preferred that I support the president no matter what justice required. My taking these positions was perceived to be undermining the micronation's prospects to retain the presidency. Several of my constituents told me point-blank that I should have supported the president notwithstanding the circumstances, and that they now considered me a traitor.

It is not that communities aren't capable of recognizing the effects of good or bad policies on the ground. However, the strong sense of trust that micro-nations have in their leaders often predominates. Communities may not have enough information to know that the person may be the wrong leader (that they may, indeed, be traveling in the wrong bus), and they may refuse to hear other perspectives that are critical of them. Such may have been the case in this instance.

As it turned out, my fears that the country had become polarized since the 2002 elections were proven right. In 2007 the voters of Kenya were genuinely divided. Perhaps the most tangible indication of how they had expressed themselves was that the number of MPs on the ODM party's side were many more than those on PNU's. (However, while the number of voters is, of course, a good indicator, the fact that an area had an MP did not necessarily mean that the constituency had a significant number of voters. During the previous regime a considerable amount of gerrymandering had been done in creating parliamentary constituencies, so that areas supporting Mr. Kibaki, for instance, had heavily populated constituencies with relatively few MPs.)

Not long after Mr. Kibaki's swearing-in on December 30, 2007, several electoral commissioners revealed their doubts about the accuracy of the presidential vote tally. In my own Tetu constituency, I had already written letters to the ECK indicating that I had reasons to suspect that irregularities had taken place.

For example, the forms that tallied the votes were meant to be signed by both the returning officer at the polling station and the agents (or representatives at the polling place) of the candidates. However, some of the forms that I saw were not signed; others I never received. It was also reported that on the day of the voting some representatives of the candidates, including my own, had been asked by the local ECK official to leave the polling room. Each candidate had two representatives (agents)—one to relieve the other if they had to use the bathroom or wanted to get a cup of tea. The ECK official should have ensured that one of the candidates' representatives was at the polling station at all times so that no irregularities with the ballot boxes could occur or suspicion of such irregularities could be raised. That both representatives had been sent away at the same time left the system open to abuse. Even though these problems concerned the parliamentary vote, it did not take much to persuade me that there might well have been malpractice with the votes for local councils and the presidency as well.

The apparent manipulation of votes began at the location where they were to be tallied. The first people who knew there were discrepancies were the returning officers, who informed leaders of the opposition and government parties of their concerns. These leaders began speaking out, and as the pressure and complaints continued, suspicion increased that votes were being misappropriated. Other accusations began to pile up. For instance, it was reported that in particular districts more votes had been cast than there were eligible voters, and recorded local vote counts differed from those presented to the electoral commission.

In some polling stations it was said that kerosene and candles by which to count the votes had run out, and when poll workers returned the next morning to continue counting, they found that new votes had materialized overnight. The chairman of the ECK was under pressure to announce the results even before he was ready. Kenyans watched and listened in disbelief. Had the country's nascent democracy been dealt a huge setback? Had the electoral process been interfered with?

In the eyes of some politicians, the misfortune of the 2007 Kenyan election was not that irregularities occurred, but that they were discovered. This is an all-too-common feature of elections in Africa: one African president is even alleged to have asked his colleague how he could lose an election he had organized. Given this history, the challenged performance of the ECK and the hurried nature of the swearing-in ceremony, it is understandable that many people in Kenya began to wonder whether there was something to hide. This unease was only enhanced over the next few days as impartial observers both within Kenya and in the international community—including the head of the European Union observer mission—detailed serious voting irregularities. When, several days after he had declared the result, the chairman of the ECK was asked who he thought had won the presidency, he replied that he didn't know. (A commission that later looked into the irregularities of the voting came to the conclusion that it may never be known who legitimately won the 2007 presidential election.)

On that same Sunday in December, only hours after the presidential result was announced, Kenya plunged into a war with itself, and the country, long considered one of the most stable in Africa, experienced perhaps the greatest level of violence since the time of the Mau Mau uprising against British rule fifty years before. Unfortunately, some citizens took their anger about the outcome of the presidential contest out on their neighbors—nearly all of whom were as poor and powerless as they. The police seemed ill-prepared to deal with the growing mayhem and even contributed to the death toll by firing live ammunition into crowds and engaging bands of young men in running battles through the streets. Tragically, some police were reported to be partisan and therefore unwilling to stop the killing and destruction if members of their own micronation were committing the crimes.

The attackers knew perfectly well that it was not their neighbors who were responsible for their anger and frustration, and that the only "crime" those neighbors may have committed was that they belonged to or voted for a different micronation or candidate—but that was enough for them to be assaulted. Some of the violence appeared preplanned. Reports circulated that some politicians not only were stirring up people along ethnic lines to attack their opponents, but were also paying young people to kill or burn down people's houses. It became clear that behind the agenda of gaining power, there was another one: to drive from the Rift Valley members of one micro-nation whom the attackers, from another micro-nation, considered "foreign settlers."

Tragically, however, violence begets violence. No matter how orchestrated the protests may have been in the beginning, eventually the leaders lost control, and, as could have been anticipated, atrocity piled on atrocity—even to the extent that gangs of young men blockaded roads and demanded passengers in passing buses to show their identity card, which in listing a person's name also usually reveals his or her ethnic origin. Or passengers were required to speak their mother tongue, another way of determining their ethnicity. If they were from the "wrong group," they were attacked and many were killed.[1] It is estimated that between 1,200 and 1,500 people lost their lives; many others were scarred and wounded by machetes or bows and arrows wielded against them. Over half a million people were forced to flee from their homes, some of which were looted or razed to the ground. Women were raped, and, in one terrible incident, as many as fifty people, mainly women and children, were burned to death when a church they had taken shelter in was set on fire.

While the violence may have been shocking, what came as no surprise to Kenyans—and, no doubt, other Africans—was that what emerged on the night of December 27, 2007, and plunged the country into turmoil for weeks reflected the challenges to genuine democracy that have plagued Africa ever since most of its nations achieved independence. As is almost always the case, it was the innocent who suffered from the vanity and obstinacy of their leaders. Many people paid the ultimate price for their leaders' refusal to consider dialogue and mediation. In such conflicts, the African peoples always lose. From Liberia and the Ivory Coast in the west to the Democratic Republic of the Congo, Zimbabwe, and Rwanda in the heart of Africa, to Sudan and Somalia, two of Kenya's neighbors, it is women, children, and the poor who have been the main victims of leaders' or would-be leaders' stubbornness, corruption, and divisiveness.

The impression of a lawless and ungovernable Africa is, undoubtedly, what the outside world has come to expect from the continent. What is rarely reported on in the global media are the many individuals who look beyond their own communities to embrace their fellow citizens. Stories usually do not focus on civil society groups who are promoting conflict resolution rather than ethnic chauvinism, or employing dialogue rather than the machete or the gun as a way of sorting out grievances.

(It is also hard to determine in news reports which actions have nothing to do with the community someone belongs to but are either the basest forms of thuggery and extortion or a desperate reaction to seemingly hopeless poverty—the marginalization many people experience when it appears that nobody cares about their thoughts or their lives.)

Indeed, notwithstanding the risks, during the strife after the 2007 elections, groups of men and women from different micro-nations throughout Kenya, in some of the poorest as well as richest neighborhoods, came together to call for peace. Religious leaders, businesspeople, editorial writers, bloggers, and ordinary citizens spoke out against violence and voiced their hope that politicians would begin serious discussions to end the conflict for the good of the country and the region.[2]

Echoing former UN secretary-general Kofi Annan, whom the African Union appointed to mediate the electoral dispute, the Green Belt Movement repeatedly called for a power-sharing arrangement between Mwai Kibaki and Raila Odinga that would be ratified by parliament and placed within the constitution so it could not be easily dismissed—as the memorandum of understanding had been after the 2002 elections. On the grounds of the GBM headquarters in Nairobi, we erected a "peace tent," where concerned individuals as well as victims of the violence could come to convey their sorrow for those who had died or been displaced and express their hopes for a peaceful resolution of the crisis.[3]

Some members of Green Belt Movement groups, as well as staff, were victims: one's house was burned to the ground, and another's extended family was forced to flee their home. Some of the tree-planting programs and seminars on Civic and Environmental Education were disrupted for a time, and thousands of young trees in the nurseries had to be abandoned. We were lucky that the Kenyan army, under the leadership of Chief of

General Staff Jeremiah Kianga, was able to rescue some one hundred thousand seedlings and take care of them. (The army has an initiative to plant trees in the barracks and in the forest.)

When the dialogue between the two sides finally started and the violence subsided, I felt as a Nobel peace laureate that it was incumbent upon me to visit those who had been displaced and were living in makeshift camps, and others who had sought refuge in towns. Staffers from GBM's peace tent and I wanted to bear witness to their suffering and console them, as well as urge them toward reconciliation; to encourage them to forgive, but not forget. It was difficult to see such misery and destruction and to realize that so many people had died or been displaced in a conflict that could so easily have been prevented if Kenya's leadership had listened and engaged in dialogue during the preceding years.

I had already discovered that perceived disloyalty to one's own ethnic community was politically dangerous; I was soon to discover that it could be physically dangerous as well. When, in the wake of the 2007 electoral standoff, I urged the president to be less recalcitrant and to engage Raila Odinga and his team in dialogue, the government I had only recently left was not pleased. The day after I lost my seat in parliament, two of my police bodyguards were reassigned. Fair enough: I was no longer a member of the government, so no longer entitled to such protection. But when I began urging the two sides to find a resolution, the last of my bodyguards was withdrawn. He had been assigned to me specifically after the awarding of the Nobel Peace Prize. The government did not wish to share power, and by removing the final bodyguard its principals were seeking to punish me for my perceived rebellious behavior—not supporting the position of my micro-national leader. Not long after, death threats were sent to me via text message. When I made these public, the government reinstated the bodyguard (in its

own time), and pleaded ignorance about why he'd been reassigned in the first place.

Whatever their source, death threats are always unwelcome
and very disturbing. I have never been physically harmed by
members of any of the forty-two distinct micro-nations that
live in Kenya, and count people of many ethnicities as friends
and colleagues. The sending of such serious threats with no
fear of the consequences was a sign to me of how polarized
things had become in Kenya.

The violence that rocked Kenya in the aftermath of the 2007
elections did not happen in a vacuum; nor was it without
precedent. In the run-up to the elections at the end of 1992,
and until 1997, the same area where the 2008 violence was
concentrated—the Rift Valley—was roiled by similar, politically instigated disturbances. At that time, the cry from the
one-party government, which had ruled Kenya virtually since
independence, was that the country was not ready for multi-
party democracy—because, they said, it would inevitably lead
to "tribalism" and discord. To prove their point, elements in
the administration stirred up the very ethnic violence they
stated would occur. Communities fought each other over land
and political power. Then, as in 2008, hundreds were killed and
thousands were displaced. Many still haven't returned to their
homes.

In 2008, however, there was a notable difference from the
period between 1992 and 1997. In 2008, the international community, remembering how it had ignored the warning signs
and done nothing as hundreds of thousands of people were bru-
tally killed in Rwanda in 1994, resolved to act. Mediators such
as Archbishop Desmond Tutu, three former African presidents
(Kaunda of Zambia, Chissano of Mozambique, and Quett
Masire of Botswana), John Kufuor, then president of Ghana and
chairman of the African Union, and President Yoweri Musev-

eni of Uganda, U.S. assistant secretary of state Jendayi Frazer, and Secretary of State Condoleezza Rice all made efforts to bring the two parties to the negotiating table. Finally, the AU deployed Kofi Annan as its chief mediator. He was joined by Graça Machel, the former first lady of Mozambique and wife of Nelson Mandela, and the former president of Tanzania, Benjamin Mkapa, to form a team of eminent Africans to facilitate dialogue.

After six weeks of active diplomacy, Mr. Kibaki and Mr. Odinga agreed to share power and then hold elections in 2009. The post of prime minister was created and the cabinet shared between the president's party and the ODM coalition. In addition, they agreed that the long-standing constitutional and political problems that had ended the coalition in 2005, and the pressing issues of land ownership and distribution, would be addressed.

Naturally, like all Kenyans I was relieved when this deal was signed in March 2008. But like many, I was also mystified and appalled as to why this agreement—which many of us had recommended from the outset of the electoral impasse, and which indeed had formed the bones of the 2002 memorandum—could not have been reached before so many Kenyans had died, been displaced, or had property destroyed, not to mention before so much ethnic hatred had been unleashed. In this regard, the accommodations and compromises for which many had been calling for more than five years could have been made (in 2005) without dismissing the cabinet or even, perhaps, the vote for a new constitution devolving into a battle between constituencies over who would retain power.

Although there were moments when I was genuinely fearful for Kenya's future, I was hopeful that the country would not descend into the horrors of a Rwandan-like genocide—precisely because of the efforts of the AU, other African nations, and the large international community to bring the two protagonists to the dialogue table. Nevertheless, the image of Kenya as a stable democracy, a place where business could invest safely and from where humanitarian missions could be launched to other countries—in other words, a place where persecuted people fled *to* and not *from*—was shattered. A country I thought could provide a model of the peaceful transfer of power in Africa had been plunged into the sort of senseless bloodletting that the outside world all too often associates with Africa.

Ironically, in the end, perhaps no community suffered more losses of land and lives because of the recalcitrance of the leaders they supported than those who belonged to the president's micro-nation: the Kikuyus. And after so much bloodshed and displacement they were forced to share the very power they were so fearful of losing. In the refrain of "Where Have All the Flowers Gone?" Pete Seeger's anthem against militarism and the Vietnam War, "When will they ever learn? When will they ever learn?"

PEACE AND RECONCILIATION

In the midst of negotiating the power-sharing deal that ended Kenya's postelectoral crisis in 2008, Kofi Annan offered his observation that Kenya needed its own Truth and Reconciliation Commission. This kind of commission, pioneered in South Africa under the auspices of Archbishop Desmond Tutu after the formal end of apartheid, is an approach that has also been adopted in Liberia, Sierra Leone, and Rwanda.

In the case of South Africa, everyone who took part in the post-apartheid process knew that simply having the victims of wrongs confront the perpetrators would never be enough to balance the unquantifiable horrors of apartheid or recompense the generations whose lives were thwarted by its pitiless laws and practices. But the commission gave voice to those whose suffering had been silenced. It returned a portion of dignity to those who had been dehumanized, and in turn pricked the conscience of a nation, and indeed the world. More important, the commission understood that only when the truth was known and justice received could wounds begin to heal. Only then could reconciliation start and the people as a whole look to the future with hope.

In Kenya, it will take more than the realignment of constitutional powers and access to land to heal the wounds that were opened by this most recent conflict. People were forced to move to their ancestral homelands, even if they had never lived there, as groups of young men incited by their leaders sought both to kill, and to avenge killings perpetrated by other groups of young men. The Kenyan economy lost over a billion dollars, much of it in the area of tourism, which dropped by a third in the first half of 2008.[4] However, the greatest loss is in those who died, as well as the destruction of the goodwill and comradeship that Kenyans from a majority of micro-nations had for each other in 2002. It has yet to be recaptured.

Indeed, even as I write, it is clear to me that the trauma that Kenya experienced is still present, and the price of a settlement has been exorbitant. The two main political blocs created an enormous government cabinet, Kenya's largest and costliest ever, with an unprecedented forty-four ministers, which, given that each minister has at least one assistant minister (and some have two), means that nearly half of all MPs are either ministers or assistant ministers. To run these ministries will cost, between 2008 and 2009, according to Kenyan government estimates, 563 billion shillings ($8.66 billion). The total budget is 760 billion shillings ($11.7 billion), which means that the cabinet alone will consume three-quarters of the entire government's budget. By contrast, the government has apportioned 31 billion shillings ($476 million) for reconstruction in the aftermath of the 2008 violence.[5]

On April 1, 2008, I along with other members of civil society and the clergy met at Freedom Corner in Uhuru Park in downtown Nairobi. Freedom Corner has long been a location where people could speak their mind and, in the years before the 2002 elections, had been where the Green Belt Movement and others had protested against human rights violations, poor governance, corruption, land grabbing, and deforestation. This day, we were there to call upon the main protagonists of the postelectoral conflict to put the Kenyan people foremost by agreeing to a small, efficient cabinet that could govern effectively and not consume a disproportionate level of national resources. We also had gathered to memorialize those who had died in the conflict and to plant a tree to encourage the peace and reconciliation that was so essential.

That day in April, an open letter was read out to the three hundred or so assembled citizens and journalists, calling upon the president, Mwai Kibaki, and the prime minister designate, Raila Odinga, to place the needs of Kenyan citizens before theirs or their parties'. Speakers noted the pressing need for funds to resettle those displaced by the violence, and that a substantial portion of the budget would be required to rebuild property that had been destroyed. But when the organizers of the gathering tried to march to the building where, it was said, Kibaki and Odinga were meeting, to present the open letter, the police reacted with tear gas as a way to disperse the crowd. Their actions were an unhappy reminder of the incivility of the Kenyan government toward the citizens it claimed to represent: the arrogance and contempt were palpable.

The panic of people running, the tear gas stinging the eyes and burning the lungs, the police chasing people through the park with their batons at the ready—all this a response to the peaceful exercise of democratic rights—were a sad reminder to me of decades of similar assaults by the authorities. That it was happening again, and that the police were receiving orders from the same government for whose inauguration many of us had gathered in jubilation at the same location just five years previously, was deeply disappointing. Equally depressing was the fact that, when elected, the same government had promised genuine change and to honor the same rights it was now denying.

The events of that morning—indeed, of the entire election and the six years between 2002 and 2008—reminded me that democratic space can never be taken for granted. It must always be defended against those who would accrue money and power to themselves at the expense of their peoples and the long-term health of the nation and the environment on which it depends. It caused me to reflect upon the terrible consequences when politicians foment rivalries between micronations, and how all too rarely these tears in the fabric of the nation-state are repaired by genuine leadership. It also fortified my belief that those who care about good governance, and believe that leaders should serve their people, can never give up.

Ten

EMBRACING THE MICRO-NATIONS

PERHAPS NOWHERE ELSE in the recent history of Africa has a genuine attempt been made to create an inclusive national culture, drawn from the richness of the many micro-nations within national borders, more than in post-apartheid South Africa. Recognizing the extraordinary complexities of the country's history, current and past racial dynamics, economic disparities, and climatic and geographical diversity, South Africa's post-apartheid leaders have chosen to upend the absurd racial markers and segregationist mentality that were the essence of the apartheid system in favor of honoring people's micro-national identity within the broader concept of the macro-nation as the guarantor of basic democratic rights.

In the early 1990s, the fate of South Africa was not so clear-cut. Apartheid policy had divided the country's micro-nations into tribal homelands in an explicit policy to forestall the formation of a united South African opposition. Post-apartheid, the country could have descended into a factionalized state, divided by race and atomized by ethnicity. Such fears were very real in the lead-up to, and the time soon after, the historic 1994 elections.

The fact that there was not widespread violence is in large measure due to the vision and commitment of Nelson Mandela, who, from the time he was released from prison, continually referred to South Africa as the "rainbow nation." He and other African National Congress (ANC) leaders eschewed any appeal to ethnicity despite the provocations of Afrikaner-based parties and the Zulu-identified Inkatha Freedom Party. The ANC seems to be organized, as I believe all political parties should be, around a set of principles and values rather than race, ethnicity, or a personality cult centered on a leader. Mandela and his colleagues found ways both symbolic and substantive to acknowledge South Africa's micro-nations as equals, while creating a milieu where a national identity also could be forged. It is an experiment I hope will work over the long term.

In 1995, when South Africa was due to host the Rugby World Cup, President Mandela saw an opportunity to knit the country together after decades of racial division. To many at the time, this would have seemed preposterous. The years after the formal end of apartheid leading to the elections of 1994 had been difficult. Episodic violence between supporters of the ANC and Inkatha flared around the country, while white separatists such as Eugène Terre'Blanche and the Afrikaner Weerstandsbeweging (Afrikaner Resistance Movement, or AWB) sought to sow mayhem in defense of what the AWB called the "white tribe," through a campaign of bombings and even an invasion of a tribal homeland.

South African rugby was then highly polarized: both the game and the national team—the Springboks—were intimately connected with Afrikaner identity. Most blacks loathed the sport and the team with equal passion, choosing to both follow and play soccer. Nevertheless, President Mandela held numerous meetings with the team's captain, the rugby authorities, and his supporters, encouraging all of them to think of the tournament as an opportunity for South Africa to embrace the future rather than as a cause for further division and polarization. The president trumpeted the slogan "One Team, One Country," and made sure it was marketed heavily. As the Springboks moved through the tournament, excitement began to increase in the country at the team's prospects, even among the black majority.

When the team reached the final, President Mandela put on the green-and-gold jersey and cap of the Springboks and strode out onto the pitch before the game to shake hands with the all-white squad. After a moment of stunned silence, the enormous crowd—nearly all of whom were Afrikaner—broke into applause. When South Africa won the game, President Mandela returned to the pitch, still dressed in the Springbok colors, and presented François Pienaar, the team captain, with the tournament trophy. "Thank you for what you have done for our country," the president is reported to have said. "No, Mr. President," replied Pienaar. "Thank *you* for what you have done."

This gesture of President Mandela's proved a turning point for the young, post-apartheid nation; it "did wonders" for South Africa, said Archbishop Desmond Tutu. Pienaar himself related how on the streets the night of the Springboks' victory, "for the first time all the people had come together and all races and religions were hugging each other." Another member of the team, Joost van der Westhuizen, recounted: "Seeing Nelson Mandela . . . and [to] think about what that guy did for this country, and now suddenly we did something for this country. It's quite a lesson for everybody, that we can do things together."[1]

President Mandela recognized that both the micro-nation and the macro-nation matter, and that culture has an essential role in creating a transnational identity. By aligning himself explicitly with rugby, this one man—who had been president for only a year and free from prison for only five—not only challenged his fellow blacks, who had suffered so much under white oppression, to acknowledge that they, too, could feel pride in the achievement of their national team. He also indicated that the Afrikaner love of rugby was a valued expression of white culture while simultaneously turning on its head their overidentification with the sport.

The point was not to honor Afrikaner culture because it was *Afrikaner* culture, but to transform rugby from a symbol of exclusivity and the dominance of one group over all the rest into a celebration of national pride, and in so doing absorb a separatist minority into the majority. Through his actions, Mandela showed how honoring a key aspect of the culture of a small micro-nation—in this case, the love of rugby—didn't have to lead to the fragmentation or weakening of the macro-nation, but could, instead, serve to strengthen it.

REIMAGINING COMMUNITY

Well-considered, carefully planned initiatives such as Mandela's that bring communities together, foster dialogue, and achieve long-term reconciliation could allow Africans to rise above competitive, and often petty, politics at the level of micro-nations and address the pressing larger issues confronting the nation-state.

This does not mean that ethnicity is nonexistent or that Africa will not have to address the problems of "tribal" identity and ethnic nationalism that exist independent of political machinations. But the different micro-nations would be much more secure and likely to flourish if they accepted who they are and, at the same time, worked together. In my view, it is essential that Africa's citizens and leaders embrace a revival of their micro-national cultures, languages, and values, and then bring the best of these to the table—that is, the nation-state. In so doing, a national or even transnational identity could be created that is at once forward-looking and relevant to contemporary needs, and securely grounded in the heritage of Africa's peoples.

In this way, African nation-states, which now for many people merely serve to issue necessary documents such as a passport and an identity card, will more fully represent the diversity and the achievements of their distinct peoples. Anything less will perpetuate the cultural deracination that has left millions of modern Africans lacking self-identity, self-confidence, self-knowledge, and, therefore, the ability to take charge of their lives. Failure will also lead to the kind of violence that is too often seen in Africa.

It is important to acknowledge that the difficulty of this transformation of what it means to be an African cannot be underestimated. Even though the boundaries of the macronations laid the groundwork for conflict, and Africans had no say in the demarcations of their countries, the macro-nations that Africans were bequeathed are now an accepted fact. And, as far back as the founding of the OAU, African leaders agreed to accept the boundaries drawn by the colonial powers. It is within these parameters that Africans must reconstitute their nations, despite the fact that they didn't name them, and that the inhabitants often do not share a common language or heritage. Africans cannot change the past; they can only manage it and determine the future.

Indeed, a related task is to reimagine what it means to be a community—whether a micro-nation or the network of micro-nations that are countries, regions, and the continent itself. As nations become more integrated within the global economy, the pressure to expand effective political and economic blocs— such as in eastern and southern Africa and eastern and southern Asia—will grow in such a way that national borders may no longer be so relevant. If, for instance, Africa becomes united in the future along the lines of the European Union, then, while it may still have troubles, borders won't be among them.

Certainly, some African countries—particularly, for instance, Tanzania and Senegal under presidents Julius Nyerere and Léopold Senghor—deliberately and consciously worked for a more cohesive nation-state by downplaying micro-national identity. Nyerere drove through policies that emphasized the importance of being Tanzanian. He did this despite Tanzania's heterogeneity; the country is comprised of over 120 micro-nations. Nyerere also stressed the importance of speaking one language—Kiswahili—above all others in order to unify the country. The result currently is a remarkably harmonious nation, with much less of the "tribalism" that affects other parts of Africa. It is an experiment whose durability will be tested by time, and dependent on the future leadership of the country.

Tanzania is one model, but there could be others that embrace micro-national identity. I don't doubt that if at the outset of independence in Kenya a conference had been held of the forty-two micro-nations and they had all negotiated a constitution under which they agreed to coexist and work together, while honoring a set of agreed-upon rights, the communal violence that has periodically wracked Kenya since then might not have occurred. Instead, Kenyan leaders, like others throughout Africa, simultaneously trivialized what it meant to be a distinct micro-nation and overemphasized—and continue to exploit—real and imagined barriers between communities. Of course, some people believe that through the process of submerging one's micro-nationality they are fighting "tribalism." In my conception it is really the opposite. The simple truth is that more than a century has passed since the colonial authorities and then postindependence leaders began to force Africans to transcend their micro-nations, and far from being buried, "tribalism" has been entrenched.

Today in Rwanda it is illegal to define oneself as either Hutu or Tutsi. While I fully understand why the government wanted to end ethnic identification after the horrors of the 1994 genocide, the truth is that, while individuals may not make their identity public, they surely know whether they are Hutu or Tutsi. This kind of impulse for self-identification can be suppressed only for a time. While it may appear that the micro-national "marker" has been removed, it cannot truly be extinguished. It will have to express itself one way or the other. Our different identities are part of a natural diversity. Instead of all attempting the impossible task of being the same, we must learn to embrace our diversity. Indeed, human beings are stronger for it. Of course, it is my fervent hope that no more ethnically based violence erupts in Rwanda or anywhere else. But its prevention will depend heavily on the action or inaction of competing political leaders.

The European Union is moving in a promising direction: uniting its individual nation-states into a larger macro-nation. Much as the EU recognizes the multitude of different cultures and countries within its larger political structure, and tries more or less successfully to accommodate the varied impulses and concerns of the communities, African countries, too, could acknowledge the composite nature of their nation-states and do likewise. It is clear that in order to have greater cohesion within nation-states, African political leaders will have to devote time, energy, and resources so that universal freedom, security, and equitable distribution of assets are assured.

Principally, the elites—the 10 to 20 percent of the population that speaks the language of the former colonial power and in large measure has adopted Western culture as its own—ought to be more in touch with the genuine wishes of the 80 percent who perceive themselves as Igbo or Yoruba first, and Nigerian second; or Luo or Kikuyu or Maasai first, and Kenyan second; or Dinka and Fur first, and Sudanese second. The elites need to recognize that most of the ordinary people whom they have been groomed to lead, by universities at home or abroad, are still bound by family relationships stronger than their ties to where they live or who their neighbors are. Connections to family and territorial nationality have sometimes been the only means whereby individuals can cope with the turbulent uprooting of their traditions since colonization. But just as one can simultaneously be a Welshman and a Briton or a Tamil and an Indian, Africans, too, can remain both loyal members of a micro-nation and loyal citizens of a nation-state. This is what it should mean to be an individual in a multicultural and multi-ethnic country today.

To ground this concept, I believe it would be a vital, boundary-breaking step if a nation established a forum for representatives of micro-nations that could be incorporated into the governance structures of the macro-nation. A sense of collective responsibility could thus be instilled among citizens throughout the country. The representatives would gather and debate and agree on a set of actions to benefit not only their micro-nation, but also the greater society. They could draw on indigenous traditions of fairness, justice, deliberation, and representation. This might, for example, take the form of an assembly, rather like the United Nations or the U.S. Senate—where all micro-nations are represented equally, no matter how many citizens they have. The members of the collective would meet as equals and discuss the affairs of the nation and how that nation should relate to other nations for the common good of the region.

The value of such a forum would be that a government body existed with the express purpose of making sure that all communities felt they had a stake and a voice in how the country was managed; that no matter how small, these micro-nations would know that their rights would be respected and their safety guaranteed. Here, some of the most pressing and long-unanswered questions could be addressed: What does "equity" mean? How should disputes over landownership that have simmered since the beginning of the colonial era be resolved? How will nations and communities protect their forests and watersheds while still enabling development? With this forum, the checks and balances would be weighted and realigned constantly. It would enshrine a central tenet often neglected by developed nations when they urge democracy on developing ones: that democracy is not just about one person receiving one vote; it is about effective representation and inclusion.

For many African societies—which were fragmented by colonialism, interfered with during the Cold War, torn apart by decades of ethnic favoritism and dissension, burdened by underdevelopment for far too long, and have too few mechanisms for government accountability—this forum would provide an opportunity for the flourishing of genuine democracy. The transformation I envision would require citizens to face the truth about the genesis of "tribal clashes." It will also depend on principled leaders who stop playing the "tribal" card to hold on to power. (Because of the negativity that is associated with "tribes" and ethnicity in Africa, it is not uncommon to find Africans preferring to use their Christian name rather than their African name, or using a foreign language, in an effort to hide their identity.)

To propel these ideas forward, in their families and from their first day at school on, African children should be taught that the peoples of their country *are* different, but that because of Africa's historical legacy they need to work together. In schools and universities, students should be encouraged to learn more fully about the cultures of other micro-nations within the macro-nation. These measures would offer the possibility of creating a new elite that is not so narrowly partisan and have the potential to develop leaders with not only greater knowledge of their countries, but greater responsibility toward all of a country's micro-nations as well as the macro-nation.

Politicians in Africa know that micro-national identity is important. When they campaign, they do not address their micro-nation in the language(s) of the macro-nation, which is often that of the former colonial master. They are often anx-

ious to speak to other micro-nations in their mother tongues—
if only a few words, such as "Hello" or "How are you?" But
their interest in that language is superficial; they are attempting to flatter the people in the hope that they will support them
at the ballot box. What is needed is a genuine recognition by
leaders that micro-nations value aspects of their identity that
they still possess, such as their languages.

SPEAKING MOTHER TONGUES

Language is an important component of culture and an essential means of binding the micro-nation together. In many
African states during the colonial administration, the government's local representative was a native. He would speak the
micro-nation's language, as well as the European language of
the administration, and interpret between the local people and
higher-level administrators, who were citizens of the colonial
power. One of the legacies of the colonial era is that in many
African nations, the governance, justice, and education systems are conducted in foreign languages, as is most media.

Even if another national language has been adopted, such as
Kiswahili in the case of Kenya, the great mass of rural populations neither speak nor understand it fluently. It is my belief
that denying someone the ability to communicate with their
government, at least at the local level, is one of the strongest
forms of discrimination and, indeed, means of oppression and
exclusion.

Most African elites speak and manage in a foreign language
that's spoken and read only by a tiny minority and not understood at all by a large majority of their peoples. The elites communicate with each other in official languages, which are
European, such as English and French, or national languages,
like Kiswahili. Their grammar, pronunciation, and sentence
structure are not at the level of a native speaker. However,

since those they speak with are also speaking imperfectly, they don't know they are making mistakes. By and large, neither the elites nor the masses know each other's mother tongues, and rarely do we make an effort to learn them. As a result, we have a very limited reach in being able to spread our ideas, or listen to others'.

For most people, especially in the rural areas, the local government representative is still the expression of the nation-state's government in their lives. If people are not allowed to communicate with, at a minimum, their local government in their own languages, it is almost as if they are living in a foreign country or being governed by a foreign power. Since they do not understand well, if at all, the official or national language, they are, in effect, completely alienated from the governance structures of their nation. This language divide is a crucial way of further distancing the government from its people. Throughout Africa, a country's managers speak to themselves, while those in whose name they govern don't understand them. The people may clap after they are spoken to by the person in authority, but for the most part, they haven't caught enough of what he or she has said to understand its meaning or relevance. If the nation is being run by a group of people that the mass of citizens can't understand, and when its leaders address only themselves, how can it move forward?

Micro-nations should have the opportunity to communicate effectively among themselves, by learning in schools to read and write fluently in their mother tongues; likewise, the government at the local level should communicate with micro-nationalities in their own languages. If the micro-nations were allowed to speak their languages and be addressed in them as well, it would encourage patriotism and a connection to the government and indeed the larger nation-state.

The Green Belt Movement has always insisted that the people participating in its programs be able to speak in their local languages. GBM's rationale is that because many Kenyans, especially those in rural areas with limited formal education, don't fully comprehend Kiswahili—and even less so English—they often sit silently when meetings are conducted in these languages. GBM staff wants to hear what the communities have to say and be sure that they can understand what GBM is saying, too. If no GBM staff member speaks the local language, someone from the community who knows the mother tongue as well as Kiswahili or English is asked to translate. Such a practice is still not common, even among those organizations doing development work, including NGOs, and indeed is sometimes criticized as "promoting tribalism."

Within Africa, one notable exception to the states' reliance on foreign languages is the Republic of South Africa, which has acknowledged its diversity by enshrining in its constitution no fewer than eleven official languages—including Setswana, Afrikaans, English, isiXhosa, and isiZulu. In doing this, South Africa has established a bedrock upon which it can build a multiracial society that both respects its diversity and encourages identification with the country as a whole. South Africa is at an advantage because it is a relatively wealthy country, and therefore can afford to have multiple languages taught and represented in official documents. Whether or not the cost of having such a polyglot state of robust micro-nations outweighs the intangible benefits of a country that understands itself may be difficult to say at this time, but I believe it is worth the wager.

To encourage better communication among Africa's micro-nations, African states could decide that every child would study his or her own language in school until the fourth or even the eighth grade. This would enable them to read literature, or the Bible, in their mother tongue, helping ensure not only literacy, but also a sense of their identity through their language. In the higher grade levels, the government could mandate that each child learn one or even two international languages, as well as a language of one of the other micro-nations. In this way, each citizen would know their own culture more deeply, and also be able to communicate effectively with fellow citizens elsewhere in their country.

In Nigeria, for instance, while four hundred languages are spoken, about half of the population speaks one of three: Hausa, Igbo, or Yoruba. So a Yoruba child in Nigeria could learn Yoruba well enough to read, write, and speak it fluently, plus Igbo or Hausa, the languages of the other major Nigerian micro-nations, or another, less commonly spoken language. He would also learn English. In Senegal, a child who grew up speaking Pulaar, the language of the Peul and Toucouleur micro-nations, could choose to study Wolof, the language of Senegal's largest micro-nation and the "lingua franca" of the capital, Dakar. She would also learn French and, if she wanted, English, too.

In Kenya, I could envision a Kikuyu child choosing strategically to learn Luo, since Luos are the third-largest micro-nation (after Kikuyus and Luhyas). Since Kikuyus can understand the Kambas, learning Luo would broaden the mind and the cultural references of the Kikuyu child, so that she would be as comfortable in Nyanza Province on the shores of Lake Victoria as she is in Nyeri in the Central Highlands. Likewise, if as an adolescent or adult she walked into a market in Kisumu and found the majority of people speaking Luo, she would not feel out of place, even though she was raised as a Kikuyu. She could visit a local restaurant and order local food, and nobody would feel embarrassed that the food is not the sort served in Hilton hotels or in New York, but is native to the region—and as worthy a cuisine as any other. Her life would be enriched by the experience; the local community would understand that a Kikuyu had made an effort to understand their cultural and linguistic reality; and possibilities for mutual cooperation will have been enhanced. The same would be true of someone raised in the Senegalese countryside speaking Pulaar and spending time in Dakar; or a Yoruba from southwest Nigeria traveling to, or even settling in, the Hausa-speaking north.

Smaller communities might be at a disadvantage, because children and their parents might decide that it would be more valuable to learn a language belonging to a larger micro-nation. This, however, might be an opportunity for greater political and linguistic coordination within or between micro-nations that could enable communities to join together to express their identity more effectively.

If instituted, such policies in Africa have the potential to bind nations not merely through the promotion of national or official languages that people don't know well, but because self-confident micro-nations would develop, with their own cultures and languages. It is, of course, possible that wider knowledge of languages might encourage people to travel and settle elsewhere, which could, as it has in the past, lead to conflict with local communities; but it's also possible that a greater sense of self would make individuals more creative and confident within their own communities, and less likely to be hostile to outsiders. Indeed, this mobility could create greater cohesion, since members of micro-nations would not only be found in their traditional homelands. This could help reduce the ethnic identification, implicit or explicit, of many African political parties. Such "melting pots" of micro-nations are already the norm in African metropolises.

A relatively inexpensive and direct way of communicating in Africa is through the radio. In the 1990s, many African states refused licenses to independent media outlets, including radio stations. They kept dissident voices out of the media or employed the state-run television and radio stations in propaganda efforts. Since then, as part of the (albeit often slow) opening of democratic space, the media have become notably freer and more diverse in Africa. State monopolies have loosened, and the Internet and satellite communication have created new channels for information and opinion.

In my view, local radio is a crucial means for micro-nations to reclaim their languages and cultures, as well as to bring greater cohesion to the nation-state. Not only can people listen to national news and opinion, but increasingly they can find radio programming in their mother tongue. Some critics rightly point out that local radio can be used to promote hate and incite violence. This was the case in Rwanda in 1994, when Radio Télévision Libre des Mille Collines actively called upon Hutus to murder Tutsis and moderate Hutus. In Kenya in 2008, charges that they magnified ethnic tensions were leveled at local-language radio hosts.

Distressing as these examples are, the answer is not to shut down this avenue of communication by closing all local-language radio stations. It is the attitudes of those speaking into the microphones in the studios that need to be addressed. National media codes of conduct and legislation banning hate speech and incitement to violence could be considered to ensure that these outlets are used to inform and explain, not for broadcasting the rants of demogogues and bigots. The danger, of course, is that such structures of governance could be used by the leadership to squelch dissenting voices, but the media could be proactive in this area: for instance, by engaging the government in a dialogue about the media's behavior, so as to avoid freedom of speech being compromised by too much government control.

One individual who would have benefited from the expansion of local-language radio was my mother, who died at the age of ninety-four a mere three months before the first Kikuyu-language FM radio station opened. She would have loved to listen to that station—speaking to her in a language she would have understood. As it could for millions of other Africans, especially the elderly and those who do not have access to newspapers or television, it would have opened and enriched her world. That is what I would like to see happen for the millions like her across Africa.

Eleven

LAND OWNERSHIP: WHOSE LAND IS IT, ANYWAY? ·

THE RATE OF urbanization in Africa is the highest in the world, with city populations doubling every twenty years.[1] Sprawling cities and slums have gobbled up vast tracts of forest and agricultural land. Nevertheless, most Africans are still rural and directly dependent on the land for their income. In addition, many African countries have significant populations of pastoralists, most of whom can no longer migrate across long distances with their herds of cows, goats, sheep, or camels the way they did before national borders were established and land throughout Africa was bought, sold, and fenced. With the onset of climate change, arable or grazeable land is likely to become even more precious. According to the United Nations Environment Programme (UNEP), degradation of land is a serious concern in thirty-two African countries, and 65 percent of the continent's farmland has sustained damage.[2]

Across much of Africa, landownership and distribution remain volatile issues. In many nations, colonial governments forcibly displaced large numbers of native Africans to make way for European settlers. When the colonial authorities arrived, they also brought with them a concept of landownership that was alien to much of the African continent. They insisted that land be controlled by a title deed, and when such deeds were bestowed, the authorities would provide them only to "the head of the household," which was the man. Traditionally, land was owned not by an individual but by the family or the community. The new rules disenfranchised women, who no longer had a right to land but who, instead, accessed land at the pleasure of the father or the husband, whose name was written on the title deed. (Advocates for women's equality are challenging this state of affairs in many African countries, and as a result laws are changing.)

At independence, land changed hands, but in many cases the details of those transactions—who owned what, who bought what, and how much of it—remain unresolved to this day. Land (the promise and the loss of it) has been a battleground—used, much like ethnic identification, by unscrupulous leaders as a way to gain political advantage. Over the past several decades, community-held and individually owned lands in Africa have been lost to a variety of forces, both man-made and ecological. Deserts have spread, topsoil has been washed away as forests and other vegetation have been cleared, and the land's fertility has been reduced through too many cycles of planting, grazing, and the application of chemicals. Much farmland has been subdivided into ever-smaller parcels as populations have grown and land has passed from one generation to the next.

Governments, too, have assumed control over land, often displacing communities in the process, for infrastructure projects (some beneficial to the nation at large, some costly "white elephants"), to accommodate sprawling urban settlements, or for national parks and reserves. Many Africans today have too little land, and some have too much, often as a result of the colonial past. In 2005 in South Africa, for instance, 96 percent of arable land was still owned by white farmers.[3] In Namibia, white farmers own around 50 percent of arable land,[4] and in Zimbabwe, where attempts to reapportion land have riven the country for years, as of 2000, 4,500 white farmers still owned 70 percent of the prime land.[5]

But it's not only the descendents of white settlers who

control vast tracts of land—nor do redistributed lands always revert to small-scale farmers or the landless. Too often, prime lands in Africa end up in the hands of ruling elites or their inner circle.[6] The issue of land distribution will continue to roil African nations until politicians stop using land as a political tool, and just settlements to controversies over land are agreed upon.

POACHERS, CONSERVATIONISTS, AND TOURISTS

The conundrum of land in Africa and its relationship to the economy, agriculture, and prospects for poverty reduction was brought into sharp relief in Kenya in 2005 when Thomas Cholmondeley, the great-grandson of Lord Delamere of Britain (1870–1931), shot to death Simon Ole Sasina, a Kenya Wildlife Service game warden investigating suspected poachers. A year later, he shot and killed a second man, Robert Njoya, who was alleged to have been poaching on his property.

Lord Delamere was a major figure in the first three decades of British rule in Kenya. He controlled land, purchased from the Maasai for a pittance, that extended over hundreds of thousands of acres in the Central Highlands and the Rift Valley. Today, the family remains among Kenya's largest landholders; the Delamere estate—Soysambu—encompasses 100,000 acres, including a 48,000-acre wildlife conservancy. Since independence, the descendents of Lord Delamere have remained close to some members of Kenya's political elite. Although he was not charged with Sasina's killing, Cholmondeley was with Njoya's murder, and the case has fascinated Kenyans and Europeans alike, as it encapsulates the racial, class, and land divides that still grip parts of Africa, more than forty years after Kenyan independence—when Nairobi's main thoroughfare was changed from Delamere to Kenyatta Avenue.

To the Delameres, the land and the animals on it are right-fully theirs, and trespassers on their property, whether those chasing poachers or poaching themselves, risk being shot. While the Delameres own beef and dairy operations, the income the estate generates from wildlife watching is considerable—an ironic reversal, given that many of the reserves established in Africa in the colonial area were set aside for white trophy hunters.

Until Europeans settled and converted a great deal of land into commercial farms, wildlife across Africa was abundant. But as the human population has increased and commercial farming has expanded, wildlife has been pushed into national parks. The only people who can have wildlife on private land are those like the Delameres, who own huge tracts. They don't need to hunt these animals for food, and many have joined the conservation and tourism sectors.

For traditional herders, separating land where their cattle, sheep, and goats can graze from wildlife reserves where they can't is an artificial construct: traditionally, in their micro-nations, no one can "own" land that has been held as a common resource by all the community's members. For Njoya and those like him who are not pastoralists and who are living in areas where wildlife is no longer present, wild animals on a neighboring large-scale estate are potential food—either for his or his family's consumption, or to sell in the market. Bushmeat markets, legal and not, are thriving in Kenya, as they are in other parts of Africa, encouraged by demand from tourists who want to eat exotic game, and from the elites who emulate them. Njoya can neither afford nor directly benefit from con-servation and wildlife watching.

Njoya's experience is not unusual. Most Africans do not see wildlife in the same light as tourists do—if they see the ani-mals at all. Indeed, many ordinary Africans who don't live near national parks or reserves see wild animals only in a zoo or safari park. Many fewer animals still exist where most Africans live than when I was growing up. Then, it was not unusual to disturb a rabbit or an antelope while walking along a path and see them run away into the bush.

The tourism economy, while an important sector in a number of African countries, is often conducted at a remove from the African peoples themselves: the tourists arrive on planes owned by foreign companies, and often stay in hotels or lodges owned by foreign corporations; they exchange money at foreign banks and may be transported to wildlife reserves on buses or in taxis also owned by foreign companies. Few revenues from this sector reach ordinary Africans. The only local people who may make money directly from tourism are guides, or staff in the lodges, hotels, and restaurants that serve the tourists. After the private companies, the second-largest beneficiary of tourism are governments. If the revenues are managed well, of course, they will reach Njoya and his family in the form of services. Unfortunately, this is all too rarely the case. For Njoya, therefore, wildlife conservation is a foreign luxury.

My aim here is not to disparage the tourists or those who package the safaris. Both are important. My point is that Africans—and their leaders—need to develop their tourism industries for the benefit of the African people. Africans—not foreign corporations—should provide affordable and clean hotels for guests; reliable and comfortable transportation to and from the national parks; hygienic and safe restaurants where tourists can eat, perhaps offering indigenous foods; tea stalls that are attractive and clean enough for tourists to drink at; and professional cultural programs (not the usual kitsch that many visitors experience) that would engage visitors in the rich heritage of the continent's micro-nations.

Much more revenue from tourism thus would stay in Africa, generating wealth and opportunities for citizens who are willing to be entrepreneurial and work hard to make a success of their businesses. The African people need to see that not only can tourism and conservation support their children's education, repair roads, and expand health facilities, but they can be part of the industry, too. With this, the sense of ownership individual Africans feel for the tourism industry would be strengthened. I don't mean just material ownership, but also ownership at a deeper level: taking responsibility for, and pride in, protecting wildlife and the environment, and the sharing of their nation and its cultures with visitors from around the world.

In nurturing this attitude and directing the revenues from the industry more equitably, government policies would encourage people like Robert Njoya to move away from subsistence living to, for instance, opening a clean, inviting kiosk selling high-quality Kenyan tea to tourists and passersby. Not enough of these exist, which is why people have a choice of drinking a cup of tea at a run-down stall or paying several dollars for one at a high-end hotel. A Robert Njoya might no longer need to poach, because he could buy food instead, and in the process could see wildlife as having more value to him alive than dead. It is important to note that, traditionally, Njoya's micro-nation did not eat wildlife, but only domestic animals. He has, however, been deculturated and encouraged to embrace bushmeat, and as a result is now helping accelerate the destruction of species that in the past he would not have harmed.

It is also clear that environmental education needs to be part of the academic curriculum in African schools. This would assist the peoples of Africa to recognize that they have an extraordinary resource in their wildlife, and that they need to protect and sustain it, and to spread the benefits of such a commitment broadly and fairly. If an African child grows up understanding the place an antelope has in the ecosystem, and that the animal has intrinsic as well as utilitarian value in terms of tourism revenue, he or she will be less likely to see it simply as meat, and will not empty the forests and parks of the biodiversity that is a crucial piece of his or her cultural and spiritual inheritance.

DIFFERENT WAYS OF WORKING THE LAND

The different perceptions and concepts about the uses and ownership of land held by pastoralists, conservationists, and farmers are aspects of the ever-present concerns over ensuring food security and reducing poverty in Africa. As the farmers in Yaoundé made evident, genuine reform and an overhaul of agriculture are a matter of urgency—especially given that, as the effects of climate change intensify, growing sufficient amounts of food will become even more challenging in many African nations. Per capita food production in Africa has already declined by 12 percent since 1981,[7] and by 2020 yields from rain-fed agriculture could be reduced in some countries by up to 50 percent.[8] The climate has become more unpredictable, increasing the irregularity of rainfall, uncertain harvests, and, as a result, the risks of food insecurity. The UN Intergovernmental Panel on Climate Change estimates that, as rainfall patterns shift, revenues from crops in Africa could fall by as much as 90 percent by 2100.[9] Anticipated changes in climate will only make subsistence living more difficult for the 60 percent of Africans who still farm and graze animals as their primary livelihood.

Food security in Africa is also increasingly in danger due to skyrocketing food prices in world markets. They have been pushed to new highs by rising oil prices and growing demands for grains and certain plants to produce biofuels, as well as meat and dairy products, in the industrialized world, Asia, and Latin America.

Food emergencies in Africa have risen threefold each year since the mid-1980s. Although the proportion of undernourished people in sub-Saharan Africa has fallen to just below one-third in the last few years, the absolute numbers have risen, from 120 million in 1980 to 206 million in 2003. In 2004, forty countries in sub-Saharan Africa received almost 3.9 million tons of food aid, almost double the level provided between 1995 and 1997.[10] By 2080, the number of people defined as undernourished in Africa is expected to triple, notwithstanding world food prices.[11]

Some of these challenges find their source in the colonial era. Traditional farming cultures, foods, and even storage methods, such as granaries for grains and beans at each homestead, were discouraged, and then disappeared. Once they stopped growing food for the household, people began buying their food—much of it processed—in shops, and with the establishment of a cash economy, they had to earn money to pay for it. The bananas, root crops, and green vegetables that had been common in people's fields, especially between harvests, gave way to cash crops (such as coffee, tea, nuts, sugarcane, and horticultural products). As they did, household and community food security became a state matter.

At independence, governments assumed the responsibility for feeding the nation. But despite statements at international conferences and roundtables of development agencies about agriculture, food security, farming techniques, and public health, postindependence governments gave little attention to agricultural policies that would have supported the growing of food crops for both home consumption and sale in local and regional markets. This neglect may be partially due to the fact that in Africa women and children produce the majority of this food. For the most part (and this is not a phenomenon exclusive to Africa), women's work, including in food production, is neither highly valued nor made a policy priority, nor are women adequately compensated for their labor.

Many national agricultural policies have relied on buying "cheap food" (such as corn, wheat, and white rice) in international markets, usually from large producers in industrialized nations. But such food is no longer cheap, and was never particularly healthy—and, indeed, is much less nutritious than the beans, grains, greens, root crops, and fruits that formed the basis of many traditional diets. Since, as has already been described, many cash crop producers are subsistence farmers who receive very little for their harvests, with payments often delayed, the result of all these policies taken together is that throughout Africa farming families experience hunger and malnutrition where their own parents and grandparents had surplus food.

For decades, the African elites have ignored agriculture because of an attitude that working the land is only for the uneducated.[12] Even those with agricultural degrees in Africa generally prefer to work in an office in a capital city rather than provide agricultural extension services to farmers. Contrast this with the work that land-grant universities in the United States have undertaken for almost 150 years. They helped to professionalize farming, supporting those with land who wanted to farm but didn't have the knowledge to do so, and educated the waves of immigrants who came to the United States possessing only rudimentary farming techniques.

How can Africa maximize the potential of subsistence farmers—such as the woman I saw on the hillside in Yaoundé, those whom I represented as a member of parliament, and those who form the bulk of the communities the Green Belt Movement works with? Clearly, African governments need to invest in making agriculture—and farmers—more productive. As the actions of the farmers on the hillside of Yaoundé suggest,

African agricultural extension services have been underfunded. At the same time, other regions outside Africa have increased food production in scale and efficiency, and have used subsidies, fertilizers, and mechanization that have allowed them not only to feed themselves but to produce food so cheaply that it undercuts local African markets. Because of corruption and the uncertainty of international commodities markets, the cash crop economy has not enriched ordinary Africans.

At the beginning of this book I suggested that we need to focus development efforts where Africans are, and that much of Africa is with that woman farmer on the hillside in Yaoundé. At the very least, I would like to see not poor farmers scrabbling to produce tea or cassava on a piece of land that long ago lost its productivity, but rather cooperatives that provide farmers with accurate and timely information about their crops and weather conditions, affordable essential inputs, and vibrant local and regional food markets. Governments will need to institute and enforce policies that ensure fair prices for their farmers in the global economy—for both commodities and products with added value. This will also entail a commitment to rooting out corruption in parastatal agencies that, as in the case of the coffee farmers in my constituency in Kenya, further exploit and impoverish small farmers.

Africa needn't intensify its farming sector so that it takes on the character of the industrial-style agriculture that dominates the West and, increasingly, parts of the East. As we are learning, industrial farming may be efficient, but it has enormous downsides for the environment—from destruction of biodiversity to heavy dependence on fossil fuels and chemical fertilizer, to massive water use and runoff that fouls rivers and creates marine "dead zones." Indeed, a recent UN assessment concluded that this method of farming is no longer viable in a world of resource constraints and climate change. The report's authors recommend a rapid shift to more ecological and sustainable ways of producing food.[13]

Africa does have options: only 7 percent of arable land is under irrigation.[14] While there may be opportunities to increase this, so that the majority of African farmers aren't wholly dependent on rain to water their crops, irrigation systems are expensive and inappropriate for regions where water is already scarce. Governments in Africa, as well as individuals, need to do all that they can to improve land and water management—by, for instance, preventing erosion by covering the soil with vegetation and trees, avoiding overgrazing, harvesting water, and retaining essential nutrients in the soil.

African leaders also need to address the way they look at land—and to employ it equitably for their people's benefit. There are many small-scale farmers in Africa who are not using their land in the most efficient way. If, for example, someone like Njoya had been a better farmer, and the government had provided him with an agriculture extension service, he would have had no need to be on another person's land.

Given the inequitable distribution of land in many countries in Africa, and the inequities perpetuated by governance and economic systems that are inherently unjust, it is difficult to wholly avoid incidents of people or peoples fighting for access to resources—especially when politicians use land to incite violence. Furthermore, those without land will find it difficult to accept that some in their country may own thousands of acres. Despite the passions and ongoing controversies inflamed by land ownership in Africa, however, there can never be any excuse to take another's life.

The ultimate goal cannot be simply to make subsistence farming easier. While some redistribution is important, it is my belief that not every African needs, or must have, a parcel of land they can call their own. Given population growth, not enough land is available without drastic encroachment into forests and reserves. If Africans did try to utilize entire land-masses for crops or grazing, they would destroy the complex natural systems upon which agriculture, and indeed all life, depends. Therefore, while it is important that Africa's farmers thrive, Africa cannot just rely on agriculture and commodities to develop. Once again, governments need to increase the capacities of their peoples in other areas.

In so doing, they could encourage the growth of sustainable industries that provide good employment in well-managed cities and towns—not the crowded, filthy slums with virtually no infrastructure that blot too many African cities and too many Africans' lives. Africans can also, like citizens in other regions of the world, work to reduce their dependence on fossil fuels and harness renewable energy sources to industrialize in a way that provides work for the millions of Africans migrating to cities, and allows some of those currently practicing sub-sistence agriculture to move off the land. While it would be preferable for Robert Njoya to grow his own food rather than poach wild animals, ownership and exploitation of land cannot remain the only way to become wealthy in Africa in the twenty-first century.

Twelve

ENVIRONMENT AND DEVELOPMENT

CLIMATE CHANGE will bring massive ecological and economic challenges. In such a context, therefore, alleviating dehumanizing poverty—and achieving the UN Millennium Development Goals (MDGs)—will become even more difficult. The MDGs, agreed upon by the UN General Assembly in 2000, increasingly guide global development policies, practices, and aid flows around the world. As some observers have noted, they are imperfect measures—not least because, when they were announced, different regions of the developing world had made more progress toward achieving the goals than others; sub-Saharan Africa was, overall, the furthest behind. Nevertheless, the MDGs offer a useful heuristic device not only as a tool to analyze development in general, but as measures against which the commitment of leaders in both the rich industrialized countries and the developing world to progress in human welfare and sustainable development can and should be judged.

The eight MDGs, to be met by 2015, are: 1) eradicate extreme poverty and hunger; 2) achieve universal primary education; 3) promote gender equality and empower women; 4) reduce child mortality; 5) improve maternal health; 6) combat HIV/AIDS, malaria, and other diseases; 7) ensure environmental sustainability; and 8) develop a global partnership for development.

Achieving each of the eight MDGs depends heavily on healthy ecosystems; but this fact is often overlooked, and the seventh MDG has not received as much attention as the others. In my view, however, it is the most important, and all of the other goals should be organized around it. What happens to the ecosystem affects everything else, as is illustrated by an example from the Central Highlands of Kenya.

The environment on and around Mount Kenya and the Aberdare mountain ranges has gradually degenerated, and the biological diversity that led Mount Kenya to be designated a World Heritage Site by UNESCO is threatened. The Aberdares serve as one of Kenya's main water towers—a system of natural reservoirs that hold moisture in snow and mist, in soil and vegetation, and in aquifers above- and belowground. For decades, these mountain ecosystems have been ravaged by deforestation, illegal logging, nonindigenous plantations, overcultivation, and other forms of human encroachment. Yet within the mountains' forests lies some of the most fertile soil in Kenya, and the glaciers and rainfall the forests attract feed hundreds of tributaries of the largest river in Kenya, the Tana. The Tana flows 440 miles from the Central Highlands to the Indian Ocean and provides drinking water for millions of Kenyans in major urban centers, including the capital, Nairobi. These water resources, and the forests, are essential for Kenya's agriculture, livestock, tourism, and energy sectors, as well as household water and fuel.

If the mountains' ecosystems continue to be degraded, it will become impossible to achieve the MDGs in Kenya. With the destruction of the mountains' forests and the gradual disappearance of glaciers (apparently due to climate change), the Tana's water flow is reduced. Simultaneously, massive deposits of river-borne silt reduce the lifespan of the dams built across the river. Both lead to lost capacity for hydropower, which provides 60 percent of Kenya's energy.[1] Without this (clean) energy, Kenya is unable to provide electricity to a very large part of her rural and urban populations.

The dearth of adequate and reliable sources of energy sty-
mies the possibilities of further rural electrification as well as
national industrial growth. Demand for power in Kenya is
growing by an average of 7 percent per year.[2] Due to shortfalls in hydropower that go back many years, Kenya has been
forced to buy power from Uganda—with money that should
have been used for development. In so doing, the government
sacrifices other priorities like combating HIV/AIDs, malaria,
and other diseases (MDG 6) and improving maternal health
(MDG 5). Shortages of electricity also mean that poor people in
rural and urban areas use wood fuel for energy, furthering
deforestation and limiting prospects that MDG 7 will be
achieved.

Agriculture in Kenya, as in most of Africa, is watered by
rain, not irrigation systems. With the destruction of the mountain forests, rainfall patterns are affected, and with them, yields
from cash and food crops. Small-scale farmers working degraded
soils are among the poorest people in Kenya. For them and
their families, not having enough nutritious food to eat is a
common phenomenon. The lack of regular rainfall, therefore,
also undermines prospects for eradicating extreme poverty and
hunger (MDG 1) and reducing child deaths (MDG 4) from
causes associated with malnutrition.

The loss of the forests also means that no vegetation
remains to hold the soil in its place. As a result, enormous
amounts of valuable topsoil are swept or blown away. When
rainwater runs downstream through lands that are extensively
cultivated, it can cause massive soil erosion and sometimes
flooding, which not only damages farms and food crops, but
can displace people from their homes. When the rains fail, and
subsequently crops, aid in the form of food, clothing, and shelter from the government or donor agencies becomes necessary.
In 2005, three million people, or nearly 10 percent of the popu-

lation of Kenya, were dependent on government food aid. In such an unsettled—and at times desperate—situation, children's schooling is disrupted, and in this context governments cannot hope to achieve universal primary education (MDG 2).

As deforestation gathers speed, women are forced to walk longer and longer distances to find wood for cooking and heating and clean water. In times of environmental difficulty, children, particularly girls, may be taken out of school to help with harvests and the collection of wood and water, or to look after their younger siblings as their mother's workload increases. Thus, protecting the mountain forests would help achieve gender equality (MDG 3) and improve the chances that all girls complete primary school, and as a result have a chance to continue their education to a higher level (MDG 2).

In addition, many of Kenya's national parks, and the wildlife within them, benefit from the Tana River and the rainfall from Mount Kenya and the Aberdares. (The presence of two species of monkey, more commonly found in Uganda and Congo, in the Tana basin is a reminder of the rainforests that once covered much of Africa from west to east.) If the mountains' ecosystems are destroyed, the savannahs will not be sustained. Tourism then will be a thing of the past, even though it's one of the most important sectors of the Kenyan economy and a major generator of employment, which, of course, contributes to poverty reduction. It goes without saying that city dwellers also depend on the environment's capacity to provide food, sources of energy, and water.

All of these challenges to human development could be avoided or their intensity reduced if the government managed the forested mountain ecosystems more sustainably. As it is now, the impact of the forests' destruction is felt by many economic sectors, and it is frustrating efforts to realize all but one of the MDGs, number eight, which calls for "a global partnership for development." But when a country has been unable to realize the other MDGs, how can it form a partnership for development? The very basis for such development is absent.

Likewise, Ethiopia, which had 40 percent forest cover at the turn of the twentieth century, has only 3 percent today—a result of a cash crop economy, overgrazing, and the use of trees for fuelwood, all of which have contributed to the threat of famine. This is holding its own development back.[3]

As it currently stands, Africa's economies will need to grow by upward of 7 percent per year if they're to keep pace with efforts to halve extreme poverty (MDG 1) by 2015.[4] Even though it's true that Africa had further to go in 2000 to meet the MDGs than other developing regions, it should be a cause of some embarrassment to the peoples of Africa that most countries on the continent are unlikely to have met a majority of the MDGs by the target date.

THE ESTABLISHMENT OF MONOCULTURES

The situation in Kenya is not helped by the establishment of monocultural plantations of exotic species of trees (a scheme until recently known as the *shamba* system). During the 1930s and '40s, the British colonial authorities deemed large sections of the five "water towers" (Mount Kenya, Aberdare, Mau complex, Cherangani hills, and Mount Elgon) suitable for commercial plantations of fast-growing species of pines from the Northern Hemisphere and eucalyptus from the Southern. The eucalyptus and pines were intended to provide timber for the then-emerging building industry and firewood for steam engines. Local flora were considered slow-growing and economically less exploitable than imported species of trees, and, therefore, large sections of indigenous forests were clear-cut and replanted with the imported tree species.

To manage the plantations of nonindigenous trees that were established, the colonial administration introduced a farming method—called *shamba,* which means "field" in Kiswahili—whereby the forestry department allowed communities living near the forests to cultivate food crops while nurturing the commercial seedlings, for free. As one might imagine, the *shamba* system worked very well for the colonialists and for the peasant farmers, who were hungry for land to grow crops. The trees thrived in the cool environment (Mount Kenya is seventeen thousand feet above sea level) and in the then-virgin soil. Unfortunately, as the human population grew, the demand for land to grow food crops likewise expanded. As government foresters authorized more and more forest to be converted into farmland, more indigenous trees were felled for more plantations and for farmers to grow food crops—a situation exacerbated by increased demand for timber. I remember as a child seeing huge bonfires in the forests as the indigenous biodiversity was burned to make way for the commercial tree plantations.

Shamba plantations are harvested every thirty years or so. The continuous planting, harvesting, and replanting of the same commercial monocultures of trees, along with the long-term cultivation of food crops by farmers, drastically minimizes the prospects for local biodiversity to return. The *shamba* system is also rife with opportunism and corruption from farmers, who benefit from growing food crops on forest land, and government officers, who are tempted to sell trees, lease land, and allow charcoal burning and illegal grazing. Foresters, who control access to the public lands, are eager to allow people back into the forests. The remuneration for facilitating some of these activities ends up in the pockets of some foresters rather than in the national treasury.

I have opposed the continuation of the *shamba* system for many years. I don't consider plantations of exotic monocultures of trees to be forests, but rather tree farms. Unlike indigenous forests, plantations destroy local biodiversity, leaving the land bare except for the monoculture of trees. Plantations lack the ecological and biological systems to retain and conserve rainwater: the extensive leaf system, the intensive and varied vegetation, the debris of biological materials that accumulate and form a sponge at ground level. In forests, a not insignificant amount of water is retained on leaves, bark, and in the soil. When it evaporates, it creates the humidity that feeds other ecological systems and the rainfall cycle. All these are removed when the forest is clear-cut, cultivated, and planted with food crops and plantations. It is partly for that reason that the plantations lack the capacity to receive and conserve rainwater. When it rains, much of the water rushes down the slope and is lost and many rivers either dry up or have their water levels greatly reduced.

When the NARC government came into power in 2002, it was more committed to conserving the environment than the previous administration and it banned the *shamba* system. While environmentalists in Kenya applauded this decision, it was greeted with dismay by many MPs and the public whose parliamentary constituencies border the forest. Many Kenyans lack an appreciation of the difference between an indigenous forest and what I call a tree farm. Kenya's forests are worth far more intact than they are fragmented or converted into tree farms.

For the first time as a partner of the Kenyan government (the new NARC administration), the Green Belt Movement launched a project to restore degraded forests in the Aberdares. Local women grew indigenous tree seedlings and planted them in the forest. For each seedling that survived, the women (and some men who joined them) were compensated with a small financial incentive to continue their work. If a woman planted many trees and ensured that they survived, she could earn a decent income to pay for school uniforms, books, and fees; nutritious food; or health care for herself, her husband, and their children. It is through this kind of approach that the Green Belt Movement addresses the MDGs in a holistic and sustainable way.

Nature has an extraordinary capacity to regenerate, especially in the tropics, and the benefits of a revitalized natural system don't have to take years to manifest themselves. By the end of 2007, it was clear that the Aberdares had begun to rehabilitate. Although the areas of the forest that had been cleared previously still did not have significant numbers of trees, many bushes had returned. More important, it was possible to see how, when the rains fell, water no longer ran off; instead, it was absorbed by the new vegetation, made its way to their roots, and replenished the underground reservoirs. As a result, rainfall patterns improved, some streams that had dried up returned, and the water levels in the rivers that emerged were noticeably higher. The rivers themselves were cleaner, and in some, fish had returned. Even the quality and quantity of tea produced in the area were reported to have greatly increased.

Many of my constituents told me that they saw that the rivers were healthier and appreciated that more water was available to them for washing, drinking, and cooking in their households. They had gained a greater understanding of the role that forests play in providing water. They were also, through much environmental education, aware of the alternatives to encroaching on the forests: that there was no reason why Kenya could not establish *shambas* and exotic plantations in the two-thirds of the country that is arid or semi-arid.

In addition, they were aware that crops could be cultivated in *shambas* outside the forest, or in the many tracts of land that Kenyans do not fully use. They also knew the Green Belt Movement had recommended that Kenyans with land should plant 10 percent of it with trees, which could supply the timber industry and allow the land to be used much more economically than it is at present. In all these ways, pressure from communities on the government to cultivate crops in the forests would be reduced, or ended altogether; indeed, people who lived near the remaining indigenous forests could participate in their restoration by, like the Green Belt Movement groups, replanting native tree species and, in turn, bringing back the indigenous biodiversity.

In spite of these arguments, a substantial number of the same people who welcomed the return of the rivers and the regrowth of the forest informed me, as their MP, that they would still prefer to return to the forests to cultivate food crops because of the high demand for and cost of food. Even though the benefits of ensuring that the rivers were full and clean were evident, my constituents were unable to think beyond their immediate needs.

They forgot or chose to ignore the dry riverbeds and the degraded soil, and concluded that they were unwilling to sacrifice their current desire to grow potatoes, carrots, cabbages, and other such foods in the forest in favor of long-term survival. This is food they could have farmed on their own plots, if they had invested in fertilizer or used manure from animals and biomass to improve the quality of the soil; or food they could have bought in the markets, if their coffee and tea were better managed and they received their due income from its profits. In a sense, the forests were victims of the corruption both in the management of the forests and in the cooperatives that the farmers belonged to.

Under pressure from foresters and communities, the Kenyan government is now planning to bring back the *shamba* system, under a new brand: the Plantation Establishment and Livelihood Improvement Scheme (PELIS). PELIS opens the door to the possibility of further destruction of remaining forests. If the government offers the poor an opportunity to cultivate crops in the forests through the PELIS program, I doubt the people will say no for the sake of the forests' long-term health (and their own).

This short-term thinking reflects the failure of people and their governments to look too deeply into the root causes of environmental decline. When a river dries up in Kenya or a crop fails, people tend to pray to God for more rain and food. They will wonder if food aid will become necessary if the harvests fail, or worry whether the boreholes and wells will be similarly affected. What they don't do as much as they should is ask *why* the river has dried up or crops have failed— questions that involve a deeper analysis and a more holistic approach to the management of ecosystems.

This only intensifies the need for responsible governance from those who do have an understanding and are entrusted with the long-term welfare of both the people and the resources that they need to survive. Given this mandate, it is extraordinary that the Kenyan government should even consider reintroducing the *shamba* system in a country where only 2 percent of forest cover remains. Moreover, why would any African government pursue such a policy in light of the projections of the toll that climate change will exact on the continent?

THE MARCH OF THE DESERT

The challenges facing agricultural communities throughout Kenya are mirrored throughout Africa and many of the poor countries in underdeveloped regions. In these regions, concern for environmental issues is treated as a luxury. But it is not: protecting and restoring ecosystems, and slowing or reversing global warming, are matters of life and death. The equation is simple: whatever we do, we impact the environment; if we destroy it, we will undermine our own ways of life and ultimately kill ourselves. This is why the environment needs to be at the center of domestic and international policy and practice. If it is not, we don't stand a chance of alleviating poverty in any significant way. Nor will we create for the African people a continent where security and progress can be realized.

Indeed, if we are serious about engendering cultures of peace in Africa, protection and rehabilitation of the environment must be a priority. This is partly because at the heart of many of the conflicts that continue to challenge Africa are degraded land, depleted water sources, lack of rain, poor soils, and desertification.

The recognition that underlying almost every conflict is either a struggle for control over resources or a scramble to access them after they have become scarce is clear in almost every conflict on the continent, from Chad to Somalia, Sudan to Ethiopia and Kenya. When I flew north to visit Chad in August 2008, I looked out of the plane windows over the landscape and saw, over and over again, the remnants of abandoned villages: as many as fifty huts spread out in a circle and, all around them, desert. These people had not left their villages after being attacked. They had come to the area when it was fertile, established farms, and cultivated their crops. Then the land had become completely degraded and they were forced to move on, to the next fertile area and the next village.

I could only ask myself: *Where could these people go next?* The Janjaweed militias who attack citizens from the neighboring region of Darfur may have many political and economic justifications for their actions, but it seemed clear to me that they were pushing farther south in search of new grazing grounds for their livestock for the same reason the villages had been abandoned: the relentless march of the Sahara Desert. The result is conflict, rape, violence, hundreds of thousands of deaths, and vast numbers of refugees.

To reverse the process of desertification requires massive

investment, and yet this does not appear to be a priority of many African governments. The ordinary people who live in the villages may not always fully comprehend what is happening to their environment; they just keep moving on. And if their governments understand, they don't seem to care or seem to be doing much about it.

I am often asked whether a trade-off is required between the environment and development. I always say no. We need and must have both; what is important is a good balance between the two. Africa is still rich in natural resources that can be used sustainably and equitably for the benefit of her peoples. Up until now, however, most African governments have not prioritized the environmental sector in terms of budget allocation, nor made it a central focus of parliamentary discussion or policy development. Even when policies are in place, they are rarely enforced to their full effect.

The results of this lack of prioritization are evident in the serious ecological decline throughout the continent. According to the UN Food and Agriculture Organization, between 2000 and 2005 Africa lost about ten million acres (or 1 percent) of its forests a year—a rate more than three times the global average.[5] Loss of forest was significant in Angola, Cameroon, the Democratic Republic of the Congo, Nigeria, Sudan, Tanzania, Zambia, and Zimbabwe. According to a recent UNEP study, the current pace of deforestation is a concern in thirty-five African countries, while significant loss of biodiversity affects thirty-four. Overgrazing and other poor farming practices have led to the expansion of the Sahara Desert south into northern Nigeria and northern Kenya. Malawi has been almost wholly deforested.[6] And the list goes on.

THE CHANGING CLIMATE

According to UNEP's *Global Environment Outlook 4* (2007), which compiled data from scientists and international agencies on the entire range of environmental and social indicators, by the middle of this century climate change could affect growing seasons in northern Africa, because less rain will water semi-arid systems. On the coasts of western and central African nations, rising sea levels and flooding could result in the disruption of coastal settlements, while the further destruction of mangrove swamps and coastal degradation could have negative impacts on fisheries and tourism, with some estimates pointing to a 2 to 4 percent loss of agricultural GDP in that region.

Southern and western Africa, as well as the Sahel region, may become more parched, including in the drylands that skirt expanding deserts. Similarly, the Kalahari through to the arid regions in northern South Africa, Angola, and Zambia may experience larger sandstorms and more dynamic dune fields (that is, shifting desert landmasses), because less moisture and higher winds will lead to a decline of the vegetation that binds sand to the ground.[7]

Scientists are predicting that some regions in Africa will receive more rain, particularly in the tropics and some parts of the east. This may allow the cultivation of new crop varieties. However, previously malaria-free highland areas in Ethiopia, Kenya, Rwanda, and Burundi could increasingly see the presence of malaria-carrying mosquitoes, especially by the 2080s. Southern Africa, too, may see the southward expansion of the transmission zone for malaria-bearing mosquitoes. Mountain biodiversity could be impacted, and there is the possibility that fish stocks in some major East African lakes could decline.[8]

Climate change threatens to eliminate or severely reduce the glaciers on Mounts Kenya and Kilimanjaro, as well as those in the Rwenzori Mountains of Uganda.

A world where climate shocks become more common will also ratchet up risk factors for conflict between and within countries. Researchers found that when shortfalls in seasonal rains led to drought and economic distress in forty sub-Saharan African countries between 1981 and 1999, the likelihood of civil war rose by 50 percent.[9] Millions of Africans may become environmental refugees this century because of the effects of climate change. This is in spite of the fact that, at 4 percent of the world's total, and one ton of carbon dioxide a year per person on average, Africa's collective and individual greenhouse gas emissions are negligible—in contrast to those of the emerging economic giants of China and India, and Europe. And North America, home continent of the United States, one of the world's top emitters of greenhouse gases, consumes over 24 percent of total global primary energy despite having only one-twentieth of the world's population.[10]

The argument over whether climate change is or is not exacerbated by human activity has, to all intents and purposes, been settled. What remains for the world to decide is what actions it will take to reduce the intensity and scale of those changes. While it isn't yet possible to pin specific meteorological events on global warming, it is evident that for the poor of the developing world, the effects of climate change are already being felt and the threats to human well-being caused by environmental degradation are neither abstract nor localized.

These changes would be hard to adjust to in and of themselves even if they were not compounded by the problems already facing the African continent. Almost half of Africa's land area is vulnerable to desertification—particularly the Sahel and southern Africa.[11] In addition, the Sahara continues to spread by thirty miles a year,[12] and the pace of desertification has doubled since the 1970s.[13] Within three generations, by the 2080s, the proportion of arid and semi-arid lands in Africa is likely to increase by 5 to 8 percent.[14]

Climate change will also have social and economic effects. Millions more poor people from rural areas are likely to relocate to cities, or to seek to flee their countries altogether, joining other environmental refugees. Coastal areas may become less habitable, forcing people living there to find other means of earning an income or to migrate inland. Women will be disproportionately affected by climate change, because across Africa they are most directly dependent on natural resources. They collect the firewood and draw the water; they plant the seeds and harvest the crops. However, women's voices have been largely absent from policy discussions and negotiations over global warming. Their experiences, creativity, and leadership should be part of the solution to the climate crisis.

THE EXPANDING FOOTPRINT

Scientists are only just beginning to understand the depth and range of services provided by Earth's ecosystems.[15] In 1998, a team of economists and scientists estimated that the life systems of the planet provided an astonishing $33 trillion worth of benefits,[16] or even as much as $54 trillion.[17] Yet the Millennium Ecosystem Assessment, a global effort undertaken between 2001 and 2005 involving nearly 1,500 researchers worldwide, found that a majority of both land and marine ecosystems throughout the planet are degraded, some critically.[18] If these trends are not reversed, many livelihoods will be threatened.

Of course, the cavalier attitude toward the Earth is not only an African problem: the danger we collectively face—of not paying sufficient attention until too much has been lost—challenges all human societies. Indeed, according to the 2005 Footprint of Nations report, humanity's collective ecological footprint averages out at 21.9 hectares (about 54 acres) per person, although the planet's biological capacity can support only an average footprint of 15.7 hectares (about 39 acres) per person. (The footprint analysis measures the combined natural resources—such as water, energy, land, and forests—used to support a person's lifestyle.) Although the average ecological footprint in the developed world far surpasses the size of that in Africa (less than one hectare, or 2.5 acres, per person),[19] the fact that humanity's current use of resources is outstripping the planet's ecological capacity should give all of us reason to pause. It is simply not sustainable for the rest of the world to mine, log, drill, build, dam, drain, and pave in a rush to achieve the standards of living of the industrialized countries, which themselves depend on massive resource extraction from the global South.

Given these realities, it continues to baffle me that African leaders do not educate their people so they understand the enormous threat likely to face them and how important it is for them to use the resources within their borders to mitigate this threat and adapt to the inevitable changes in climate. States are custodians of these resources, and citizens have an interest in how these resources are managed on their behalf. Throughout Africa, the budgets of environmental ministries are dwarfed by those of defense ministries or national security, even in countries where the major threat to security is desertification, poverty, and unemployment. It further astonishes me that those concerned with or working for the development agenda in Africa still don't acknowledge that the environment must be at the center of all solutions, just as neglect of it is at the root of our most pressing problems. The continent must wake up.

It is this prevailing mind-set that explains, in part, why Africa lags behind other developing regions in progress toward the Millennium Development Goals. If Africa does not change, not only will it not achieve the MDGs, it will also further degrade or destroy the resource base on which development depends, and in so doing exacerbate and entrench the challenges that the continent faces. No amount of advanced weaponry can fight the desert. But the problem can be overcome by planting trees and other vegetation to curb soil loss and harvest rainwater, and it is in repulsing the sands of the desert as they encroach on arable land and in fighting deforestation and climate change that the genuine battle for national and human security lies.

SAVING THE FORESTS

Just as natural resources provide the basis for human development, they also serve as a buffer against the worst effects of climate change. There is a cruel irony in the fact that the negative effects of climate change will be felt most keenly by those least responsible for creating global warming. As major polluters, the industrialized countries have a responsibility to deal with climate change at home, but also to assist Africa and the rest of the developing world to address its effects. They are in a position to share their technological know-how to reduce vulnerability and increase adaptive capacities. Mechanisms ought to be established—quickly—to raise steady and reliable funds for the prime victims of the climate crisis, who will be poor and rural, very young, and, more often than not, female. And many of them will be African.

Africans cannot reverse global warming, but they can, while calling for urgent action by the largest emitters of greenhouse gasses, do their part. Right now, most governments' forest policies are not helping matters. Africa is home to about 17 percent of the world's forests. However, around half of the planet's global deforestation has taken place on the continent, and Africa has the highest rate of deforestation in the world—currently losing approximately half a percent of its forests annually.

Industrialized countries should accept their moral duty to assist Africa and other poor regions to find alternative and renewable sources of energy—such as biomass, wind, hydropower, and solar—and enable the global South to participate in the carbon market so Africa can develop industries based on renewable energy sources. In 2007, global investors plowed $148 billion into new wind, solar, and other alternative energy initiatives.[20] But those funds were almost wholly concentrated in the industrialized countries, along with some in China, India, and Brazil. Almost none of this investment is coming to Africa, despite the continent's vast energy poverty and abundant sun and wind. Africa's challenge lies in making herself a relevant beneficiary of these resources.

One exception, however, may be Algeria, which is already planning to export solar power.[21] A huge $70 billion "supergrid" in the Sahara could provide Europe with up to one hundred gigawatts of clean electricity by 2050,[22] while also supplying electricity for local consumption.[23]

Aside from further research into and development of these and other sources of energy, all nations must work to reduce their energy consumption and move beyond fossil fuels, to cut their greenhouse gas emissions from all sources, and to adopt policies so that corporations operate more responsibly wherever they are and individuals can live more sustainably. Otherwise, Africans will suffer even more from the consequences of overconsumption from peoples across the oceans. In the meantime, Africa must do her part. Indeed, it may be a good time to remind Africa that the United Nations Conference on New and Renewable Sources of Energy was held in Nairobi in 1981. It is a measure of the commitment to these issues that neither the hosts nor the continent followed through with investments in research and implementation. Instead, they waited for technology and the means of mitigation and adaptation to be developed in continents that needed them least. Nearly three decades later, Africa finds itself in an even more vulnerable position. This trend is clearly unacceptable.

While the industrialized world can help mitigate the effects of climate change by supplying Africa with appropriate technology, the continent itself can do its part by prioritizing the protection and rehabilitation of its forests. All governments must make a concerted effort to stop unsustainable logging and find mechanisms, such as reforestation programs, whereby the poor can secure a livelihood by protecting and not degrading their environment. Well-managed, participatory tree-planting programs that serve as carbon offsets for industrial-country emissions are an important mechanism to support responsible global warming mitigation efforts in developing countries.

The Green Belt Movement, for example, is working with the World Bank's BioCarbon Fund through an Emission Reductions Purchase Agreement (ERPA) to continue reforestation efforts in Mount Kenya's and the Aberdares' forests, the *shamba* system notwithstanding. The trees that the Green Belt Movement groups plant will, according to World Bank estimates, capture 375,000 tons of carbon dioxide by 2017. In addition, these trees will restore the health of the soil, offer habitat for biodiversity, help regulate the local climate, support regular rainfall, and provide poor, rural people with a small income.

Partnerships such as this also present a challenge to NGOs when they work with international institutions or private-sector companies, some of which may have undertaken activities that harm the environment. It is my belief that, while it would be preferable to work with partners who are holistic in their approach to the protection of the environment, the reality is that many corporations, organizations, and governments are not always doing the right thing. It is therefore necessary to work to assist in actively making a difference to the daily lives of the people in the region and, in so doing, preserving more forest.

One such project was formulated in 2006 at the annual meeting of the UN Framework Convention on Climate Change in Nairobi. The Green Belt Movement, UNEP, and the World Agroforestry Center (ICRAAF) launched the Plant for the Planet: Billion Tree Campaign to encourage tree planting as a means of mitigating global climate change, while restoring habitats and ecosystems. Prince Albert II of Monoco and I served as patrons of the campaign. From the outset, the partner organizations were aware that for the project to succeed, a wide variety of participants, from the government through to the private sector, as well as individuals and citizen groups, would have to cooperate. The sheer scale of the action—planting one billion new trees by the end of 2007—necessitated the engagement and participation of governments, organizations, and millions of individuals. By October of that year, we had achieved our goal.

Initiatives like the Billion Tree Campaign, while essential, shouldn't provide an excuse for industrialized countries not to take serious and immediate steps to reduce their greenhouse gasses. Both developed and developing countries must take action to deal with the negative impacts of emissions. To me, this is a matter of environmental justice and the price for peace. It should be addressed more responsibly by all.

The world's forests are its lungs. Thick, healthy stands of indigenous trees absorb huge amounts of carbon dioxide, a major greenhouse gas, and hold vast reserves of carbon. As these forests are cleared for timber, agriculture, mining activities, human settlements, or commercial development, a vital element in slowing, and ultimately reversing, global warming is lost, and local, regional, and global climates will be further destabilized. In a vicious cycle, as climate change continues, forests will become more vulnerable: soils may dry up and trees die on a mass scale. At the 2007 meeting of the UN Framework Convention on Climate Change in Bali, Indonesia, both government officials and NGOs signed on to the "Forests Now Declaration." Its main tenet: If we lose forests, we lose the fight against climate change.

Thirteen

SAVING THE CONGO FORESTS

THE EARTH is enriched by the rain forests of Amazonia and Borneo and the taiga of northern Canada, Russia, and Scandinavia. Africa, too, has the great forests of the Congo Basin in central Africa. Nowhere else in Africa is there a greater abundance of remaining forest, or is the threat to it more pressing, than here. Conserving this region presents an extraordinary opportunity to African heads of state, the international community, and the peoples of the basin. It also requires a reimagining of what "development" means—not only across Equatorial Africa, but throughout the continent and, indeed, the world. If the three legs of the African stool are re-created here, and the seat of the stool is made broad and strong by national and international policies and action, this region could be a model for governments, international agencies, civil society, and the private sector. It is perhaps the ultimate challenge to Africa, and the world.[1]

The Congo Basin Rainforest Ecosystem is a vast expanse of seven hundred thousand square miles, parts of which are present principally in Cameroon, the Central African Republic, the Democratic Republic of the Congo (DRC), Equatorial Guinea, Gabon, and the Republic of the Congo (Congo-Brazzaville). The ecosystem constitutes a quarter of the world's remaining tropical rainforest, and provides almost a third of all of Africa's vegetation cover. The basin includes a large number of forests, as well as savannah, woodlands, and aquatic and riverine habitats. The forest and marine ecosystems of the Congo Basin contain the most biodiversity in Africa, while the region as a whole has more United Nations Natural World Heritage sites than the rest of Africa put together.

The basin holds ten thousand species of plants, of which 30 percent are endemic; over a thousand species of birds; nine hundred varieties of butterflies; four hundred mammal species; and more than two hundred species each of reptiles and amphibians. It is home to both lowland and mountain gorillas, around four thousand elephants, and nine thousand chimpanzees. It is also home to the bonobo, a highly endangered primate, and the threatened okapi, a cousin of the giraffe, and new species are still being discovered.

In addition to its wide range of biotic life, the ecosystem provides a home for perhaps up to half a million Batwa (the Pygmies), whose culture has been traced back some twenty thousand years. Indeed, evidence suggests that humans have occupied the forests of the Congo Basin for at least fifty thousand years. Today, around 50 million people from more than 150 distinct micro-nations live in the ecosystem, including small-scale farmers and hunter-gatherers; however, more than 100 million depend on the Congo Basin forests for their livelihoods, food, and shelter.

Scientists estimate that somewhere between twenty-four and thirty-four billion tons of carbon are contained within the region's forests (equivalent to four years of the current production of man-made carbon dioxide). Through their natural cycle of degradation and regeneration, the forests already release 237 million tons of carbon into the atmosphere annually. If the forests were wholly destroyed, an astonishing 135 billion tons of carbon dioxide would be released.

The science of forests here, however, is inexact. The extent of any large forest is hard to measure, not least because it contains different types of forest, with different densities and thus different masses of trees. It is also not clear how forests will respond to climate change. Should the climate become drier and warmer, a forest may release more carbon because of the decrease in moisture, but increased photosynthesis from the higher temperatures may allow forests to grow more quickly or denser, and thus store more carbon. Finally, not all forests are used in the same way—they may be clear-cut, partially logged, or sustainably harvested. If the land that was once forest is reforested, it may be able to reabsorb carbon once more, and perhaps even more efficiently.

The Congo Basin forests' effect on the climate is also not limited to the reduction or increase of carbon dioxide in the atmosphere. The forests play a major role in determining weather around the continent. Here, too, our understanding of global climatic patterns is still evolving, as are our models for determining just how the climate will change in the forthcoming decades. Here, too, the Congo Basin provides a good example of the complexities and interconnections of the planet's weather systems.

What we know is that while up to 95 percent of the rain that falls within the Congo Basin region stays there, the basin's convection systems—the movement of moisture as it rises into the atmosphere from the transpiration and evaporation of water generated in the forest canopy and the soil—mean that the basin's rainfall patterns affect a much broader area. Indeed, scientists have discovered that Central Africa provides much of the rain for West Africa.

Just as deforestation in West Africa has affected rainfall in Central Africa, so deforestation in the Congo Basin has an impact on weather patterns, not merely locally but also throughout the continent and even beyond its shores. Scientists estimate that the cutting down of trees in the Congo Basin has led to an average 5 to 15 percent drop in the amount of rain that falls in the Great Lakes region of the United States—reaching a peak of 35 percent less each February. At the same time, rainfall has been reduced by as much as a quarter immediately north of the Black Sea.

Some models suggest that, should the entire basin be deforested, monsoon rain patterns could be affected worldwide and there would be both drier and wetter weather over the American Midwest and the southern part of central Asia, as well as central Europe. In Africa itself, experts forecast that less rain would fall over eastern and western Africa, but more over the southern areas of the DRC and southern Africa. Temperatures would rise in the region by perhaps five degrees Celsius. Some studies indicate that there would be a 30 percent increase in rainfall in East Africa and the Arabian peninsula. Within the Congo Basin itself, decreased rainfall patterns may result in the vegetation of some of its forests shifting to woodland or even savannah ecosystems, bringing about collapses in local biodiversity.

Forests also play an important role in regulating the global albedo—the amount of light that is reflected off the Earth's surface and which can either increase or decrease temperatures. Once more, scientists are only just discovering the complex role that trees, whether in temperate or tropical climates, play in the albedo; research suggests that deforestation in the tropics, including in the Congo Basin, will likely increase temperatures and decrease albedo.

Over half of the Congo Basin forests are located in the Democratic Republic of the Congo (formerly Zaire). During the late 1990s and early 2000s, armies from nine surrounding countries, along with numerous militias, fought for control over the abundant reserves of natural resources such as timber (and wood products such as charcoal), gold, copper, diamonds, coltan, cobalt, zinc, and other minerals. That this was truly an international war, beyond the reaches of central Africa, was confirmed by a report that experts prepared for the UN Security Council, which found that up to eighty-five multinational corporations from the United States, Europe, and South Africa had done business with criminal networks operating in the DRC.

The war was, in many ways, merely the latest fight to utilize the forests' resources stretching back to the days of Mobutu Sese Seko, who as the president of Zaire enriched himself and his coterie for three decades at the expense of his people. This conflict mirrored the exploitation of the Belgian colonial administration that preceded Mobutu, and the Belgian king Leopold II, who ran the Congo as his personal estate in the late nineteenth and early twentieth centuries.

For the poor who live in the Congo Basin, hunting for bushmeat and the collection and burning of firewood for charcoal are the highest sources of income. Wood and charcoal constitute four-fifths of the energy used in the households of the DRC, while bushmeat has provided the peoples of the Congo forest with a vital source of food for centuries. Recently, however, the subsistence-level hunting in the forest that sustained the local communities has expanded and intensified to threaten the wildlife that populates the entire basin. Some one million tons of bushmeat is now consumed annually, and around thirteen thousand pounds (most of it in the form of primate flesh) arrive in Europe and North America every month, where it is consumed as a delicacy by expatriate Africans and others.

The increase in the number of animals killed for bushmeat is directly correlated with the opening up of the forest to logging companies. Penetrating the parts of the forest previously unreachable by mechanized transport, the timber trucks literally make inroads and, as they do, allow easier access to the animals. The results can be dramatic. A mere twenty days after a logging company arrived in one of Congo's forests, the density of animals there declined by more than a quarter.

About a quarter of the rain forest area of the Congo Basin has been divided up into timber concessions. The irony is that timber itself has an economic value far below the other products that come from the forest—such as medicines, plant foods, and condiments—even though it is the sector where there is the greatest danger of the misuse or plundering of public resources. Penetration of the forest brings about its own risks as well. Increased contact with the animals of the forest has enhanced the possibility of exposure to diseases, such as Ebola, that can cross the species barrier.[2] Such tropical diseases, along with HIV/AIDS and malaria, only further complicate, and in some cases hinder, efforts to conserve the forest.

MOVING BEYOND THE YAOUNDÉ DECLARATION

In a recognition of the importance of the Congo Basin to their countries' forest ecosystems, the heads of state of six surrounding countries issued the Yaoundé Declaration in 1999, in which they agreed to establish a framework for new conservation efforts throughout the region. Because of the conflict in the DRC, however, little was implementable at that time. In September 2002, at the UN World Summit on Sustainable Development in Johannesburg, South Africa, the United States and South Africa joined with twenty-seven other partners, both public and private, to launch the Congo Basin Forest Partnership (CBFP), to conserve the basin through economic development, poverty alleviation, better governance, and the establishment of a network of protected areas. The CBFP also issued a code to try to ensure that any contracts awarded to private corporations by the region's governments seeking to exploit the forests' resources were well managed.

This last provision—which, among other stipulations, mandated that all companies should consult local people, allow them to keep all their rights as traditional users of the forest, and ensure that 15 percent of the concession area was protected—was long overdue. It sought to address the concessions for many millions of acres of forest that had been handed out or bought both before and during the war. In spite of efforts to establish a moratorium on new concessions, a number of new contracts have been offered to logging and mining companies since 2002. Instructively, perhaps, these corporations are headquartered, or have offices in, Belgium, Liechtenstein, Portugal, Germany, Great Britain, Sweden, Switzerland, China, Canada, Singapore, and the United States, as well as Côte d'Ivoire, Congo-Brazzaville, and the DRC. Some of them have received investment funds through the International Finance Corporation of the World Bank, which was instrumental in supporting the 2002 moratorium.

In the past few years, a welcome measure of peace has come to the DRC and its neighbors, and in June 2006 Congo held elections under UN supervision. Nevertheless, not all conflicts in the region have been resolved, especially in the eastern part of the country where civilians are still being threatened, displaced, and even killed by continued fighting between the government and militia. And under the protection of heavily armed warlords who continue to fight the Congolese government, charcoal syndicates are threatening the Congolese section of Virunga National Park. The park also stretches into Rwanda and Uganda, both countries that have seen internal conflicts spill over into Congo. About one hundred thousand people displaced by Congo's wars have settled on the park's boundaries. With no other sources of energy for heating or cooking, the refugees rely on illegally harvested charcoal—up to four thousand sacks of it a day. Takings from the trade are $30 million a year, and the charcoal merchants protect their turf fiercely. In 2006, seven of the park's endangered mountain gorillas were killed (not poached—no body parts were taken), an act that was widely interpreted as a warning from the charcoal syndicates not to interfere with their business.

As I have argued repeatedly throughout this book, Africa is a rich continent, and should be able to improve the standards of living of its peoples by their utilizing the resources around them sustainably, especially when those resources (such as oil, gold, diamonds, and minerals) garner high prices on the world market. Additionally, the potential to derive energy from the Congo Basin remains enormous. Indeed, water-generated electricity alone, if developed, might amount to almost a sixth of the global total.

All such endeavors, of course, come with possible dangers. The extraction of oil and minerals not only leaves the environmental cost of lost future earnings from the ecosystem in question, but also contains the potential for long-term and perhaps irreversible pollution (as Nigeria's Niger Delta bears witness to). Mining creates waste in the form of slag heaps and rock piles, as well as dust from detonation, the silting of rivers, and toxins from chemical leaching and smelting. Once the mining has been finished, the areas will need to be reseeded, recontoured, and fenced in so that chemicals do not leak and there are no hidden pits or shafts. While hydropower does not add to the carbon footprint, there are environmental impacts of building dams, including habitat destruction, displacement of local populations, deforestation, and soil erosion.

Here, the principles of sustainability, accountability, and equity need to be made real and tangible. In a manner that is likely only to become more vivid as the decades pass, sustainability entails recognizing that the destruction of the Congo's forests has *global* implications—not simply in further destabilization of weather patterns that may mean reduced harvests in the American Midwest and increased desertification in central

Asia, or the increase of carbon dioxide in the atmosphere; but also perhaps in the loss of critical medicines and minerals that may allow for human development in the future, both in Africa and beyond.

Accountability must mean local, regional, and international institutions working in concert to ensure that the industrialized countries do not repeat the sins of the colonial period, and extract without genuine recompense or an eye to protecting the resources of the future. This will require international efforts to bolster government and civil society institutions to ensure that private interests—which have a role to play in developing the region—do not do so at the expense of local citizens and the short- and long-term survival of central Africa and beyond.

It is a tragic irony that it may be the area's political instability that has allowed the Congo Basin ecosystem to remain as intact as it has. With the emergence of peace and opportunities for development, conditions may suit the increased exploitation of the basin's resources. Once the militias are disarmed and the roads are repaired or built, small-scale and subsistence-level businesses have a chance to grow. Likewise, with prices for certain minerals continuing to rise, companies that previously prospected only in the savannahs or the riverine areas may feel it is worth the cost and the difficulty to go deeper into the woodlands and forests for those resources, potentially threatening delicate ecosystems.

In both cases, it is likely to be the large multinational corporations, with their capital and economies of scale, that will gain the most. It is up to the governments of the region, and indeed the world, to make sure that the Congo Basin's peoples, too, benefit from these investments and are lifted out of poverty.

This is why the third element—equity—is essential. In order for the ecosystem to be protected, it is vital that the people who live in and around the forests of the Congo Basin feel they have a stake in its protection. This means acknowledging that the peoples of these forests have had a centuries-long relationship with the area's flora and fauna, and need both to be included in any decision making about its future and to benefit from its development. For instance, it would be important to establish governance systems to make sure that local communities prosper from the commercial use of as-yet-undiscovered medicinal and other properties of the biodiversity of their region.

The multinationals and the relevant governments must recognize that it is in the companies' own best interests that the forests' essential ecosystem functions are maintained. Equity will also mean international cooperation at an unprecedented level to ensure that effective institutions are established that will collect data, map and monitor existing concessions, and ensure transparency and a sound basis for future development.

All of this will be difficult—not least because mechanisms for this kind of multicountry, multistakeholder approach are not yet in place in many parts of the world, let alone a region that has seen the displacement and killing of millions of people, the near total infrastructural and institutional breakdown of governance associated with a failed state, and, preceding that, a century and a half of exploitation, corruption, and mismanagement on an unimaginable scale. Combine this history with the sheer size of the area and the diversity of its natural and human ecosystems, and the challenge becomes all the greater.

CARBON AND CONCESSIONS

Nevertheless, there are a number of policies that could and should be implemented. First, it is clear that no more resource concessions should be granted until there has been a thorough review of all the contracts, and effective mechanisms are in place that will allow those contracts that are awarded to be monitored and policed, by those who are capable of monitoring and policing them.

Second, the collection of revenues from the taxes levied on companies gaining access to these forest concessions must be made more transparent, and a sizeable portion of the monies returned to the areas where the concessions have been made, so that local communities benefit directly from the exploitation of their natural resources. This will, of course, mean ongoing monitoring of contracts to make sure that the Congo Basin Forest Partnership's forest code requirements are implemented.

Third, it is important to support small-scale ventures, ensure that they are sustainable, and encourage local communities to work to preserve and even rehabilitate areas of the forests that are especially vulnerable. Here, the Green Belt Movement model may be applicable.

Ultimately, of course, all stakeholders should be encouraged to move away from viewing the forest as a seemingly endless source of extractable minerals and various carbon-based life-forms, and instead look at it holistically. Efforts are already being made in this area. The Coalition for Rainforest Nations, which includes Costa Rica, Indonesia, and the DRC, among others, is working to persuade governments in the global North and South to accept the idea that a forest has value by *not* being exploited, in that it stores carbon in the ground, and if left undisturbed will continue to do so into the future. In this way, nations such as the DRC with large tracts of intact forest would receive remuneration for protecting their forests, so that carbon is not released into the atmosphere.

Ongoing research indicates that, assuming a market rate of $4 per metric ton of carbon dioxide, the DRC could generate around $200 million a year by selling carbon credits. According to the U.S.-based Association for Tropical Biology and Conser-

vation, the forests found in the fifteen countries that are part of
the Coalition for Rainforest Nations could have a value in
carbon credits of over $1 trillion. Private companies have an
opportunity to act as good global citizens and help existing
forests by buying credits to offset their carbon emissions as
part of their corporate social responsibility policies. Of course,
it is vital to make sure that the revenues raised by such carbon
concessions in the Congo Basin are managed transparently, and
that the benefits are shared equitably, particularly with poor
communities who depend on the forest.

Scientists estimate that the clearing of forests throughout
the world currently amounts to about 20 percent of total greenhouse gas emissions. Protecting intact forests has become an
important element in a comprehensive approach to addressing
global climate change, which is a welcome development. Governments have agreed that in the next treaty to guide national-
level action on global warming (the successor to the Kyoto
Protocol), protecting standing forests and avoiding further
deforestation and forest degradation must be a priority. A mechanism is being developed that would compensate developing
countries that have significant forest cover if they slow rates of
forest clearing, reverse these trends, and manage these forests
sustainably.

While the details of establishing, regulating, and ensuring
the fairness and transparency of a global market for such carbon credits are not fully resolved, it is an enterprise I support.
The markets, though, must serve the forests, and not solely
the other way around. It is also essential that any such system
for selling carbon credits be part of a national framework and
coherent policy of sustainable use and conservation, rather
than a mishmash of piecemeal actions that do not protect the
ecosystem as a whole, or provide a front for further indiscrimi-
nate exploitation of the natural resources. This is why there
must be multisectoral involvement and cooperation at every

level between NGOs and advocates for environmental conservation, indigenous peoples' rights, human rights, and private
and public institutions.

Nations, particularly in Africa, will also need assistance to
develop their capacity to negotiate more effectively within
global climate change policy-making bodies, particularly the
UN Framework Convention on Climate Change) as well as
with the private sector.

In 2005 in Brazzaville, Republic of the Congo, the heads of
state of the ten countries that have within their borders parts
of the Congo Basin asked me to serve as the goodwill ambassador for the Congo Basin Rainforest Ecosystem. In that role,
I have been seeking to raise awareness of the importance of
the region and its biodiversity. In 2006, the UK government
pledged $116 million to establish the Congo Basin Forest Fund.
Housed at the African Development Bank in Tunis, the fund
will accept proposals from the region for initiatives that both
protect the forests and support livelihoods that don't depend on
their destruction. Former Canadian prime minister Paul Martin and I are the fund's cochairs. At the fund's official launch in
London in June 2008, the Norwegian government donated a
further $100 million.

The first project to receive funding is focused on monitoring:
to track forest loss—and seek to arrest it—cameras mounted
on satellites will provide precise, high-resolution images of
forest cover. The use of technology is essential, since, for instance,
there are only thirty-four Central African botanists who have
been trained to study, monitor, and protect the diversity of
plants in the basin. It is also a good example of utilizing international funds to enhance local knowledge and capacities.

As both the founder of an NGO and a cochair of the Congo
Basin Forest Fund and goodwill ambassador for the forest basin,

I am aware of concerns about the extent to which the governments in the region, the international community, and corporations active in the Congo Basin are committed to the protection of the forest ecosystem. Many have other interests, and some may at times try to hoodwink those who are indeed committed. This makes it even more necessary for genuine leadership to be shown by heads of state and their foreign and environment ministers in Central Africa, Asia, Europe, North America, and elsewhere; similar will and commitment needs to be evident from civil society, and at the community level. It also means that international institutions, such as the World Bank, must ensure that their stated aims are not in conflict with their actions.

Therefore, while the more positive engagement of the international community and African heads of state in the Congo Basin is essential, I am also eager to encourage the engagement of regional NGOs and local communities. They are urging that the monies provided by the Congo Basin Forest Fund be subjected to careful scrutiny. It is a call that former prime minister Martin and I welcome, and to which we are committed.

Fourteen

THE AFRICAN FAMILY

AFRICA IS A PARADOX. It is one of the richest continents on the planet, endowed with oil, precious stones and metals, forests, water, wildlife, soil, land, agricultural products, and millions of people. Yet most Africans remain poor. Unable to add value to raw materials so they can sell processed goods in local and international markets and negotiate better prices along with better trade rules, they are trapped in a vicious cycle of poverty.

In addition, when international debts are not canceled, when trade barriers are raised, or when foreign assistance is given to governments who do not dispense it to their people responsibly; and when political leaders fail to invest in their citizens, do not protect their interests, and do not model service for the common good, the conditions are set for the underdevelopment that has held back Africa.

In any examination of the challenges of Africa, one natural resource often goes underappreciated: Africans themselves. As I have said, the disempowerment of ordinary people, especially at the grassroots, underlies Africa's gravest problems. In all of their incredible diversity, Africans share common bonds that tie them together and that they must cherish in their communities, nations, regions, and across the continent. It is fundamental that Africa's leaders create the conditions under which their peoples gain confidence, dignity, and a sense of self-worth—with the citizens themselves actively participating in this effort.

NURTURING THE FAMILY

As in other regions of the world, the base of African society is the family. A critical element in promoting and sustaining development in Africa is to keep African families intact. Achieving this will involve what we might call the "reintroduction" of the African man to his family. Since the earliest days of slavery, through colonialism and beyond, virtually the entire economic system of sub-Saharan Africa has depended on uprooting the African man and forcing him explicitly or by default to seek employment away from his home. Men have gone to work on commercial farms they didn't own; they have gone down mines and into quarries often at considerable distances from their families.

From the perspective of the colonial administration, separating men from their families may not only have been a necessary evil for the provision of labor, but it was also testament to the colonial administration's insensitivity to the African man's need to provide emotional and physical security to his family. This practice of sending civil servants to work away from their families was extended to teachers and even the clergy, and continues to this day. Yet the purposes for which the system was created by the colonial administration are no longer relevant to the African government. Even as the integrity of the settlers' family was given priority—the white man was supposed to be virtuous and responsible to his wife and children—that of the native Africans was undermined. Either through economic policies or administrative fiat, the colonial powers created conditions under which it was almost guaranteed that African men would be irresponsible toward, and increasingly removed from, their families. They could neither parent nor provide security for their children.

Such decisions, made out of convenience and opportunism

on the part of the colonizers, and accepted out of need and insecurity on the part of the African man, have had long-term negative consequences that may not have been considered at the time. Even today, geographically separated from their families and only able to visit occasionally during the year, many men throughout Africa have been unable to be effective partners in their marriages, parent their children adequately, and be part of the extended family. Indeed, the whole concept of extended family in Africa is rapidly being lost, as many Africans adopt the model of the western nuclear family. Cases of women-headed households and single parenthood have not only greatly increased, but it is also socially acceptable for women to raise families alone and give their last names to their children. A challenge for Africa is that the nuclear family on the continent is often dysfunctional, because the man is so often separated from his wife and children or, as is increasingly the case, absent from the outset.

A further threat to the extended family is that it was to a large extent sustained by aspects of indigenous cultures—the ceremonies, songs, and stories. With the loss of that culture, the extended family has also been uprooted and replaced by, for instance, membership in churches or mosques, and newer organizations and societies generally associated with houses of worship.

The physical separation of men from their families has led to other pressures, in both the family unit and societies at large. For instance, women have been forced to labor long hours in fields or offices, *and* look after their children, leaving many exhausted. Many men have spent so much time working in urban centers that they have developed independent lives away from their families. When they visit (or leave their jobs and retire), they are unable to adjust to the new environment away from the comforts and familiarity of urban life: they are psychologically separated from their wives, their children, or other relatives, and are often unable to cope in the unfamiliar surroundings, where they have nothing to do or no clear role. Away from home, many men become lonely, and may seek comfort with other women, including prostitutes, from whom they might contract a sexually transmitted infection, such as HIV, that they risk spreading when they return to their wives.[1]

What can African governments do to address the deeply entrenched labor system that has led to this state of affairs? Surely, one approach could be that governments appreciate the role of the family and work to create a society that provides men with employment opportunities where their families are, or allows parents who have to move for their jobs to bring their families with them. In this way, a century-old pattern of partnerless migrant labor across Africa could come to an end.

To me, the absence of men within their families is a major contributor to the lack of dynamism that is evident in many African societies, particularly in rural areas. These disrupted families make children more vulnerable. One of the most devastating experiences for any African—especially those who are parents themselves—is to see street children or child soldiers; or youth addicted to drugs, engaged in prostitution, afflicted with HIV/AIDS; or young men and women languishing in a state of alienation or torpor. Where men do not take their family responsibilities seriously, how can a strong society be created or raise secure and confident children?

This is why I believe passionately that African governments and individuals also must demonstrate the value of, and love and care for, Africa's children—by making every effort to provide young people with a good education, available opportunities, and encouragement so they can develop skills along with their talents that are modeled by their parents, elders, and leaders.

Babies with distended bellies and children wielding guns or high on drugs are all symptoms of a disintegrating society—

and intact families are a means of remedying the fissures. By "reintroducing" men to their families, I do not mean reverting to the norms of a traditional, patriarchal society, even if that were possible. Instead, I am suggesting that in modern Africa what is needed is genuine partnership in raising and parenting children in an atmosphere where gender equity is respected, and men and women share responsibilities fairly. To a degree, this is now occurring with younger, upscale couples—who can afford conveniences and are dividing more of the housework and child rearing—although women are still doing more than their share. If African parents fail to prepare the next generation, what is all the work in their lifetimes for? It will be in vain.

THE BRAIN DRAIN

The dislocation of the African family is writ large in the emigration of Africans overseas. Leaders in Africa need to ask themselves why they cannot make the continent more hospitable so citizens do not risk life and limb to flee their nations. They must take an honest look at the fact that some of their most promising men and women are being lured away to Europe, North America, or elsewhere because of greater professional and financial opportunities, improved security, and a better quality of life.

Many other Africans are running from a rich continent only to live hand-to-mouth elsewhere, where the costs of living are often higher and life faster and more competitive, doing menial work even when they have been trained in professions. This situation can only wreak havoc on the African psyche. If one espouses the principles of human rights and freedom of movement, then one cannot blame individuals for wanting to seek their fortune or professional development anywhere: in their own country, elsewhere on the continent, or overseas.

On the other hand, it is worth asking why the World Bank and, more pointedly, donor countries would be giving or lending Africa funds to improve its medical facilities and universities to train personnel, only for the donor governments to then lure these newly trained individuals away. Of course, this flight is not only an African phenomenon; many people from other continents are knocking at the doors of the rich countries in Europe and North America for the same reasons. Since some of these nations were the colonial administrators of many African nation-states and because they speak the same languages and have adopted the culture, many Africans feel more at home in these countries than elsewhere. Lower population growth in developed countries also means that there are employment opportunities for immigrants who will take the jobs that the more privileged locals do not wish to do.

This state of affairs is a continuation of the dynamic whereby the industrialized world provides Africa with assistance on the one hand and removes its natural capital on the other. Unless African governments are sufficiently wise, or committed to changing the rules of the game, the contest will remain one-sided. The only solution, as I see it, is to improve the quality of life and governance in Africa so people can enjoy basic freedoms. Is it too much to ask for someone to have a decent house, be able to send their children to good schools, and have access to preventative and curative health care? Or to live on a safe street where public transportation works, and walk along paved paths on roads lined with plants and flowers and where there is no dust or mountains of trash?

Another facet of leadership that would be welcome from African governments would be to deepen and strengthen relationships with those who *do* leave Africa. Every African outside the continent should be considered an ambassador for it. Many emigrate and make great successes of themselves, demonstrating the potential they would have had if the opportunities available to them in their adopted countries were open to them at home. But there are others who carry with them what might be called the burden of Africa—the perception that the continent is dysfunctional and that Africans, compared to peoples of other regions, are backward and unable to take advantage of the opportunities available.

Africans abroad often begin to accept the perceptions that they see reflected in many of the images of Africa they encounter. They become unable to overcome the challenges they may meet: discrimination, lack of acceptance, the quick judgment, and no allowance for any errors. If an African makes a mistake, the risk for him or her is that others will think, *Well, what else do you expect?* These prejudices can become overwhelming, and the immigrant can fail, further entrenching an already skeptical view of Africans in other regions.

While it is true that Africans don't have the latitude to make mistakes, sometimes, it seems to me, they give the world too many reasons not to give them the space to do so. Heads of state, politicians, businesspeople, those working in civil society, and ordinary Africans surely must be able to raise the bar for themselves—not primarily in order to persuade the rest of the world that they don't always have to operate below par, but for their own sense of self.

There ought to be a collective effort, particularly through the embassies of African states, to provide systems and institutions to support Africans outside of the continent, so they can adjust successfully to their new environment. The government of India has done this with their own diaspora. It has a ministry for expatriate Indians (or NRIs), which helps them get travel documents easily and supports them culturally and economically so that they may succeed and reinvest part of the money they make outside the country in India. It would be a very positive step if African governments were similarly conscious of the fact that African emigrants face challenges and help them to become good ambassadors—and thereby proactively shape (rather than have shaped) the image of Africans abroad.

Certainly, Africans abroad are doing their part. Between 2000 and 2003, remittances to Africa as a whole ($17 billion a year) outpaced average annual foreign direct investment ($15 billion). The estimated 3.6 million sub-Saharan Africans living in the diaspora also increased their remittances, from $1.8 billion in 1990 to $6 billion in 2003.[2] By 2007, this figure had doubled to $12 billion.[3] Remittances are invaluable additions to family income, and are more likely to reach poor households than aid or indirect government spending; they also bolster national income.[4]

The fast pace of the increase in remittances in recent years exemplifies the burgeoning wealth of the African diaspora. While they have yet to see success along the lines of NRIs, many of whom have thrived overseas and brought expertise back to India, Africa could in the future likewise lure back its professionals, carrying their exposure, skills, and experiences with them. One practical way of achieving this would be to give Africans dual citizenship with conditions that give them confidence and a sense of security. This would assure Africans that, should they ever want or need to return home, they would be able to. There needs to be one place in the world where it is okay to be an African—and that is Africa.

When Africans do come back, they shouldn't be apologetic that they left their countries in the first place, to seek an environment where their talents could flourish. What is important is that they do the best they can where they are: either supporting Africa from abroad or, when the time comes, returning to help their nations prosper.

African governments must also make it easier for returning Africans to start a business or put into practice what they learned outside of their home country. It's all the more important, then, that these entrepreneurs—whether social or economic—should not feel frustrated by an incompetent, corrupt system that makes starting or running a business or organization extremely expensive or unnecessarily bureaucratic. After all, why should anyone return to their mother country with a skill that could help the nation and find it impossible to start a business or school or IT company because of red tape, or because they have to visit the minister of science and technology, for example, and provide him with a kickback?

As I know myself, traveling out of the continent is a *big* learning experience, providing you with perspective, opening you to new ideas, and stimulating you to look at your society with fresh eyes. The same can be said for traveling *within* the continent. It has not been easy to do this—not only for Africans of my generation, but even for those who live in Africa now.

The difficulty of traveling within Africa itself is not merely a result of the limited air and other transportation links. It is also a function of the often negative perceptions that Africans have of each other, which makes getting the travel documents one needs a laborious process—even for an African to visit another country in Africa. If Africans could travel more easily inside Africa and not be subject to the endless delays of acquiring the documents, it would help them understand each other, know the continent better, and recognize the issues it is facing.

Despite the numerous challenges confronting the African peoples as a whole, individuals, both in the diaspora and at home, are taking some piece of Africa's present and future into their own hands. The Beninese singer Angelique Kidjo has established the Batonga Foundation to provide girls with primary and secondary educational opportunities in several sub-Saharan African countries. Liberian soccer star and UNICEF special ambassador George Weah is using sports to encourage children in Liberia to stay in school. Somali-born human rights activist Ayaan Hirsi Ali is a strong advocate for women's rights and freedom of thought in the Horn of Africa and throughout the world.[5]

After decades when all that was heard from Africa were the echoes of its rhythms in American, Caribbean, and Latin music, the sounds of Africa themselves are now heard and expressed around the world: Youssou N'Dour of Senegal, Hugh Masekela and the late Miriam Makeba of South Africa, Salif Keita from Mali, Femi Kuti of Nigeria, Papa Wemba from the Democratic Republic of the Congo, and many others have continued the tradition of expressing the aspirations of their peoples, their languages, and a common humanity. In literature, to name a very few, the words of African giants such as Léopold Senghor of Senegal; Chinua Achebe and Nobel laureate Wole Soyinka of Nigeria; John Kani, Winston Ntshona, and Athol Fugard, and Nobel laureate Nadine Gordimer from South Africa; and Ngũgĩ wa Thiong'o of Kenya—whose novel *Wizard of the Crow* captures in surreal, satirical detail the absurdities of African politics—continue to give voice to a continent fighting to realize its possibilities.

Quietly and out of the spotlight of international attention, the conferences, and the concerts, Africans are organizing themselves. Over the past two decades, following droughts in the 1970s and '80s, women farmers in Niger have planted trees covering 3 million hectares (7.5 million acres), not only holding back the desert sands but re-greening parts of the Sahel. While keeping the trees alive, they also provide themselves with food, fuel, and income as they sell off branches for firewood.[6]

Women in Lesotho are not waiting for international agencies to provide food; they are creating extraordinarily productive "keyhole gardens" in their neighborhood, growing large amounts of green vegetables, and protecting themselves from hunger.[7] Committed individuals have adapted traditional processes to form sustainable businesses: solar drying cookers for fruit in Uganda, ethanol-fueled stoves in Ethiopia, and biomass ovens in Tanzania.[8]

The West Africa Network for Peacebuilding is attempting to promote peace and prevent future conflicts after years of civil war, warlordism, and the widespread use of child soldiers.[9] Rangers in Virunga National Park in the DRC are fighting to protect the wild animals, including the endangered mountain gorillas, that live there—despite the fact that in the course of a decade more than 150 of their men have been killed and some abducted.[10]

In Zambia, Hammerskjoeld Simwinga, the head of the North Luanga Wildlife Conservation and Community Development Programme, has campaigned to protect biodiversity while helping villagers in the region through education, rural health and women's empowerment initiatives, and micro-lending programs. In Mozambique, musician Feliciano dos Santos is touring remote villages in Niassa Province to promote the importance of sanitation and water conservation using compostable toilets. In Liberia, Silas Kpanan'Ayoung Siakor's documentation of human rights abuses in the logging sector, and the use of proceeds from logging to fund the country's civil war, led to a UN Security Council ban on the export of Liberian timber.[11]

In Kenya, Dekha Ibrahim Abdi, a Muslim woman, has worked for peace in the troubled north of the country and has established the Oasis of Peace Centre in Mombasa to foster mediation.[12] In 2006, Alfred Taban from Sudan, Zainab Hawa Bangura of Sierra Leone, Immaculée Birhaheka from the DRC, and Reginald Matchaba-Hove from Zimbabwe received awards from the United States' National Endowment for Democracy for "their contributions to the advancement of democracy, human rights, gender equality, government transparency and free and fair elections in their homelands."[13] Zackie Achmat's Treatment Action Campaign is working to make access to antiretroviral treatments along with HIV/AIDS care and prevention available all across South Africa.[14] Kenyan marathoner Tegla Loroupe is using her worldwide fame to promote peaceful coexistence and development in eastern Africa.[15]

These actions, undertaken by individuals—some of whom are well known, others not, but all extraordinary—don't necessarily involve multimillion-dollar aid grants or governmental approval. Nonetheless they are changing perceptions and realities on the ground. As these people and countless others illustrate, it is ultimately Africans themselves who have to determine their future. Where there is poverty and environmental degradation, Africans must work with what they have and join together to solve their immediate needs while increasing their chances of future prosperity by regenerating forests, protecting watersheds, and practicing efficient agriculture. Where there are business opportunities and abundant natural resources, Africans must use them wisely and for the good of Africans, developing their own industries and circulating capital within their countries. Where there is a need for foreign investment and partnership, Africans must behave shrewdly, and encourage honesty and transparency, and not give away what they have so cheaply through ignorance or corruption.

And, of course, where there is poor leadership, Africans need to stand up for the leaders they want and not settle for the leaders they get. Too many African leaders have been the narrow heroes of their micro-nations rather than genuine statesmen for the whole macro-nation. They have played upon people's desire to follow someone who will lead them from their difficulties to immediate riches rather than joining with them to solve their own problems by exploiting their own talents.

In their unwillingness to share with other micro-nations,

micro-national leaders have precipitated many of the past, and current, conflicts that bedevil Africa. When everyone fights to have all of the pie, all that anyone is left with are crumbs. If African leadership cannot or will not prevent the leaders of their countries' micro-nations from fighting each other, how can they stop conflicts between their nation-states, let alone hope to realize the African Union's vision of a united continent?

What is necessary is for these leaders (and the people they claim to represent) to recognize that, even within the context of democracy, all the micro-nations have a right to play a role in the macro-nation. This is the case no matter how large or small in numbers a micro-nation may be, or how well or how poorly they are represented in parliament or national administration. Majority rule is not sufficient. Even the smallest micro-nation and its leaders need to participate in governance—and not fear that their grievances about being left out are evidence of "tribalism."

The watchwords for Africa must be accountability, responsibility, equity, and service. With these in the hearts of every African, it will be more likely that their children will go to school rather than become soldiers or be forced to work in the fields; citizens will feel empowered to challenge leaders before they co-opt the army or the police to become tyrants; the integrity of women's bodies will be honored, and they will have a chance to bring about the kind of change that enhances the strength of the voices, rights, and, indeed, lives of men and women in African societies across the continent.

And finally, we will have a generation of Africans who embrace a set of values, like service for the common good, and commitment, persistence, and patience until a goal is realized. They will live their lives for something larger than themselves. Like Nelson Mandela, Desmond Tutu, Julius Nyerere, and Kwame Nkrumah—who are known and admired for the tasks they undertook that were beyond their narrow self-interests, who had a vision for their continent, and who were often scorned or ignored—they will not accept the status quo. But with honesty and integrity and resilience they will keep working. Like these heroes, they will understand that they can no longer wait for the forces that have held Africa in check to move out of the way.

RESTORATION

When the Norwegian Nobel Committee decided to award me the Peace Prize in 2004, they were sending a number of messages. The prize wasn't only a call for the environment to be at the center of work for peace; it was also an acknowledgment for the African people in general, for the struggles they face every day. It was a demonstration of how important the environment and natural resources are in making sure we survive; and it was a message of hope for the continent.

It was also saying to African women, in particular, that women can make an impact, although their ideas and actions are often dismissed. In addition, it was a recognition of the many citizens around the world who had been working on a set of similar issues—the environment, human rights, democracy, women's rights, and peace-building—and had not perhaps seen the connections between them. I was honored to be the symbol for that collective.

Over the years, it has become clear to me that in advocating for the environment, and seeing the manifold ways that a degraded environment harms the life of the smallest community and the entire continent of Africa, the connection between who I am as an African and the abstractions of peace, democratic space, and development is deeper than words can say. In seeking restoration for my continent, I am quite literally restoring myself—as, I believe, is every African—because who we are is bound up in the rivers and streams, the trees and the valleys. It is bound up in our languages, rich in aphorisms from the natural world and our fragile and almost forgotten past. We are fighting for the future of our children, and the children of the men and women who grew up with us, and the future generations of other species.

In looking at the vast riches of the Congo Basin forests, for instance, it is possible to see that, in the peoples' dependence on the natural resources around them, all of us can reach a deeper appreciation of the fact that it is what is *not* human that ensures that we continue to exist. Without human beings, the creatures and plants and trees would flourish; but without those species, human beings have no hope of survival. This is why in thinking about *human* rights, we need to reach another level of consciousness to appreciate that these other species, too, have a right to their existence and their piece of the Earth.

This struggle to preserve what they have and hold it close to them is one that all Africans—indeed, all peoples—should engage in. Because if the soil is denuded and the waters are polluted, the air is poisoned, wildlife is lost, and the mineral riches are mined and sold beyond the continent, nothing will be left that we can call our own. And when we have nothing to call our own, we have nothing to reflect back to us who we truly are. Without the mirror that the natural world presents to us, we will no longer see ourselves, and we will forget who we are.

This is why our work is reclamation—bringing back what is essential so we can move forward. Planting trees, speaking our languages, telling our stories, and not dismissing the lives of our ancestors are all part of the same act of conservation—all constituent elements of the broader ecosystem on which human life depends. We need to protect our local foods, remember how to grow and cook them, and serve and eat them. We must remember how to make our clothes and wear them with pride; we need to recall our mother tongues and, literally, mind our language. Let us practice our spirituality and dance our dances, revivify our symbols and rediscover our communal character. Without these cultural acts of recreation, we are merely fashion victims, food faddists, going through empty rituals and employing pointless markers to get ahead in a world devoid of depth or meaning. We are vulnerable to anyone who wishes to exploit us.

Africans must make a deliberate choice to move forward together toward more cohesive macro-nations, where all can feel free, secure, and at peace with themselves and others, where there is no need for any group to organize violence against their neighbors. Then, everyone would begin to reap the benefits of unity in diversity.

Acknowledgments

First of all, thanks must go to Mia MacDonald of Brighter Green and Martin Rowe of Lantern Books for their dedication, intelligence, skill, and hard work in the development and execution of *The Challenge for Africa*. I want to express my appreciation to my editor, Erroll McDonald, for his great interest in, and enthusiasm for, this book and for bringing it into the world. I would also like to thank Sangamithra Iyer for providing research assistance, and Serge Bounda for his considerable expertise on the Congo Basin ecosystem.

I also acknowledge all those in my constituency of Tetu who worked so hard to make the Constituency Development Fund and other projects a success; the staff and members of the Green Belt Movement and Green Belt Movement International, who continue to strive to fulfill our mission; and our friends and supporters in Kenya and around the world, too numerous to mention here, but who provide me with continual inspiration and encouragement.

As always I would not have been able to complete this book without the unswerving support of my children—Waweru, Wanjira, and Muta. They are both Africa's and my future.

The Challenge for Africa is a call for genuine leadership that puts peoples' welfare first, places the environment at the center of development, and maintains a vision of the future founded on justice and sustainability. To that extent, it would be remiss of me not to acknowledge the millions of people who have labored without recognition for the future of the African continent—including all who have stood up for freedom and demanded accountability, responsibility, and respect from those who have claimed to be their leaders. We may never know their names, but the freedom and dignity they strove for must never be forgotten.

Notes

One THE FARMER OF YAOUNDÉ

1 Arthur Bright, "South Africa's Anti-Immigrant Violence Spreads to Cape Town," *Christian Science Monitor*, May 23, 2008.
2 "Poverty Rates in Sub-Saharan Africa Steadily Declining Over Last Ten Years: Report," Ethiopian News Agency, August 28, 2008.
3 "The State of Africa's Children, 2008," UNICEF, May 28, 2008.
4 Cathy Majtenyi, "Women Have Strong Voice in Rwandan Parliament," Voice of America, July 16, 2007.

Two A LEGACY OF WOES

1 See Pakenham, *The Scramble for Africa.*
2 See Hochschild, *King Leopold's Ghost.*
3 "Zambia: Rise of African Nationalism (1945–1964)," EISA, www.eisa.org.za.
4 See Meredith, *The Fate of Africa,* p. 176.
5 For the history of Africa in precolonial times, see Wikipedia entries for "Ashanti," "Benin," "Dahomey," "Great Zimbabwe," "Kongo," "Mali," "Songhai," "Sankore," "Zulu" (accessed on September 2, 2008).

Three PILLARS OF GOOD GOVERNANCE

1 See Meredith, *The Fate of Africa,* p. 142.
2 Elsa Artadi and Xavier Sala-i-Martin, "The Economic Tragedy of the XXth Century: Growth in Africa," NBER Working Paper #9865, July 2003.
3 Table 6:1, "Africa's Growth Tragedy: An Institutional Perspective," *Economic Growth in the 1990s: Learning from a Decade of Reform,* World Bank, 2005 p. 275.
4 See, for instance, "Timeline: Democratic Republic of Congo," BBC News, April 30, 2008.
5 See Stiglitz, *Making Globalization Work,* p. 11.
6 See "War Against Women: The Use of Rape as a Weapon in Congo's Civil War," CBS News, January 13, 2008; and "IRC Study Shows

Congo's Neglected Crisis Leaves 5.4 Million Dead," International Rescue Committee, January 22, 2008, www.theirc.org.

7 See Theo Mushi, "IMF Optimistic About Africa Development Prospects," IPP Media, February 19, 2008.

8 Martin Ravallion and Shaohua Chen, "The Developing World Is Poorer Than We Thought but No Less Successful in the Fight Against Poverty," World Bank, August 26, 2008.

9 "Sub-Saharan Africa Spring 2008 Regional Economic Outlook: Growth Expected to Remain Robust but Global Developments Cloud Prospects," International Monetary Fund press release, April 12, 2008.

10 *Economic Report on Africa*, 2008, Economic Commission on Africa, p. 62.

11 See AVERT, www.avert.org/aidsbotswana.htm (accessed on September 2, 2008).

12 UN Human Development Report 2007/2008, pp. 229–30.

13 "Reducing the Global Incidence of Civil War: A Discussion of the Available Policy Instruments," Inwent—Capacity Building International, Germany, October 8, 2004, www.inwent.org/ef-texte/military/collier.htm (accessed September 2, 2008).

Four AID AND THE DEPENDENCY SYNDROME

1 The session is viewable at www.youtube.com/watch?v=R8CF4E0XjDo.

2 See Larry Elliott, "Elephant in the Room Can't Leave It All Up to Sharon," *The Guardian*, January 31, 2005. The initial amount pledged was thought to be $1 million.

3 Mark Sundberg and Alan Gelb, "Making Aid Work," *Finance & Development*, International Monetary Fund, December 2006, vol. 43, no. 4.

4 "Global Fund Money Will Make Mosquito Nets Widely Available in Tanzania," Global Fund to Fight AIDS, Tuberculosis, and Malaria press release, December 2, 2002.

5 "Malaria—Facts & Figures," 2004, Global Fund to Fight AIDS, Tuberculosis, and Malaria; see also "The Impact of Malaria, a Leading Cause of Death Worldwide," U.S. Centers for Disease Control and Prevention, www.cdc.gov/malaria/impact/index.htm (accessed September 2008).

6 "Malaria: The Impact of Malaria, a Leading Cause of Death Worldwide," U.S. Centers for Disease Control and Prevention, www.cdc.gov/malaria/impact/index.htm (accessed September 2008).

7 See Easterly, *The White Man's Burden*, pp. 4–5.

8   "AIDS Epidemic Update 2007," Joint United Nations Programme on HIV/AIDS and the World Health Organization, 2007.

9   James Whitworth, "Malaria and HIV," HIV inSITE Knowledge Base Chapter, May 2006, http://hivinsite.ucsf.edu/InSite?page=kb-05-04-04#S2X (accessed September 2008).

10 See Sachs, *The End of Poverty*, pp. 227–38; and www.millennium promise.org.

11 "The Magnificent Seven," *Economist*, April 27, 2006.

12 Eliza Barclay, "How a Kenyan Village Tripled Its Corn Harvest," *Christian Science Monitor*, June 17, 2008.

13 See "Tackling the Silent Killer: The Case for Sanitation," Water Aid, July 2008; and Gumisai Mutume, "Rough Road to Sustainable Development," *Africa Renewal* 18:2 (July 2004).

14 All data in this paragraph is from "Regional Economic Outlook: Sub-Saharan Africa, April 08," International Monetary Fund; G-8 Aid: DATA [Debt, AIDS, Trade, Africa], June 2008.

Five DEFICITS: INDEBTEDNESS AND UNFAIR TRADE

1   Lydia Polgreen, "Angolans Come Home to 'Negative Peace,' " *New York Times*, July 30, 2003; and "Angola: Towards Peace and Democracy (2002–2007)," EISA, www.eisa.org.za/WEP/angoverview10.htm (accessed September 2008).

2   United Nations Economic Report on Africa, 2008, p. 49.

3   Sharon LaFraniere, "As Angola Rebuilds, Most Find Their Poverty Persists," *New York Times*, October 14, 2007.

4   UN Human Development Report 2007/2008.

5   "Angola: Thousands Forcibly Evicted in Postwar Boom," Human Rights Watch, May 17, 2007.

6   See Richard Black, "Africa Fish Fall Blamed on Japan," BBC News, June 24, 2008.

7   UN Integrated Regional Information Networks, "And Then There Were No Fish," November 21, 2007.

8   "The Crisis of Marine Plunder in Africa," *ISS Today*, October 2, 2007, www.iss.co.za.

9   "Africa Moves to Stop Fish Theft," BBC News, July 2, 2008.

10 "Crisis in African Fish Supplies Looms, Experts Warn Africa Leaders," World Fish Center, August 21, 2005.

11 "Fisheries Link to Bushmeat Trade," BBC News, November 12, 2004.

12 Lydia Polgreen, "Once a Bright Point, Senegal Teeters Toward a Crisis," *New York Times*, June 18, 2008.

13 Hilaire Avril, "Overfishing Linked to Food Crisis, Migration," Inter Press Service, August 11, 2008.

14 Paul Fauvet, "Fisheries Ministry Has Just One Patrol Boat," Agencia de Informação de Moçambique, May 31, 2008.

15 "Poverty, Search for Status Driving Migration to Europe," UN Integrated Regional Information Networks, July 4, 2007.

16 See "And Then There Were No Fish" and Sharon LaFraniere, "Europe Takes Africa's Fish, and Boatloads of Migrants Follow," *New York Times*, January 14, 2008.

17 "Why Drop the Debt?" Jubilee USA Network, www.jubileeusa .org/truth-about-debt/why-drop-the-debt.html (accessed September 2008).

18 See "The Dirty Dozen," Trace Aid, http://traceaid.com/media/ looting_index1.pdf; and http://traceaid.com/pages/media/briefs/pre-2004-briefs-archive.php (accessed September 2008).

19 See Jubilee Debt Campaign, www.jubileedebtcampaign.org.uk/ Malawi+3481.twl (accessed September 2008), and "Unfinished Business: Ten Years of Dropping the Debt," Jubilee Debt Campaign, May 2008.

20 *Global Environment Outlook* (GEO) 4, p. 200.

21 United Nations Economic Commission for Africa, 2008, p. 6.

22 Figure and Johnson-Sirleaf quotation from "Africa Action Stands with African Voices on Debt Cancellation," Africa Action, July 12, 2007, www.africaaction.org.

23 Sam Olukoya, "Nigeria Makes Progress on Stolen Cash," BBC News, July 2, 2008.

24 Data on commodities from Cheru, *African Renaissance*, particularly pp. 11–13 and 129–33; and Ayittey, *Africa Unchained.*

25 "World Economic and Financial Surveys: Regional Economic Outlook: Sub-Saharan Africa, April 2007," International Monetary Fund.

26 Economic Report on Africa, 2008. See Fig. 1.1, p. 22.

27 Economic Report on Africa, 2007, p. 22.

28 Ibid., p. 127.

29 "Regional Economic Outlook: Sub-Saharan Africa, April 2008," International Monetary Fund, p. 3.

30 Collier, *The Bottom Billion,* p. 39.

31 Ibid., pp. 140–46.

32 "Norway: An Oil Nation," see the government of Norway's website at www.norway.org.uk/policy/trade/oil/oil.htm (accessed September 2008).

33 UN Human Development Report 2007/2008, p. 229.

34 "Norway: Economy," Wikipedia.

35 Darren Foster, "Nigeria: The Corruption of Oil," *Frontline*, May 1, 2007.

36 "Nokia and Nokia Siemens Networks Prepare for Growth of Telecommunications in Africa at CTO Roundtable," Corporate Social

Responsibility Newswire, May 29, 2007, www.csrwire.com/News/8692.html (accessed September 2008).

37 "Regional Economic Outlook, Sub-Saharan Africa, April 2008," International Monetary Fund.

38 "On the Frontier of Finance," *Economist*, November 15, 2007.

39 See Collier, *The Bottom Billion*.

40 See Cheru, *African Renaissance*, p. 127. For an article on NEPAD's achievements and challenges, most notably the call for strong leadership, see Wiseman Nkuhlu, "NEPAD: A Look at Seven Years of Achievement—and the Challenges on the Way Forward," January 23, 2008, www.africafiles.org/article.asp?id=17138 (accessed September 2008).

41 CIA Factbook: European Union, see www.cia.gov/library/publications/the-world-factbook/geos/ee.html (accessed September 2008).

42 Thomas J. Christensen and James Swan, "China in Africa: Implications for U.S. Policy," U.S. Department of State, June 5, 2008, www.state.gov/p/eap/rls/rm/2008/06/105556.htm (accessed September 2008); see also Alden, *China in Africa*, pp. 12, 18, and 22.

43 See Alden, *China in Africa*; see also the thoughtful essay by George Esunge Fominyen, "China in Africa: Invasion or the New Face of Globalisation?" www.gefominyen.com/2008/06/china-in-africa.html (accessed September 2008).

44 Joseph Kahn, "China Courts Africa, Angling for Strategic Gains," *New York Times*, November 3, 2006.

45 Howard W. French, "Behind the Reluctance of China and Africa to Criticize Mugabe," *International Herald Tribune*, July 3, 2008.

46 Matt Schroeder and Guy Lamb, "The Illicit Arms Trade in Africa: A Global Enterprise," *African Analyst*, #1, Third Quarter 2006, pp. 69–78.

47 Richard Grimmett, "Conventional Arms Transfers to Developing Nations, 1998–2005," Congressional Research Service Report for Congress, October 23, 2006.

48 "Did 'Ship of Shame' Complete Mission?," Yahoo News, May 8, 2008.

49 Christof Maletsky, " 'Ship of Shame' Cargo Delivered to Country," *The Namibian*, May 20, 2008.

Six LEADERSHIP

1 "Prize Offered to All Africa's Leaders," BBC News, October 26, 2006.

2 "Chissano: Mo Ibrahim Prize for Achievement in African Leadership Acceptance Speech," November 26, 2007, www.polity.org.za/article.php?a_id=122204 (accessed September 2008).

3 Cited in Sarah Childress, "In Africa, Democracy Gains Against Turmoil," *Wall Street Journal*, June 19, 2008.

4 Ayittey, *Africa Unchained*, pp. 389–91.

5 See the website for the Ellen Johnson-Sirleaf Market Women's Fund at http://smwf.org.

Seven MOVING THE SOCIAL MACHINE

1 Ben Onyasimi, "Govt Sets New Conditions for CDF Teams," *Kenya Times*, August 13, 2008.

2 "Integrating Tree Cash Crops in Agricultural Production Systems, Kenya," by Mr. Y. Sato, managing director, Kenya Nut Company, and Mr. J. H. G. Waithaka, consultant, Eureka Agritech Limited, World Bank Group.

Nine THE CRISIS OF NATIONAL IDENTITY

1 See Jeffrey Gettlemen, "Official Sees Kenyan Ethnic Cleansing," *New York Times*, January 31, 2008; and Simiyu Barasa, "Kenya's War of Words, *New York Times*, February 12, 2008.

2 See, for instance, Najum Mushtaq, "Kenya: Writing for Peace," Inter Press Service, August 5, 2008; "A List of Bloggers Covering the Kenyan Elections and Its Aftermath," January 2, 2008, http://whiteafrican.com/2008/01/02/a-list-of-bloggers-covering-the-kenyan-elections-and-its-aftermath/; Generation Kenya, http://generationkenya.co.ke/main/; and Peace in Kenya, www.peaceinkenya.net/ (accessed September 2008).

3 "Peace and Reconciliation," Green Belt Movement website, www.greenbeltmovement.org/c.php?id=18 (accessed September 2008).

4 "Kenya Tourism Down in Wake of Election Violence," Associated Press, July 30, 2008.

5 Jim Onyango, "Kenya: Spending on Police, Teachers Pushes Budget to SH760 Billion," *Business Daily Africa*, June 11, 2008.

Ten EMBRACING THE MICRO-NATIONS

1 The story is told in John Carlin, "How Nelson Mandela Won the Rugby World Cup," *Daily Telegraph* (UK), October 19, 2007; and Karen Bond, "Mandela Unites a Nation to RWC Glory," Rugby News Service, July 9, 2007.

Eleven LAND OWNERSHIP: WHOSE LAND IS IT, ANYWAY?

1 GEO 4, p. 208.
2 *Africa: Atlas of Our Changing Environment,* UNEP, 2008; for details, see "Glacial Retreat to Rapid Urbanization Chronicled in Landmark Satellite Report to Africa's Environment Ministers," UNEP press release, June 10, 2008.
3 Charlayne Hunter-Gault, "Land Ownership Elusive for South Africa's Poor," *All Things Considered,* August 7, 2006.
4 "Government Warns Namibia's White Farmers," *The Namibian,* February 20, 2008.
5 "White Farmers Under Siege in Zimbabwe," BBC News, August 15, 2002.
6 See Otsieno Namwaya, "Who Owns Kenya?" *East African Standard,* October 1, 2004; Clemence Manyukwe, "Judge Allocated Farm After 'Special Duties,' " *Financial Gazette,* June 12, 2008; and the discussion regarding South Africa at www.bbc.co.uk/blogs/worldhaveyoursay/2007/10/whose_land_it_is_anyway.html (accessed September 2008).
7 GEO 4, p. 196.
8 Ibid., p. 210.
9 Regional report of Working Group II, UN Intergovernmental Panel on Climate Change, 2007.
10 GEO 4, p. 210.
11 F. N. Tubiello and G. Fischer, "Reducing Climate Change Impacts on Agriculture: Global and Regional Effects of Mitigation, 2000–2080," *Technological Forecasting and Social Change,* 2007.
12 See "Renewed Focus on the Importance of Agricultural Extension Services," *African Agriculture,* May 4, 2008, http://africanagriculture.blogspot.com/ (accessed September 2008).
13 *International Assessment of Agricultural Knowledge, Science and Technology for Development,* www.agassessment.org, April 2008.
14 Ernest Harsch, "Agriculture: Africa's 'Engine for Growth': Small-scale Farmers Hold the Key, Says NEPAD Plan," *Africa Recovery* 17:4 (January 2004).

Twelve ENVIRONMENT AND DEVELOPMENT

1 Zeddy Sambu, "Power Suppliers Eye Thermal Sources to Bridge Deficit," *Business Daily Africa,* April 1, 2008.
2 Mwaniki Wahome, "As Power Shortage Looms, KenGen Looks to Old Dams," *Daily Nation* (Kenya), August 28, 2008.
3 "Ethiopia: Deforestation and Monoculture Plantations Behind the Fires," World Rainforest Movement, Bulletin no. 55, February 2002.

4 GEO 4, p. 203.

5 *State of the World's Forests 2007,* UNFAO, 2007.

6 *Africa: Atlas of Our Changing Environment,* UNEP, 2008.

7 GEO 4, p. 205–13; see also Sonja van Renssen, "Climate Change 'Will Set Kalahari Dunes in Motion,'" SciDev.net, June 30, 2005, www.scidev.net/en/news/climate-change-will-set-kalahari-dunes-in-motion.html (accessed September 2008).

8 GEO 4, pp. 196–213.

9 Edward Miguel, Shankar Satyanath, and Ernest Sergenti,"Economic Shocks and Civil Conflict: An Instrumental Variables Approach," *Journal of Political Economy* 112:4 (2004).

10 GEO 4, p. 201.

11 Ibid., p. 209.

12 Abraham McLaughlin and Christian Allen Purefoy, "Hunger Is Spreading in Africa," *Christian Science Monitor,* August 1, 2005.

13 " 'Pace of Desertification Doubled Since 1970s, U.N. Says,' " Africa Conservation Forums, June 16, 2004, www.africanconservation.org/cgi-bin/dcforum/dcboard.cgi?az=read_count&om=7&forum=DCForumID33 (accessed September 2008).

14 GEO 4, p. 212.

15 "Valuation of Ecological Services and Natural Capital," in "Phytotechnologies," United Nations Environment Programme, Freshwater Management Series no. 7, www.unep.or.jp/Ietc/Publications/Freshwater/FMS7/11.asp (accessed September 2008).

16 "Valuing Ecosystem Services," in World Resources, 1998–99, World Resources Institute, http://earthtrends.wri.org/features/view_feature.php?fid=15&theme=5 (accessed September 2008).

17 "The Value of the World's Ecosystem Services and Natural Capital," University of Vermont, www.uvm.edu/giee/publications/Nature_Paper.pdf (accessed September 2008).

18 *Ecosystems and Human Wellbeing: Synthesis, 2005,* Millennium Ecosystem Assessment, 2005.

19 GEO 4, p. 202.

20 "Clean Energy Investments Charge Forward Despite Financial Market Turmoil," UNEP press release, June 2008.

21 "Algeria Aims to Export Power—Solar Power," CBS News, August 11, 2007.

22 Alok Jha, "Solar Power from Saharan Sun Could Provide Europe's Electricity, Says EU," *The Guardian,* July 23, 2008.

23 "Algeria Plans to Develop Solar Power for Export," Reuters, June 19, 2007.

Thirteen SAVING THE CONGO FORESTS

Information on the Congo Basin is gathered from a number of sources:

Biodiversity, weather, and climate: "Congo Basin Forest Partnership," USAID Sub-Saharan Africa; Alison L. Hoare, "Clouds on the Horizon: The Congo Basin's Forests and Climate Change," Rainforest Foundation, February 2007; "Congo River Basin, A Reservoir of Biodiversity Threatened with Extinction," IRIN, February 15, 2005; "Congo Basin Forest Fund: Why a Fund Is Needed," see www.cbf-fund.org; "The Forests of the Congo Basin: A Preliminary Assessment," USAID/CARPE [Commission des Forets D'Afrique Centrale], 2005.

World Bank and businesses involved in the Congo Basin: Rory Carroll, "Multinationals in Scramble for Congo's Wealth," *The Guardian*, October 22, 2002, citing *Final Report of Experts on the Illegal Exploitation of Natural Resources and Other Forms of Wealth of the Democratic Republic of the Congo* [New York: United Nations Security Council, S/2003/1027, October 2003]; "Forests in Post-Conflict DRC: Analysis of a Priority Agenda," Center for International Forestry Research [CIFOR], Centre International de Recherche Agronimique pour le Développement [CIRAD], World Bank, et al., 2007; William Wallis and Dino Mahtani, "World Bank Admits Congo Omissions," *Financial Times*, December 6, 2007; Robin Heighway-Bury, "Deforestation and Double Standards," Bretton Woods Project, October 5, 2007; Andrew W. Mitchell, Katherine Secoy, and Niki Mardas, "Forests First in the Fight Against Climate Change: The VivoCarbon Initiative," Global Canopy Programme, June 2007; Erik Reed and Marta Miranda, "Assessment of the Mining Sector and Infrastructure Development in the Congo Basin Region," WWF, January 2007; "Carving Up the Congo," Greenpeace, April 11, 2007.

Politics, gorillas, bushmeat, and charcoal industry: Sharon Begley, "Slaughter in the Jungle," and "Congo's Gorilla Tragedy," *Newsweek*, August 6, 2007; also CIFOR/CIRAD, above; Keya Acharya, "Rainforest Coalition Proposes Rewards for 'Avoided Deforestation,' " Environmental News Network, August 15, 2007.

1   GEO 4, p. 208.
2   "Major Ebola Outbreak in DR Congo," BBC News, September 12, 2007; "Ebola Information," Wildlife Conservation Society, www.wcs .org/sw-high_tech_tools/wildlifehealthscience/fvp/167620 [accessed September 2008].

Fourteen THE AFRICAN FAMILY

1 See Helen Epstein, "The Hidden Causes of AIDS," *New York Review of Books*, May 9, 2002.

2 Gumisai Mutume, "Workers' Remittances: A Boon to Development," *Africa Renewal* 19:3 (October 2005).

3 "Migration and Development Brief 5: Revisions to Remittance Trends 2007," Development Prospects Group, Migration and Remittances Team, World Bank, July 10, 2008.

4 See "Remittances to Africa Overtakes Foreign Direct Investment," UN press release, December 7, 2005.

5 Batonga Foundation, www.batongafoundation.org; George Weah, www.tlcafrica.com/weah.htm; Ayaan Hirsi Ali, ayaanhirsiali.org.

6 Lydia Polgreen, "Trees and Crops Reclaim Desert in Niger," *International Herald Tribune*, February 11, 2007.

7 Peter Greste, "Lesotho Gardens Relieve Food Crisis," BBC News, June 3, 2008.

8 See Ashden International Award Winners, 2008, www.ashdenawards.org/international_winners_2008 (accessed September 2008).

9 See www.wanep.org.

10 See Stephanie McCrummen, "Rangers Battle Odds to Save Rare Gorillas," *Sydney Morning Herald*, August 13, 2007; and Ndesanjo Macha, "Conservation 2.0: Congo Park Rangers Bring Global Attention to Endangered African Wildlife," Global Voices Online, May 16, 2007, www.globalvoicesonline.org/2007/05/16 (accessed September 2008).

11 Hammerskjoeld Simwinga, Feliciano dos Santos, Kpanan'Ayoung Siakor: all winners of the Goldman Environmental Prize, www.goldmanprize.org.

12 Dekha Ibrahim Abdi, winner of the Right Livelihood Award, www.rightlivelihood.org/abdi.html (accessed September 2008).

13 Rachel J. King, "Four African Freedom Activists Honored: Recipients Chosen for Efforts to Establish, Improve Democracy in Africa," America.gov, June 28, 2006.

14 See www.tac.org.za/community.

15 See www.tegla.org.

Select Bibliography

Alagiah, George. *A Passage to Africa.* London: Time Warner Paperbacks, 2002.

Alden, Chris. *China in Africa.* New York: Zed Books, 2007.

Ayittey, George B. N. *Africa Unchained: The Blueprint for Africa's Future.* New York: Palgrave Macmillan, 2005.

Calderisi, Robert. *The Trouble with Africa: Why Foreign Aid Isn't Working.* New York: Palgrave Macmillan, 2006.

Cheru, Fantu. *African Renaissance: Roadmaps to the Challenge of Globalization.* New York: Zed Books, 2002.

Collier, Paul. *The Bottom Billion: Why the Poorest Countries Are Failing and What Can Be Done About It.* New York: Oxford University Press, 2007.

Easterly, William. *The White Man's Burden: Why the West's Efforts to Aid the Rest Have Done So Much Ill and So Little Good.* New York: Penguin, 2006.

Economic Commission for Africa and the African Union. *Economic Report on Africa, 2007: Accelerating Africa's Development Through Diversification.* Addis Ababa, Ethiopia: United Nations Economic Commission for Africa, 2007.

———. *Economic Report on Africa, 2008: Africa and the Monterrey Consensus: Tracking Performance and Progress.* Addis Ababa, Ethiopia: United Nations Economic Commission for Africa, 2008.

Eggers, Dave. *What Is the What.* San Francisco: McSweeney's, 2006.

Evans, Gareth. *The Responsibility to Protect: Ending Mass Atrocity Crimes Once and For All.* Washington, D.C.: Brookings Institution Press, 2008.

French, Howard W. *A Continent for the Taking: The Tragedy and Hope of Africa.* New York: Vintage, 2005.

Hirsi Ali, Ayaan. *Infidel.* New York: Free Press, 2007.

Hochschild, Adam. *King Leopold's Ghost.* New York: Houghton Mifflin, 1998.

Kapuściński, Ryszard. *The Shadow of the Sun.* Trans. Klara Glowczewska. New York: Vintage, 2002.

Mandela, Nelson. *Long Walk to Freedom.* Boston: Little, Brown and Company, 1994.

Meredith, Martin. *The Fate of Africa: A History of Fifty Years of Independence.* New York: Public Affairs, 2005.

Ngũgĩ wa Thiong'o. *Wizard of the Crow.* New York: Anchor, 2007.

Pakenham, Thomas. *The Scramble for Africa.* London: Abacus, 1992.

Sachs, Jeffrey D. *The End of Poverty: Economic Possibilities for Our Time.* New York: Penguin, 2005.

Stiglitz, Joseph E. *Making Globalization Work.* New York: W. W. Norton, 2007.

United Nations Development Programme. *Human Development Report 2007/2008: Fighting Climate Change: Human Solidarity in a Divided World.* New York: Palgrave Macmillan, 2007.

United Nations Environment Programme (2008). *Africa: Atlas of Our Changing Environment, 2008.* Nairobi, Kenya: Division of Early Warning and Assessment and United Nations Enviironment Programme, 2008.

———. *Global Environment Outlook 4,* Nairobi, Kenya: United Nations Environment Programme, 2007.

Index

HIV/AIDS, 10, 55, 67, 70, 75, 77,
    169, 265, 277, 285
  environment-development
    relationship and, 239, 241
  foreign aid and, 63–4
  social machine and, 130, 139,
    144–6
Houphouët-Boigny, Félix, 51, 91
human rights, 11, 18, 25–6, 187,
    192, 209, 272, 278, 287–8
  and accomplishments of
    individuals, 283–5
  Africa's historical legacy and, 30,
    33
  China and, 107–9
  culture and, 168, 178, 180
  governance and, 51, 56, 58,
    60–1
  leadership and, 112, 114, 125
Human Rights Watch, 85
hunger, 77–81, 86–7
  culture and, 168, 175, 181
  environment-development
    relationship and, 239, 241, 243
  family and, 277–8
  foreign aid and, 77, 79–81
  governance and, 54, 56
  and image of Africa, 78–81
  land and, 234–5
Hutus, 32, 216, 225

Ibrahim, Mo, 116–18
indebtedness, 5, 20, 74, 89–94, 104,
    274
  dependency and, 63–4
  governance and, 48–50, 53, 57,
    89–90, 93–4
  relief for, 10, 92–4, 101
India, Indians, 35, 54, 59, 97, 161,
    218, 252, 256, 280–1
infrastructure, 5, 50, 93, 95, 100,
    113, 142–3, 269, 279
  land and, 228, 232
Institute for Security Studies, 86

International Criminal Court
    (ICC), 188
International Monetary Fund
    (IMF), 75, 89, 92
  governance and, 50, 53
  trade and, 98, 100–1
Islam, 65, 191, 276, 284
  Africa's historical legacy and, 32,
    37, 42
  culture and, 180–2

John Paul II, Pope, 178–9, 182
Johnson-Sirleaf, Ellen, 10, 92–3
  leadership and, 126–7
Jubilee 2000 Campaign, 89, 92

Kani, John, 283
Kaunda, Kenneth, 51, 205
Keita, Salif, 283
Kenya, 9–10, 67, 80
  and accomplishments of
    individuals, 283–5
  CDF of, 133–44, 157
  coffee industry of, 146–50,
    152–3, 236, 247
  culture and, 161, 164, 166, 168,
    173–6, 178–9, 181
  development in, 72–5, 240–52,
    256–8
  GBM in, 15, 133, 144–6, 193,
    203–4, 209, 222, 245–7
  governance and, 3, 52, 54, 131–4,
    136–41, 143–4, 146–7, 149–50,
    152–3, 157, 166
  historical legacy of, 21, 28–9, 32,
    42–4, 46–7, 157, 175–6, 200–1,
    229
  indebtedness and, 89, 93
  land and, 229–32, 236
  leadership and, 115, 121, 124,
    128, 131–3, 193–5, 198–9,
    201–4, 207–8, 210
  macadamia nut farming in,
    150–4

Somalia, 9, 43–4, 86, 102, 186, 189,
202, 249, 283
governance and, 51–2, 61
South Africa, 9–10, 21, 51, 84–6,
143, 161, 228, 251, 283, 285
Congo Basin forests and, 264–5
leadership and, 112, 115–16
micro-nations and, 211–14, 222
peace and reconciliation in,
207–8, 214
trade and, 102, 109
Southern African Development
Community (SADC), 105, 110
Southern Rhodesia, 31–2
Soviet Union, 31, 33, 115
Angolan relations with, 83–5
China and, 108–9
collapse of, 50, 52, 96–7
trade and, 96–7, 104, 109
Soyinka, Wole, 283
spirituality, 233, 276, 289
Africa's historical legacy and, 34,
37–41, 46
culture and, 160, 162–3, 168–9,
171, 173–4, 176–82
leadership and, 177–9, 203
social machine and, 129, 142,
145
Sudan, 11, 32, 37, 61, 108, 116,
179, 202, 217, 249–50,
284–5
conflict between Chad and, 9,
128, 187–92

Taban, Alfred, 284
Tana River, 240, 242
Tanzania, 37, 206, 250, 284
Africa's historical legacy and,
29–30, 43–4
foreign aid and, 63–5, 81
leadership and, 112, 128
micro-nations and, 215–16
trade and, 104–5
Taylor, Charles, 91–2

technology, 11, 48, 68, 155, 282
Africa's historical legacy and, 36,
40–1
culture and, 162, 173, 182–3
environment-development
relationship and, 255, 257
trade and, 98, 102–3
Tetu, 196, 199
social machine and, 132,
135–48
Thiong'o, Ngũgĩ wa, 283
three-legged stool, 260
governance and, 56–62
leadership and, 115–17
social machine and, 139, 159
tourism, 143, 208
Africa's historical legacy and, 42,
46
of Angola, 83, 85
environment-development
relationship and, 240, 242, 251
land and, 230–3
trade and, 96–7, 100
trade, 5, 10, 16, 35, 75, 86–9,
95–110
of Angola, 83, 86, 110
Asia and, 96–7, 101–2, 104,
106–10
Congo Basin forests and, 266–7
globalization and, 101–2, 104–6
governance and, 50, 53, 95–6,
99–100, 102–3, 105
imbalance of, 95–106
protectionism and, 101, 147, 274
regional cooperation and, 104–6
social machine and, 147, 149,
151–2
in weapons, 109–10
see also slavery, slave trade
traditional healers, 180–1
transportation, 36, 71, 85, 95,
279–80
emigration and, 280, 282
land and, 231–2

the
green belt
movement
international

My life's work has evolved into much more than planting trees. Two organizations that I founded, the Green Belt Movement and its sister group, the Green Belt Movement International, demonstrate that evolution. By planting trees, my colleagues in this grassroots movement and I planted ideas. The ideas, like the trees, grew. By providing education, access to water, and equity, GBM empowers people—most of them poor and most of them women—to take action, directly improving the lives of individuals and families.

Our experience of thirty years has also shown that simple acts can lead to great change and to respect for the environment, good governance, and cultures of peace. Such change is not limited to Kenya or Africa. The challenges facing Africa, particularly the degradation of the environment, are facing the entire world. This is why the Green Belt Movement International was founded. Only by working together can we hope to solve some of the problems of this precious planet. It's my fervent hope that you will seek to learn more about the work of the Green Belt Movement and the Green Belt Movement International by visiting our website, www.greenbeltmovement.org. Please share in our message of hope.

Wangari Maathai

Printed in the United States
by Baker & Taylor Publisher Services